The Public Policy Theory Primer

SECOND EDITION

Kevin B. Smith
University of Nebraska, Lincoln

Christopher W. Larimer
University of Northern Iowa

WESTVIEW
PRESS

A Member of the Perseus Books Group

Westview Press was founded in 1975 in Boulder, Colorado, by notable publisher and intellectual Fred Praeger. Westview Press continues to publish scholarly titles and high-quality undergraduate- and graduate-level textbooks in core social science disciplines. With books developed, written, and edited with the needs of serious nonfiction readers, professors, and students in mind, Westview Press honors its long history of publishing books that matter.

Copyright © 2013 by Westview Press
Published by Westview Press,
A Member of the Perseus Books Group

Find us on the World Wide Web at www.westviewpress.com.

Every effort has been made to secure required permissions for all text, images, maps, and other art reprinted in this volume.

Westview Press books are available at special discounts for bulk purchases in the United States by corporations, institutions, and other organizations. For more information, please contact the Special Markets Department at the Perseus Books Group, 2300 Chestnut Street, Suite 200, Philadelphia, PA 19103, or call (800) 810-4145, ext. 5000, or e-mail special.markets@perseusbooks.com.

A CIP catalog record for the print version of this book is available from the Library of Congress
PB ISBN: 978-0-8133-4749-3 (alk. paper)
E-book ISBN: 978-0-8133-4750-9

10 9 8 7 6 5 4 3 2 1

The Public Policy Theory Primer

CONTENTS

This second edition of *The Public Policy Theory Primer* has the same justification, organization, and objectives as the first edition. Where it differs is in description, inference, and conclusion; simply put, policy scholarship has moved on since the first edition. That scholarly output has forced a reconsideration of some important issues. To cite just a few examples, since the first edition, implementation research has been reinvigorated by the application of public management theory, policy and impact analysis has started to incorporate newly developed methods and conceptual frameworks rooted in behavioral economics, and evolutionary frameworks of human decision making seem to have reached a tipping point that demands policy scholars begin taking seriously the notion of incorporating them into theories of the policy process. As an indication of the scholarly productivity prompting these reassessments, one hundred new studies are cited in this edition.

Just as important as the changes is the consistent motivation underlying the *Primer*. This book has its origins in the challenges of introducing upper-division undergraduates and beginning graduate students to the field of policy studies. Advanced survey courses in public policy are a standard curricular component of graduate programs in political science, public administration, and other fields, and similar courses are increasingly common for upper-division undergraduates. The field of public policy, however, is so broad, diffuse, and balkanized that imposing order on it from an instructor's perspective—let alone from a student's perspective—can be a difficult and frustrating undertaking.

In facing this challenge in our own classes, we came to the realization that the challenge was not simply the logistical and organizational demands of putting together a coherent syllabus. What lay beneath was a fundamental question, perhaps *the* fundamental question, of the field of public policy studies: Does such a field really exist? Comparing syllabi with colleagues rapidly revealed a widely divergent approach to introducing students to the study of public policy.

The differences ranged across methodology, epistemology, theory, and specific policy subject matter. These are not just variations in teaching style, but differences in the substance of what is being taught. In viewing the fractured nature of the field of policy studies, we came to the conclusion that it is not possible to provide a comprehensive and coherent introductory survey of the field until those of us who study public policy come up with some coherent notion of what that field is.

So the book still has two primary aims. First, we seek to provide an integrationist vision of the field of policy studies. In short, we mount an argument for what is at the core of the study of public policy. Our approach is to define the key research questions in the field and use them to organize policy studies into coherent and related subfields that address those questions. Second, we provide a coherent and organized introduction to the field of public policy studies. In other words, we see our table of contents as a reasonable outline for a generic survey course on public policy.

Our broader academic goal was inseparable from our pedagogical goal, in that the latter is a direct outgrowth of the former. However, we also tried very hard to ensure that the latter is useful and practical even to those less concerned with the former. In what follows we claim to contribute to, rather than just report on, the professional academic public policy research. We are fully cognizant that our integrationist argument is going to meet skepticism, and perhaps even outright opposition, from some quarters. Rationalists and post-positivists, for example, will find plenty to damn and praise in equal measure. We recognize the scope for disagreement and encourage readers to make up their own minds rather than simply accept or reject our argument. Regardless of the level of agreement or disagreement with our more theoretical goals, however, what springs from our attempt to seriously engage and answer the question "What is the field of policy studies?" is what we believe to be a coherent and logically organized survey of the field itself. Regardless of one's conclusions about our integrationist vision of the field, we believe the resulting organizational structure can be practically adopted and adapted to virtually any advanced survey course on public policy.

A book is rarely the product only of the authors acknowledged on the cover; they simply get the credit for what is very much a team effort. Thanks are due to many people for making this book possible. These include our editor, Anthony Wahl, and all the good folks at Westview Press, who helped translate the idea into reality. Kevin Smith would like to thank his kids, CC and Brian, for reminding him that there is much more to life than work, and his wife Kelly, who for reasons unknown continues to put up with him. Chris Larimer would like to thank his son, Drew, and his wife, Danielle, for their loving support; his dad, Richard, for showing remarkable patience and determination during his health battles the last three years—your courage is an inspiration.

CHAPTER 1

Public Policy as a Concept and a Field (or Fields) of Study

A common criticism of the academic field of public policy studies is that no such thing exists. The study of public policy is concentrated in no single academic discipline, has no defining research question, is oriented toward no fundamental problem, has no unifying theory or conceptual framework, and employs no unique methods or analytical tools. As the introduction to *The Oxford Handbook of Public Policy* puts it, the study of public policy is "a mood more than a science, a loosely organized body of precepts and positions rather than a tightly integrated body of systematic knowledge, more art and craft than a genuine 'science'" (Goodin, Rein, and Moran 2006, 5). Even the field's best-known scholars can be openly skeptical of its coherence; Ken Meier once described policy research as "65 variables explaining 25 cases" (Meier 2009, 9).

Yet despite the vagueness associated with the field of policy studies, there is no doubt that a lot of people *are* studying public policy. Undergraduate public policy courses are part of the standard curriculum in fields such as political science, public administration, and economics. Prestigious institutions such as Harvard University's Kennedy School of Government and the University of Michigan's Gerald R. Ford School of Public Policy offer graduate programs in policy studies. There are professional societies for the study of public policy (the Policy Studies Organization, the Society for the Policy Sciences) and entire academic journals devoted to promoting and disseminating the best of academic public policy scholarship (e.g., *Policy Studies Journal, Policy Science, Journal of Policy Analysis and Management*). Outside of academics, professional students of public policy—typically called *policy analysts*—are scattered throughout all levels of government, with staffers in the Congressional Budget Office, the Government Accountability Office, and state-level legislative reference bureaus (not to mention various executive agency policy shops), all constituting a considerable industry dedicated to producing policy studies, reports, and recommendations. Outside of government, there are plenty of think tanks, interest groups, nongovernmental organizations (NGOs), and private sector consulting firms producing cost-benefit analyses, program evaluations, decision-making methods, and alternate public policy options on everything from watersheds in Colorado to counterterrorism strategies in the Middle East.

Is there anything that ties all of this together? Is there some common thread that unites such a varied group of people and activities? In short, is there really such a thing as a distinct and definable field that can be called public policy studies? This book seeks an answer to this question. We aim to provide readers not just with an overview of how policy is studied and why, or a tour of the major conceptual models and methodologies commonly employed in the study of public policy, though we hope to squarely address these goals in what follows. The core of our effort, and the true goal of this book, is to help readers draw a reasoned conclusion about the nature, and future, of the field of public policy studies.

A central difficulty for the beginning (and often the experienced) student of public policy is gaining just this sort of coherent perspective on and orientation to the field. It is so all-encompassing, both in terms of its potential subject matter and its promiscuous attachments to wildly different academic disciplines, that it seems less a noun (I study policy) and more an adjective (I am a policy economist, or I am a policy political scientist). Studying public policy takes so many forms, from so many different perspectives, that stitching its constituents into an overall systematic pattern may seem a daunting task. Nonetheless, that is the goal of this book. In what follows, we claim that it is possible to integrate the many strands into a coherent whole and to present a systematic picture of a field that is at least as much a science as it is an art or a craft.

Defining Public Policy

A logical place to begin such an effort is to try to come to grips with what the field is actually studying. This is no easy task. Public policy is like pornography. U.S. Supreme Court Justice Potter Stewart famously commented in his concurring opinion in *Jacobellis v. Ohio* (1964) that it was unlikely he could ever intelligibly define hard-core pornography, "but I know it when I see it." Public policy is like that: an intuitive concept that is maddeningly difficult to define precisely.

A small academic industry is dedicated to defining public policy. Some definitions are broad. Policy is "whatever governments choose to do or not to do" (Dye 1987, 1); "the relationship of governmental unit to its environment" (Eyestone 1971, 18); or "the actions, objectives, and pronouncements of governments on particular matters, the steps they take (or fail to take) to implement them, and the explanations they give for what happens (or does not happen)" (Wilson 2006, 154). Such definitions are accurate in the sense that they cover pretty much everything that could conceivably be considered public policy, but they are so general that they do little to convey any idea of what makes policy studies different from political science, welfare economics, or public administration. They convey no clear boundary that isolates the intellectual quarry of the policy scholar and differentiates it from, say, the political scientist who studies institutions or even voting behavior (what elected governments choose to do or not to do is, after all, ultimately tied to the ballot box).

Other definitions are narrower. James Anderson's widely used undergraduate textbook, for example, defines policy as a "purposive course of action or inaction undertaken by an actor or set of actors in dealing with a problem or matter of concern" (1994, 5). This definition implies a distinguishing set of characteristics for public policy. Policy is not random but purposive and goal oriented; public policy is made by public authorities; public policy consists of patterns of actions taken over time; public policy is a product of demand, a government-directed course of action in response to pressure about some perceived problem; public policy can be positive (a deliberately purposive action) or negative (a deliberately purposive decision not to take action). Others seek to extract common characteristics by isolating common elements of broader definitions. Theodoulou (1995, 1–9) used this approach and ended up with a list that overlaps considerably with Anderson's, but she also added that public policy has distinct purposes: resolving conflict over scarce resources, regulating behavior, motivating collective action, protecting rights, and directing benefits toward the public interest.

Defining public policy, as Anderson and Theodoulou have done, by trying to distill a set of characteristics at the core of the underlying concept, is no doubt a useful exercise. However, this sort of approach is vulnerable to the criticism that it simply takes a different route to end up at the same conceptual destination of the more succinct "it's what government does." The list of characteristics becomes so long that taken together they still add up to the "everything and nothing" approach captured more succinctly by Dye and Eyestone. A purposive course of action or inaction to address a problem or matter of concern covers a lot of ground.

The bottom line is that there is no precise and universal definition of public policy, nor is it likely that such a definition will be conceived in the foreseeable future. Instead, there is general agreement that public policy includes the process of making choices, the actions associated with operationalizing those choices, and the outputs and outcomes produced by those actions; that what makes public policy "public" is that choices or actions are backed by the coercive powers of the state; and that, at its core, public policy is a response to a perceived problem (Birkland 2001).

Consensus on such generalities, though, does not lead easily to conceptual specifics. This lack of general agreement on what policy scholars are actually studying is a key reason why the field is so intellectually fractured. As Bobrow and Dryzek put it, the field of policy studies is "a babel of tongues in which participants talk past rather than to one another" (1987, 4). This is not so surprising. If a group cannot agree on what it is studying, it is difficult to talk about it coherently. An easy and shortsighted criticism of the field is that a policy is an identifiable output, so presumably a single theory or explanatory framework should suffice. But policy is the result of many interconnected actors, institutions, and groups, as well as independent decisions. Policies also affect the nature and design of future policies, making prediction a difficult if not impossible standard to which to hold the field. Just because we cannot define the concept beyond generalities, however, does not mean we cannot define the field (or fields) of policy studies.

Defining the Field(s) of Public Policy Studies

Lacking a general definition of public policy means the various disciplines with policy orientations can adopt their own definitions and not worry that other supposed policy scholars seem to be studying something very different, and for very different reasons. From this perspective there is not a *field* of public policy studies; there are *fields*—plural—of public policy studies. This plurality is not necessarily a bad thing. For one thing, it frees the study of public policy from the insular intellectual silos that constitute traditional academic disciplines. Policy scholars are free to jump fences, picking whatever disciplinary pasture seems most suited to the issue or question at hand. The policy sciences have been described as "a-disciplinary or trans-disciplinary," with scholars adopting and adapting theories and methods from multiple fields depending on what works best for the question at hand (Pielke 2004, 216).

Rather than defining a single concept as the core focus of different activities, then, perhaps it is better to define the field (or fields) rather than the core concept. Some may argue that this restates the definitional problem rather than solves it. The field of policy studies, for example, has been defined as "any research that relates to or promotes the public interest" (Palumbo 1981, 8). Such broad definitions make the field of policy studies as vague and general as the concept of public policy appears to be. Definitions of the "policy sciences"—for our purposes a synonym for "policy studies"—include the "application of knowledge and rationality to perceived social problems" (Dror 1968, 49) and "an umbrella term describing a broad-gauge intellectual approach applied to the examination of societally critical problems" (deLeon 1988, 219). From the field-level perspective, then, the study of public policy is about identifying important societal problems that presumably require government action to be effectively addressed, formulating solutions to those problems, and assessing the impact of those solutions on the target problem (deLeon 2006).

Under this general umbrella is a range of subfields that have developed quite independently of each other. These include policy evaluation, policy analysis, and policy process. *Policy evaluation* seeks to systematically assess "the consequences of what governments do and say" (Dubnick and Bardes 1983, 203). Policy evaluation is typically an *ex post* undertaking that uses a wide range of methods to identify and isolate a causal relationship between a policy or a program and an outcome of interest (Mohr 1995). The fundamental question in policy evaluation is empirical: What have we done?

Whereas policy evaluation is largely an empirical exercise, *policy analysis* is more normative. Policy analysis focuses on *ex ante* questions. The most fundamental of these is: What should we do? The object is to determine the best policy for public authorities to adopt to address a given problem or issue of concern.

The challenge for policy analysis is coming up with some comparative yardstick to measure what is "best." Efficiency and effectiveness, for example, are both defensible criteria for judging what is, or is not, the best policy to address a particular problem or issue of concern. Yet the most efficient policy is not necessarily the most effective, and vice versa.

If policy evaluation asks questions about what we have done, and policy analysis asks questions about what we should do, *policy process* research is focused on the how and why of policymaking. Those who study policy process are interested in finding out why governments pay attention to some problems and not others (agenda setting), why policy changes or remains stable across time, how individuals and groups affect policy, and where policy comes from.

Imposing organization and order on the field of policy studies through a taxonomy of its constituent subfields such as policy analysis, policy evaluation, and policy process can in one sense lead us back to the definitional dead ends we found when trying to squeeze specificity and clarity out of the underlying concept of public policy. Most of these fields have an intellectual history that mimics the definitional struggles surrounding the concept of public policy. Policy analysis, for example, has been defined as "a means of synthesizing information including research results to produce a format for policy decisions" (Williams 1971, xi) and as "an applied social science discipline which uses multiple methods of inquiry to produce and transform policy-relevant information that may be utilized in political settings to resolve policy problems" (Dunn 1981, ix). Parsing out such definitions leads to either loopholes (shouldn't the definition say something about who is using the information, and for what purposes? See Weimer and Vining 2005, 24) or vacuous generalities (policy analysis covers everything dealing with government decision making).

This approach, however, does provide at least one clear advantage. *By carving the field into broad, multidisciplinary orientations such as policy or program evaluation, policy analysis, and policy process, it is possible to identify within each some roughly coherent framework.* If nothing else, this approach clarifies a series of research questions central to the field of public policy studies as a whole: How do public authorities decide what problems or issues to pay attention to? How does government decide what to do about those problems? What values should be used to determine the "best" government response to a particular problem or matter of concern? What do government actions intend to achieve? Have those goals been achieved? If so, to what extent? If not, why not? These questions systematically sort and organize different policy subfields such as policy process (the first two questions), policy analysis (the second two questions), and policy evaluation (the last questions). And within each of these particular orientations identifiable conceptual frameworks have been either constructed or appropriated to provide systematic answers to the underlying questions. Even accepting the difficulties in defining the concept of public policy, most would agree that these are important questions and finding the answers is important, both to improve the lot of society and to better understand the human condition generally.

Although it is not immediately clear what connects, say, the work of a political scientist studying the formation of coalitions within a policy subsystem to, say, a program evaluator running randomized field trials on the effectiveness of a particular government activity, the connections definitely exist. For one thing, most (if not all) of the subfields under the policy studies umbrella trace back to a common historical root. There may be fields (plural) of policy studies rather than a field (singular), but the original intent was to till all with a common intellectual plow.

The Policy Sciences:
A Very Short History of the Field of Policy Studies

It is not difficult to extend the history of policy studies back to antiquity; what governments do or do not do has occupied the attention and interest of humans ever since there were governments. All advisers who whispered in the ears of princes, and their rivals who assessed and countered the prince's decisions, were students of public policy. All were interested in answering the research questions listed just a few paragraphs ago. Using these questions as a means to define its intellectual heritage, policy studies can legitimately claim everyone from Plato (who laid out a lot of policy recommendations in *The Republic*) to Machiavelli (who in *The Prince* had some definite ideas on how to exercise policymaking power) among its intellectual founders. Other political thinkers—Thomas Hobbes, John Locke, James Madison, Adam Smith, John Stuart Mill—qualify as policy scholars under this definition. They all were broadly concerned with what government does and does not do and were often interested in specific questions of what the government should do and how it should go about doing it, as well as in assessing what impact the government has on various problems in society.

Most students of public policy, however, consider the field of policy studies a fairly new undertaking, at least as a distinct academic discipline. Public administration, economics, and political science consider their respective policy orientations to be no more than a century old. Many claim a lineage of less than half of that. Systematic policy analysis is sometimes attributed to the development and adoption of cost-benefit analyses by the federal government (mostly for water projects) in the 1930s (Fuguitt and Wilcox 1999, 1–5). Others trace the roots of policy analysis back no further than the 1960s (Radin 1997).

Whereas any claim to identify the absolute beginning of the field of public policy studies should be taken with a grain of salt, most histories converge on a roughly common starting point. That starting point is Harold Lasswell, who laid down a grand vision of what he called the "policy sciences" in the middle of the twentieth century. Even though his vision has been at best imperfectly realized, most of the various policy orientations discussed thus far share Lasswell as a common branch in their intellectual family trees, even as they branch off into very different directions elsewhere.

In some ways Lasswell's view of the policy sciences was a vision of what political science should become (see Lasswell 1951a, 1956). Yet though he gave political science a central place in the policy sciences, his vision was anything but parochial. The policy sciences were to draw from all the social sciences, law, and other disciplines. The idea of the policy sciences was an outgrowth not just of Lasswell's academic interests but also of his practical experience in government. He was one of a number of high-profile social scientists who helped government formulate policy during World War II. At the time, Allied governments—particularly the United Kingdom and the United States—drafted experts from a wide range of academic fields to apply their knowledge, with the aim of helping to more effectively prosecute the war. Out of such activities was born a more rigorous and often quantitative approach to studying and making policy decisions. Lasswell was one of these experts drafted into government service. His expertise was in propaganda—he wrote his dissertation on the topic—and during the war he served as the chief of the Experimental Division for the Study of War-Time Communications. This experience helped solidify Lasswell's idea that a new field should be developed to better connect the knowledge and expertise of the social sciences to the practical world of politics and policymaking.

Lasswell's vision of the policy sciences, and of the policy scientist, was expanded and refined in a series of publications between the 1940s and his death in 1978. The foundational article, "The Policy Orientation," was published in an edited volume in 1951. Here Lasswell attempted to lay out the goals, methods, and purposes of the policy sciences. He began with a clear(ish) notion of the concept of public policy, which he viewed generically as "the most important choices made in organized or in private life" (1951b, 5). Public policy, then, was the response to the most important choices faced by government. The policy sciences would be the discipline that developed to clarify and inform those choices and to assess their ultimate impact. Specifically, Lasswell laid out the following distinguishing characteristics of the policy sciences.

Problem oriented. The policy sciences were oriented to the major problems and issues faced by government. These were not necessarily outcome focused; process is also a critical focus of the policy scientist. Under the umbrella of important problems were the formation and adoption, as well as the execution and assessment, of particular choices. The key focus of the policy scientist was not a particular stage of policymaking (analysis, evaluation, process), but rather an important problem faced by government. (What should we do to best address the problem? How should we do it? How do we know what we've done?)

Multidisciplinary. Lasswell made clear that policy science and political science were not synonymous (1951b, 4). The policy sciences were to cut across all disciplines whose models, methods, and findings could contribute to addressing key problems faced by government.

Methodologically sophisticated. Lasswell recognized that many of the important contributions social sciences had made to public policy during World War II were tied to their methodological sophistication. In his 1951 essay he specifically mentioned improvements in economic forecasting, psychometrics, and the measurement of attitudes. Advances in these areas helped government make more effective decisions about everything from allocating resources within the war economy to matching individual aptitudes with particular military specialties. Lasswell saw quantitative methods as "amply vindicated" and assumed any debate would not be about the development and worth of quantitative methods, but rather about how they could best be applied to particular problems (1951b, 7).

Theoretically sophisticated. If the policy sciences were going to help effectively address important problems, they had to understand cause and effect in the real world. Understanding how social, economic, and political systems operated and interacted was absolutely critical if government was going to squarely address problems in those realms. This meant that policy scientists had a critical need for conceptual frameworks with enough explanatory horsepower to clarify how and why things happened in the larger world of human relations. How do institutions shape decision making? How can governments best provide incentives for desirable behaviors? An effective policy science had to be able to credibly answer these sorts of questions, and to do so it would need sophisticated theoretical models.

Value oriented. Importantly, Lasswell did not just call for a development of the policy sciences. He called for development of the policy sciences *of democracy.* In other words, the policy sciences had a specific value orientation: their ultimate goal was to maximize democratic values. In Lasswell's words, "the special emphasis is on the policy sciences of democracy, in which the ultimate goal is the realization of human dignity in theory and fact" (1951b, 15).

Overall, Lasswell's vision of the policy sciences was of an applied social science, the roving charge of which was to fill the gap between academically produced knowledge and the real world of politics and problems. The operating model was that of a law firm or a doctor. The job of the policy scientist was to diagnose the ills of the body politic, understand the causes and implications of those ills, recommend treatment, and evaluate the impact of the treatment. Like a doctor, the policy scientist had to have scientifically grounded training, but would employ that knowledge to serve a larger, value-oriented purpose. Though there was no suggested Hippocratic oath for the policy scientist, his or her expertise was supposed to be harnessed to the greater good and deployed for the public good and the general betterment of humanity.

This, then, was the original vision of the field of policy studies. It was not a field built around a core concept; it did not need a universal definition of public policy to function as an independent discipline. In Lasswell's vision, policy studies (or as he would put it, the policy sciences) was a field analogous to medicine. Within the field were to be numerous subspecialties, not all necessarily tied together within a universal intellectual framework. What was to give the field its focus was its problem orientation. Yet while Lasswell gave policy studies a unifying focus in problem orientation, his vision contained the seeds of its own demise.

The Fracturing of the Policy Sciences

Lasswell's vision of the policy sciences is breathtaking in its scope, and many still find it an attractive notion of what the field of policy studies *should* be (see Pielke

2004). For good or for ill, though, this vision is not an accurate description of what the field of public policy studies *is*. Why? The short answer is that Lasswell's vision contains too many internal contradictions to support the broader project. He called for the training of a set of specialized experts to play a highly influential role in policymaking. Ceding such influence to technocrats smacks of elitism, not the more egalitarian ethos of democracy. Where does the citizen fit into democratic policymaking? It is difficult to discern in Lasswell's vision much of a role for the citizen at all. The policy scientist as physician for the body politic might produce more effective or efficient policy, might help solve problems, and might even produce policy that is viewed as being in the public interest. However, it is hard to see how this approach is democratic when it assigns the ultimate source of sovereign power—the citizen—to a passive and secondary role (deLeon 1997).

It is also hard to square the values underpinning science with the values that underpin democracy, for the simple reason that science's fundamental values are not particularly democratic. Science values objectivity and believes in an objective world that is independent of those who observe it. It is oriented toward a world in which disagreements and debates are amenable to empirical analysis. If one set of people hypothesizes that the sun moves around the earth and another group the opposite, careful observation and analysis of the universe that exists independently of either perspective ultimately decides which hypothesis is false. This is because the universe operates in a certain way according to certain laws, and no amount of belief or ideology can make them work differently. It matters not a whit if one believes the sun revolves around the earth; the simple empirical fact of the matter is that the sun does no such thing. The earth-centric worldview is empirically falsified, and no degree of faith or belief will make it otherwise in the eyes of science.

As critics of the Lasswellian project point out, it is not a particularly accurate description of the world of politics. In the political world perception is everything. Indeed, these critics argue that perception in the social and political world *is* reality; no independent, universal world separate from our own social and mental constructions exists (see Fischer 2003). It is exactly one's faith or belief in a particular part of the world that creates political reality. What constitutes a problem, let alone what constitutes the best response, is very much in the eye of the political beholder. Some believe the government should take on the responsibility for ensuring that all citizens have access to adequate health care. Others believe it is not the government's role or responsibility to provide health care; these are services best left to and controlled by the market. What resolves that difference of perspective? Whatever the answer, it is unlikely to be an objective, scientific one. Both sides have access to the same facts, but it is how those facts are filtered through particular belief systems that defines problems and suggests solutions. And indeed, empirical evidence demonstrates that coalitions on both sides of an issue exhibit strong biases in how they process information—forming partnerships with those who share their beliefs, while ignoring and not trusting those with opposing viewpoints (Henry 2011). The answers, in other words, are value based, and those values are held by particular individuals and groups—there is no independent, objective world with the "correct" set of values.

As an epistemology, that is, a method of gaining knowledge, science has few equals, and its benefits have contributed enormously to the betterment of humankind and a deeper understanding of our world. Science, however, cannot make a political choice any less political. The difficulty of reconciling knowledge with politics, of fitting values into the objective, scientific approaches that have come to dominate the social sciences, has never been resolved. Lasswell argued that facts would be put into the service of democratic values. He never seemed to fully recognize that facts and values could conflict, let alone that values might in some cases determine "facts."

These sorts of contradictions fractured and balkanized the field of policy studies from its inception. Lasswell's vision helped birth a new field, but simultaneously crippled it with logical inconsistencies. As one assessment put it, "Lasswell's notion of the policy sciences of democracy combined description with prescription to create an oxymoron" (Farr, Hacker, and Kazee 2006). Rather than a coherent field, what emerged from Lasswell's vision was the range of orientations or subfields already discussed: in other words, policy evaluation studies, policy analysis, and policy process. Each of these picked up and advanced some elements of the policy sciences, but none came close to fulfilling the grander ambitions of Lasswell's call for a new field.

Across these different perspectives were some discernible commonalities rooted in the larger policy sciences project. The methodological aspects, for example, were enthusiastically embraced and pursued. It is all but impossible, at least in the United States, to study public policy in a sustained fashion without getting a heavy dose of quantitative training. Cost-benefit analysis, risk assessment, operations research, matrix analysis—just about everything in the econometric, statistical, and mathematical tool kit of the social sciences has been adopted and adapted to the study of public policymaking. The jury is out, however, on just how much that has contributed to the study of public policy. The heroic assumptions required to make, say, cost-benefit analysis mathematically tractable (e.g., placing a dollar value on human life) justifiably raise questions about what the end product of all this rigorous quantitative analysis tells us. Critics of the development of technocratic policy studies argue that the most science-oriented aspects of policy research have a spotty historical record. Number-crunching policy scientists wielding complex causal models bombed (sometimes quite literally) in a series of big, broad-scale problems, such as the war in Vietnam, the war on poverty in the 1960s, and the energy crisis of the 1970s (Fischer 2003, 5–11; deLeon 2006, 43–47). Others counter that science-based policy analysis for at least fifty years has provided an important and highly valued source of information for policymakers and played a critical role in testing and advancing the most important and influential theories of the policy process (Head 2008; Sabatier 2007).

Whether one agrees or disagrees with their merits, there is no doubt that the methodological aspects of Lasswell's vision have been enthusiastically embraced. Other aspects, however, have been largely ignored. Lasswell's notion of the policy sciences was explicitly normative; it was the policy sciences *of democracy*. This created an internal tension within all disciplines with a policy orientation, a conflict between those who gave precedence to the values of science and those who gave precedence to the values of democracy (or at least to particular political values). Academics of a scientific bent are inherently suspicious of pursuing explicit normative agendas. Declaring a value-based preference or outcome tends to cast suspicion on a research project. Ideology or partisanship does not require science, and the latter would just as soon do without the former. With notable exceptions, academics have not been overly eager to build political portfolios, because their aim is to further knowledge rather than a particular partisan policy agenda.[1]

Those who see their job as shaping policy in the name of the public good, on the other hand, may find themselves less than satisfied with a mathematically and theoretically complex approach to public policy. The technocratic orientation of the policy sciences can be especially frustrating to those with an advocacy bent; the very notion of reducing, say, proposed health-care programs to cost-benefit ratios strikes some as misleading or even ludicrous. From this perspective, the real objective of policy study is not simply the production of knowledge. The more important questions center on values: Do citizens in a given society have a right to universal health care? What is the proper place and influence of minority viewpoints in public policy decision making? How do we know if a policy process, decision, output, or outcome is truly democratic? The answers to such questions will not be found in a regression coefficient generated by a model that assumes an independent, value-free world. To borrow from the second U.S. president John Adams, values, like facts, "are stubborn things."

Setting aside the problems in trying to get objectively grounded epistemologies to deal with normative values, coalescing the various academic policy orientations into the more coherent whole envisioned by Lasswell has also been bested by practical difficulties. Because policy scholars are almost by definition multidisciplinary, it can be difficult to find a definite niche within a particular field. Political scientists who study American politics, for example, tend to study particular institutions (Congress, special interest groups, the media) or particular forms of political behavior or attitudes (voting, opinion). These provide neat subdisciplinary divisions and organize training, curriculum offerings, and not insignificantly, job descriptions within the academic study of American politics. The problem for policy scholars is that they do not do any one of these things; they do *all* of them—and quite a bit else besides—which tends to give them a jack-of-all-trades, master-of-none reputation (Sabatier 1991b). This in turn gives rise to a widespread view that policy scholars within political science are not pulling their weight, especially in terms of generating theories of how the social, political, and economic worlds work. Instead, they simply piggyback on the subfield specialties, borrowing liberally whatever bits of conceptual frameworks they find useful, but doing little in the way of reciprocation. As we shall see, this is a central criticism of policy studies generally, one that must be creditably answered if policy studies is to make a supportable claim to be an independent field of study.

The end result of its internal inconsistencies, the friction between science and democratic or other political values, and the failure to generate conceptual or methodological coherence has largely prevented Lasswell's vision of policy sciences from taking root as an independent academic discipline. Policy sciences is so fragmented and spread out that, even within a relatively small discipline like political science, policy scholars can operate completely independent of each other, not just ignoring each other's work but largely unaware that it even exists. In 2008 some of the biggest names in policy process theory convened a conference at the University of Oklahoma to discuss potential advances in their field. One of the telling comments at that conference came from Chris Weible, who noted that three-quarters of the people in his home department—all doing public policy—did not know anyone in the room (Eller and Krutz 2009). Rather than a single field, we have the multiple, multidisciplinary orientations already discussed. Taken on its own terms, each of these orientations can provide a good deal of clarity and systematic orientation on important questions about what government does and why (a good deal of this book is devoted to making this point). But these different orientations do not seamlessly fit together, and they make for a poor vessel to hold Lasswell's vision. The gaps in the joints are so large, the policy sciences simply leak away.

Does this mean that we have managed to answer our key question before we have finished the first chapter? Is there really no such thing as the field of policy studies, just a set of marginally related academic orientations cobbled together out of bits and pieces of different social sciences, each distinguishable only by the sorts of questions it's trying to answer? Not necessarily.

The research questions at the heart of the subdisciplines that make up the field of policy studies are big ones, with large, real-world consequences. We contend in this book that if there is, or ever is going to be, such a thing as a field of policy studies, those important questions have to be pushed to the forefront, and so must the broader conceptual frameworks created to answer them. It is not just core questions, in other words, that define a field. It is some systematic, core gyroscope that serves to orient those searching for the answers. In other words, a field—a distinct, defensible, coherent discipline—needs theory. And theory, according to critics and champions of public policy scholarship, is something that policy scholars have done pretty miserably for a very long time.

Why Build When You Can Beg, Borrow, and Steal?

There is no general theoretical framework tying together the study of public policy. So how is it possible to make sense of the complex world of public policy? Sabatier (1999a, 5) has argued that there are two basic approaches. The first is to simplify and make sense of that complexity ad hoc: simply use what works in a given situation. Employ whatever lens brings focus to a particular issue or question at a particular time and place. Make whatever assumptions seem to make sense and make up whatever categories bring tractability to the analysis at hand. The second is science. This means trying to do in public policy what students of markets have done in economics. Specifically, it means assuming that underlying the highly complex world of public policymaking is a set of causal relationships. Just as assumptions about utility maximization and the law of supply and demand can explain a wide-ranging set of observed behaviors in markets, there are corollaries that explain how and why governments address some problems and not others. If these causal relationships can be identified, presumably they can be linked together logically to build overarching explanations of how the world works. These claims can be tested, the tests can be replicated, and the model can be refined into general propositions that hold across time and space. In other words, generalizable theories can be built.

The problem with such theory-building projects is that generalizability has thus far proven highly elusive; public policy is such a diffuse topic that it is hard to even imagine a single, broad conceptual model that all policy scholars could practically adopt and apply. Frameworks might work for this or that aspect of policy study, but nothing currently or in the foreseeable future provides a conceptual core to the field in the same way that, say, the model of rational utility maximization serves as a universal gyroscope for economics. This can make it difficult to assess the quality of theory in the field of public policy, because the theories are built for different purposes, to answer different questions. Comparing these theories to decide which is "best" in a scientific sense is all but impossible. As one long-time student of public policy put it, "the scholar seeking the optimal policy theory is essentially handicapping how the New England Patriots would do against Manchester United in Indy car racing" (Meier 2009, 6).

Rather than bemoan this state of affairs, the ad hoc approach embraces it, and indeed, there is good reason to recommend an ad hoc approach to the study of public policy. For one thing, it provides policy scholars with a license to beg, borrow, or steal from the full range of conceptual frameworks developed across the social sciences. It also relieves policy scholars of the pressure to shoehorn conceptual frameworks into an ill-fitting and messy reality. Analytic case studies can provide a wealth of information and detail about a particular policy or process, even if they are ad hoc in the sense that they have no grand conceptual framework proposing causal links to empirically verify. A good example is Pressman and Wildavsky's (1973) classic study of implementation, which has shaped virtually all implementation studies that followed. The big problem here is that ad hoc frameworks have extremely limited value; it is, unsurprisingly, difficult to build cumulative and generalizable knowledge from what are essentially descriptive studies (implementation studies have struggled with this problem). Using the ad hoc approach, policy scholars are destined to be forever reinventing the wheel, finding that what works in one circumstance is trapped there—the causal assumptions hold only for a particular place in a particular slice of time.

Such limitations, coupled with the policy field's penchant for poaching theories rather than producing them, have done much to sully the reputation of policy scholarship, especially in fields such as political science. Policy scholars are viewed as theory takers rather than theory makers. They swipe whatever is useful for them but rarely return a greater, more generalizable understanding of the world they study. In the eyes of many, this consigns the field of policy studies—whatever that field may or may not be—to a social science discipline of the second or third rank. It is hard to overstate this point: a central problem, perhaps *the* central problem, of policy studies is its perceived inability to contribute to a more general understanding of the human condition.

This general argument has wide currency and leads to no small amount of hand-wringing among policy scholars. Indeed, flagellating ourselves for our theory—or lack thereof—is a long-standing tradition in policy studies. Public policy "is an intellectual jungle swallowing up with unbounded voracity almost anything, but which it cannot give disciplined—by which I mean theoretically enlightened—attention" (Eulau 1977, 421). The policy studies literature, at least the political science end of it, "is remarkably devoid of theory" (Stone 1988, 3), with policy scholars making, at best, "modest contributions to developing reasonably clear, and empirically verified theories" (Sabatier 1991a, 145). This inability to provide coherent explanations of how policy is formulated, adopted, implemented, and evaluated leads to policy studies being "regarded by many political scientists, economists and sociologists as second-best research" (Dresang 1983, ix).

Some argue that the attempt to produce generalizable theories of public policy is not only pointless but hopeless. Political scientists seem to have all but given up on trying to construct systematic explanatory frameworks for policy implementation (though see Chapter 7 for some interesting new developments, and to see how other disciplines are taking up the challenge, see Saetren 2005). Though everyone agrees implementation is a critical factor in determining policy success or failure, the sheer complexity of the subject seems to defy general explanation. After spending forty years struggling to distill parsimonious, systematic patterns in implementation, political scientists found themselves making little progress from the initial observations of Pressman and Wildavsky's (1973) classic study. Many political scientists seem content to let the study of implementation return to its origins: many case studies, some of them very good, but not adding up to a comprehensive and general understanding of what's happening and why (deLeon 1999a).

Some scholars of public policy see the general failure of the project to construct "scientific" theories of public policy as a good thing, a hard lesson that has finally been learned. From this perspective, the lack of good theory exposes notions of a positivist "science" of policy theory for what they actually are—that is, Lasswellian pipe dreams. As Deborah Stone put it, the scientific approach to public policy that has occupied the attention of so many social scientists is, in effect, a mission to rescue "public policy from the irrationalities and indignities of politics" (2002, 7). The problem, of course, is that public policy is very political and not particularly scientific, so nobody should be surprised that science isn't much help in explaining the political world. Rather than pursue the "rationalistic" project (Stone's term) of building scientific theories, it's better to recognize the value-laden realities of public policy and embrace normative theories as the gyroscope of policy studies (deLeon 1997; Stone 2002; Fischer 2003). Normative theories (e.g., discourse theory, social constructivism) may not reveal universal truths—they assume there may not be any to reveal—but they can get us closer to understanding the different perspectives that underlie conflict in public policy arenas. This unabashedly political approach to organizing the study of public policy, argue its advocates, is more illuminating and ultimately more practical than quixotically tilting at scientific windmills.

There is considerable merit to such criticisms of the scientific approach (typically called post-positivist or post-empiricist). Yet as we shall see, it is not clear that post-positivism can separate itself from the dichotomous choice laid down by Sabatier. Post-positivism may reject science, but it's not clear it can duck charges of being ad hoc. We shall return to this debate in some depth in later chapters. For now let us say that it is our view that much of the criticism of the scientific approach to policy theory is overblown, at least in the sense that it highlights problems unique to policy studies. The general failure of policy studies to produce generalizable theories to explain the world and unify the field is shared by a number of other social science disciplines. Public administration, for example, has long agonized over its lack of intellectual coherence (Frederickson et al. 2012). And political scientists who criticize policy studies for its theoretical failings can in turn be held accountable for throwing stones from glass houses. The last time we checked, our home discipline (both authors are political scientists) had no unifying conceptual framework, an observation that can be verified by a glance through any major political science journal. Policy scholars, as we intend to convincingly demonstrate in what follows, have constructed a remarkable array of conceptual frameworks, some of which have been disseminated within and across social science disciplines and are usefully employed to bring order to the study and understanding of the policy realm.[2]

Economics is a social science with a central, unifying conceptual framework and a well-developed set of methods to operationalize that framework and test its central claims. Notably, that framework has come to dominate considerable areas of public administration, political science, and policy studies (usually under the rubric of public choice). Such successful, if highly incomplete, colonization of other disciplines demonstrates the power of good theory. Because economic models spring from a largely coherent, general view of how the world works, they are applicable to a wide range of human interaction, even if it does not directly involve the exchange of goods and services.

It is exactly with this sort of operation that policy scholars are supposed to have done such a poor job. Beginning in the next chapter, we intend to make the argument that the study of public policy has actually done a lot more in this area than it is given credit for. For now, however, we freely concede that the field of policy studies has nothing remotely close to a general theory of policy comparable to mainstream models of economics.[3] Although it doesn't have *a* theory (singular), we claim it has produced functional theories (plural) within a wide-ranging set of policy orientations such as policy process, policy evaluation, policy analysis, and policy design. Within each of these orientations are core research questions that have prompted the construction of robust conceptual frameworks that usefully guide the search for answers. Those frameworks can be pragmatically mined by advocates and others who are less interested in theory and more interested in making an impact in the real world of a particular policy issue. The real question for us is whether these policy orientations constitute a core foundation for a coherent field or are so different in terms of questions, frameworks, and methods that they are best considered as adjuncts to other scholarly enterprises rather than an independent discipline.

Conclusion

Is there such a thing as a field or discipline of public policy studies? There is no doubt a strong claim for answering this question in the negative. Scholars in this field, after a half-century of trying, have yet to produce a general definition of the concept supposedly at the heart of their study. At a minimum, public policy has never been defined with a degree of specificity that clearly separates what a public policy scholar is studying from what, say, a political scientist or economist is studying. It may be that such a definition is impossible.[4]

Despite the lack of agreement on what public policy scholars are studying, there seems to be no lack of interest in the study of public policy. Graduate programs, academic societies, and professional careers are supposedly dedicated to the specialist field of policy studies. Yet even a cursory inspection of these activities reveals more differences than similarities: different questions, methods used to produce answers, audiences, and purposes. How do we make sense of this? What, if anything, connects all of this activity? Does it really add up to an independent and coherent field of study?

One way to bring the field of public policy into focus is to view it in the plural rather than the singular sense. Within a range of different orientations toward the study of public policy, it is possible to identify a rough and ready coherence. This starts with a central research question (or questions) and a set of associated explanatory frameworks built to guide the systematic search for answers to these questions. An example of how this can be done is provided in Table 1.1, which describes a series of different policy orientations, their core research questions, and related frameworks.[5]

We can tackle the field(s) of public policy by taking these various orientations on their own merits. The questions they pursue are undoubtedly important, and the frameworks generated to answer them orient research toward conclusions that can have important, real-world consequences. But is it possible to go further than this, to somehow connect these pieces into a larger picture of a coherent field that can take its place as a social science in its own right?

Most policy orientations can be traced to a common root, that of the policy sciences. Lasswell formulated the policy sciences as an independent field of study, but that vision simply collapsed under the weight of its own contradictions. Stitching the various orientations together into a coherent, independent field requires what neither Lasswell nor anyone thus far has managed to supply: general theories of public policy that are not bounded by space or time. Deservedly or not, public policy scholarship has gained a reputation for doing a poor job of constructing original theories, instead preferring to borrow bits and pieces from others when it proves useful or convenient to do so. In what follows we hope to achieve two primary goals. First, we seek to provide the reader with a guided tour of the particular fields of public policy studies as exemplified in Table 1.1. In particular, we want to illuminate the key research questions and the conceptual frameworks formulated to address them. In doing this we have the explicit aim

TABLE 1.1 Fields of Policy Study

Field of Policy Study	Representative Research Questions	Representative Conceptual Frameworks	Methodological Approach and Examples	Representative Disciplines
Policy and politics	Does politics cause policy, or policy cause politics?	Policy typologies Stages heuristic	Quantitative and qualitative classification (typology and taxonomy) Statistical analysis Case studies	Political science
Policy process	Why does government pay attention to some problems and not others? How are policy options formulated? Why does policy change?	Bounded rationality (and extensions) Multiple streams (garbage can models) Punctuated equilibrium Advocacy coalitions Diffusion theory Systems theory	Quantitative	Political science Economics/behavioral economics Psychology
Policy analysis	What should we do? What options exist to address a particular problem? What policy option should be chosen?	Welfare economics/utilitarianism Behavioral economics	Quantitative/formal/qualitative Cost analysis Forecasting Risk assessment Delphi technique	Political science Economics Public administration Policy specific subfields (education, health, etc.)

(continues)

TABLE 1.1 Fields of Policy Study (*continued*)

Field of Policy Study	Representative Research Questions	Representative Conceptual Frameworks	Methodological Approach and Examples	Representative Disciplines
Policy evaluation	What have we done? What impact did a particular program or policy have?	Program theory Research design frameworks Narrative policy frameworks	Quantitative/qualitative analysis Statistics Expert judgment	Political science Economics Public administration Policy specific subfields (education, health, etc.)
Policy design	How do people perceive problems and policies? How do policies distribute power, and why? Whose values are represented by policy? How does policy socially construct particular groups? Is there common ground to different policy stories and perspectives?	Discourse theory Hermeneutics	Qualitative analysis Text analysis	Political science Philosophy/theory Sociology
Policymakers and policymaking institutions	Who makes policy decisions? How do policymakers decide what to do? Why do they make the decisions they do?	Public choice Incrementalism	Formal theory Quantitative analysis	Political science Economics Public administration
Policy implementation	Why did a policy fail (or succeed)? How was a policy decision translated into action?	Bounded rationality Ad hoc Public management/governance theories	Quantitative analysis Qualitative analysis	Political science Economics Public administration Policy specific subfields

of countering the oft-made argument that those who study public policy have done little original work in theory. Second, in doing all of this we intend to equip readers with the tools necessary to make up their own minds about the present and future of the field (singular) of policy studies. Within particular orientations to studying public policy, we are fairly confident we can make a case for coherence. But is there any possibility that these orientations can be joined together into a comprehensive picture of an academic discipline? In other words, is there such a thing as a field of public policy studies?

Notes

1. The exceptions, though, are notable. Lasswell is the preeminent example of a policy scientist who moved easily between academia and government. In a more contemporary context, there is a handful of policy scholars whose work and willingness to advocate solutions to particular problems have had an enormous impact on shaping real-world policy. Examples are James Q. Wilson (crime), John Chubb and Terry Moe (education), and Milton Friedman (everything from the best way to staff the U.S. military to creating the basic economic policies of the entire country of Chile). See Pielke (2004) for a broader discussion of the pros and cons of a pure Lasswellian framework of the policy sciences.

2. Most chapters in this book hammer on this theme, so it is not being pursued in-depth here. This contrarian claim, though, can be backed by a few examples (all discussed in-depth elsewhere in the book): policy typologies, punctuated equilibrium, and the advocacy coalition framework. Although there are some notable black holes of theory in the policy world (e.g., implementation), other areas (e.g., policy process) encompass a number of systematic, comprehensive, and empirically testable frameworks. And policy scholars are constantly trying new theoretical lights to illuminate even the black holes. As discussed in Chapter 7, public management scholarship has recently reinvigorated implementation theory.

3. Except, of course, when that model *is* mainstream economics. Public choice, for example, applies the fundamental assumptions of economics (e.g., utility maximization, individual rationality) to the political world. Such approaches have been enormously influential in explaining "why government does what it does" (e.g., Buchanan and Tullock 1962; Niskanen 1971).

4. Over the years a number of our graduate students for whom English is not a native language have pushed us particularly hard to clearly distinguish politics from policy and have mostly been less than satisfied with our answers. Several of these students have stated that in their native languages there is no equivalent word for the concept of policy as it is employed in the political science policy literature.

5. Please note that this is intended to be a descriptive rather than an exhaustive table.

CHAPTER 2

Does Politics Cause Policy?
Does Policy Cause Politics?

As detailed in Chapter 1, the field of policy studies is often criticized for its theoretical poverty. Yet though conventional wisdom regards the policy sciences as contributing few explanatory frameworks that help us systematically understand the political and social world, we believe the evidence suggests otherwise. In fact, the policy sciences have produced at least two frameworks that continue to serve as standard conceptual tools to organize virtually the entire political world: policy typologies and the stages theory.

These two frameworks are generally remembered as theoretical failures, neither living up to its original promise because of the universal inability to separate fact and value in the political realm (typologies) or failing to be a causal theory at all (policy stages). These criticisms are, as we shall see, not without merit. Yet both of these frameworks suggest that the policy field conceives of its theoretical jurisdiction in very broad terms, and that even when its conceptual frameworks come up short, they leave a legacy of insight and understanding that helps organize and make sense of a complicated world.

The stages theory (or what many would more accurately term the stages *heuristic*) is perhaps the best-known framework of the policy process. Yet by most criteria it does not qualify as a good theory, because it is descriptive rather than causal and does little to explain why the process happens the way it does. Theodore Lowi's original notion of a policy typology was nothing less than a general theory of politics—it raised the possibility that the study of politics would become, in effect, a subdiscipline of the study of public policy. Lowi (1972) posited the startling possibility that policy caused politics, rather than the reverse causal pathway still assumed by most students of politics and policy. Typologies ultimately foundered on a set of operational difficulties, quickly identified but never fully resolved. For these reasons typologies and the stages heuristic, if anything, are more likely to be used as evidence of the theoretical shortcomings of policy studies than as evidence for its worthy contributions. Despite their problems, both are still employed to bring systematic coherence to a difficult and disparate field. And even though both are arguably "bad" in the sense that they do not live up to their original promise (typologies) or are not theory at all (stages heuristic), at a bare minimum they continue to help clarify what is being studied (the process of policymaking, the outcomes of policymaking), why it is important, and how systematic sense can be made of the subject. The general point made in this chapter is that if there is such a thing as a distinct field of policy studies, it must define itself by its ability to clarify its concepts and key questions and to contribute robust answers to those questions. This is what good theory does. And as two of the better-known "failures" in policy theory clearly demonstrate, the field of policy studies is not just attempting to achieve these ends; it is at least partially succeeding.

Good Policy Theory

What are the characteristics of a good theory, and what are the characteristics of a good theory of public policy? Lasswell's (1951b) notion of the policy sciences, with its applied problem orientation, its multidisciplinary background, and its call for complex conceptual frameworks, set a high bar for policy theory. Standing on a very diffuse academic foundation, it was not only expected to explain a lot, but also to literally solve democracy's biggest problems. It is little wonder that theory in public policy, when measured against this yardstick, is judged as falling short. Such expectations are perhaps the right goal to shoot for, but no conceptual framework in social science is going to live up to them.

Daniel McCool (1995c, 13–17) suggested that good theory in public policy should exhibit these characteristics: validity (an accurate representation of reality), economy, testability, organization/understanding (it imposes order), heuristic (it serves as a guidepost for further research), causal explanation, predictiveness, relevance/usefulness, powerfulness (it offers nontrivial inferences), reliability (it supports replication), objectivity, and honesty (it makes clear the role of values). The exhaustiveness of McCool's list makes it almost as ambitious as the burdens placed on policy theory by the Lasswellian vision. Getting any single theory to reflect all of these traits would present serious challenges in any discipline, let alone one attempting to describe the chaotic world of politics and the policy process. In fact, McCool readily admits it is highly unlikely that policy theory will contain all of these characteristics. Paul Sabatier has also provided extensive commentary on what constitutes "good" policy theory (1991b, 1997, 1999a, 2007a, 2007b). At a minimum, policy frameworks should be coherent and internally consistent, be causal in nature, generate falsifiable hypotheses, be subject to empirical testing, have some explanatory power, be broad in scope, and be "fertile" ground for research (Sabatier 2007a, 8; 2007b, 322).

Policy typologies and the stages heuristic certainly do not meet all the criteria set forth by McCool and Sabatier; as this chapter discusses, both lack key traits (e.g., the stages heuristic is not predictive; policy typologies arguably have reliability problems). Yet both frameworks reflect a majority of the intimidating list of theoretical ideals, both are attempts to make broad causal claims about the policy process, and both have proven to be fertile ground for commentary and research. As such, they continue to be used to make sense of the policy and political world.

Policy Stages: A First Attempt at Policy Theory

Given the broad scope of its studies and its vagueness about key concepts, a not inconsiderable challenge for policy theory is trying to figure out what it is trying to explain. Individual behavior? Institutional decision making? Process? In his "pre-view" of the policy sciences, Lasswell (1971, 1) argued that the primary objective was to obtain "knowledge *of* and *in* the decision processes of the public and civic order." For Lasswell, this knowledge takes the form of "systematic, empirical studies of how policies are made and put into effect" (1971, 1). Given this initial focus, policy process was an early focal point of theoretical work in the field. But where in the policy process do we start? What does the policy process look like? What exactly should we be observing when we are studying public policy? What is the unit of analysis?

Table 2.1 traces the lineage of what would become the stages model of the policy process. The similarities among the models should be evident. First a problem must come to the attention of the government. Policymakers then develop solutions to address the problem, ultimately implementing what they perceive as the most appropriate solution, and then evaluate whether or not it served its purpose.

For Lasswell (1971), the policy process was fundamentally about how policymakers make decisions. His initial attempt to model the policy process was based more generally on how best to model decision processes. Lasswell identified a set of phases common to any decision process: the recognition of a problem, the gathering of information and proposals to address the problem, and implementation of a proposal, followed by possible termination and then appraisal of the proposal. The seven stages listed in Table 2.1 were meant to descriptively capture this process as it applied to policy decisions.

Writing at roughly the same time as Lasswell, Charles Jones (1970) also placed a strong emphasis on examining the process of policymaking. The focus should not be solely on the outputs of the political system, but instead on the entire policy process, from how a problem is defined to how governmental actors respond to the problem to the effectiveness of a policy. This "policy" approach is an attempt to "describe a variety of processes designed to complete the policy cycle" (Jones 1970, 4). Although Lasswell identified what could be considered stages of the decision process, it is with Jones that we see the first attempt to model the process of public policy decisions. For Jones, the policy process could aptly be summarized by a distinct set of "elements" listed in Table 2.1.

Jones's focus on the elements of the policy process is very much in line with Lasswell's interest in "knowledge *of*" that process. The process begins with perception of a problem and ends with some sort of resolution or termination of the policy. Jones, however, moved the evaluation element, what Lasswell would describe as "appraisal," to immediately prior to the decision to terminate or adjust a policy. Because public problems are never "solved" (Jones 1970, 135), evaluations of the enacted policy must be done to best decide how to adjust the current policy to fit with existing demands. Jones went on to more broadly classify these ten elements as fitting within five general categories, which are meant to illustrate "what government does to act on public problems" (1970, 11).

The phases laid out by Lasswell and Jones conceptualize public policy as a linear decision-making process of linked stages that very much reflects a rationalist perspective: a problem is identified; alternative responses are considered; the

TABLE 2.1 The Evolution of Stages Theory

Policy Scholar	Proposed Stages Model
An Introduction to the Study of Public Policy Charles O. Jones (1970, 11–12)	*Elements* Perception Definition Aggregation/organization Representation Formulation Legitimation Application/administration Reaction Evaluation/appraisal Resolution/termination *Categories* Problem to government Action in government Government to problem Policy to government Problem resolution or change
A Pre-View of the Policy Sciences Harold D. Lasswell (1971, 28)	Intelligence Promotion Prescription Invocation Application Termination Appraisal
Public Policy-Making James E. Anderson (1974, 19)	Problem identification and agenda formation Formulation Adoption Implementation Evaluation
The Foundations of Policy Analysis Garry D. Brewer and Peter deLeon (1983, 18)	Initiation Estimation Selection Implementation Evaluation Termination
Policy Analysis in Political Science Randall B. Ripley (1985, 49)	Agenda setting Formulation and legitimation of goals and programs Program implementation Evaluation of implementation, performance, and impacts Decisions about the future of the policy and program

"best" is solution adopted; the impact of this solution is evaluated; and on the basis of this evaluation, the policy is continued, revised, or terminated. In laying out this linear progression Lasswell and Jones were essentially trying to describe the policy process and organize it into coherent and manageable terms. The "phases" or "elements" are merely descriptive terms they used for patterns regularly observed by policy scholars at the time.

The major advantage of the stages approach formulated by Lasswell and Jones, as well as contemporary stages models such as that proposed by James Anderson (1974), is that they provided an intuitive and practical means of conceptualizing and organizing the study of public policy. They provided a basic frame of reference to understand what the field of policy studies was about. Various refinements of the stages model have been offered, though all retain the basic formulation of a linear process, albeit in a continuous loop (e.g., Brewer and deLeon 1983; Ripley 1985). The common patterns are clearly evident in Table 2.1; they all portray public policy as a continuous process, in which problems are never solved, they are only addressed. Although different variations used different labels for the phases or stages, the fundamental model was always a rationalistic, problem-oriented, linear process in a continual loop. The stages models seemed to impose order and make intuitive sense of an incredibly complex process, but policy scholars were quick to identify their drawbacks, not the least of which was that they did not seem to be testable.

Stages Model: Descriptive or Predictive?

Critics have cited two main drawbacks of the stages approach. First, it tends to produce piecemeal theories for studying the policy process. Those interested in agenda setting focus on one set of policy research, whereas those interested in policy analysis focus on another, and those interested in policy implementation focus on yet another aspect of the process. In other words, the stages model divides rather than unites the field of policy studies, reducing the likelihood of producing a unifying theory of public policy. Such a view also tends to create the perception that the stages are disconnected from one another, or at least can be disconnected and studied in isolation, and that the policy process is best viewed as proceeding neatly between stages. This criticism is far from fatal. A unified model of public policy is a very tall order, and it is unlikely that viewing policy from the stages perspective is a major obstacle to developing such a theory. In the absence of a unifying theory, the stages model arguably creates an intuitive and useful division of labor for policy scholars, focusing on the construction of more manageable conceptual frameworks in specific stages, such as agenda setting or implementation. Still, the stages model ultimately can be said to suffer from the process it seeks to explain, in the sense that it encompasses so much that it has a hard time tying it all together. For example, variables that serve as significant predictors for some aspect of the policy process at one stage may be insignificant at another (Greenberg et al. 1977). Recent research provides empirical support for these sorts of clear distinctions between stages, with each stage likely to evoke different political considerations. To effectively model and predict policy change thus requires paying attention to the uniqueness of each stage of the policy process. So, for example, the causal variables and processes that might explain, say, policy adoption, are not necessarily transferable to policy implementation (Whitaker et al. 2012; see also Karch 2007). The purpose of the stages models was not to provide a list of explanatory variables for policy scholars, but rather to illuminate and provide structure for the variety of steps when moving from a problem to a policy output.

A second frequent criticism is that the stages approach assumes a linear model of policymaking, discounting the notion of feedback loops between stages or different starting points for the entire process (deLeon 1999b, 23). Again, we do not see this as a fatal flaw in the stages model. If the process is continuous, disagreements over starting points and feedback loops are all but unavoidable. The most damaging criticism, especially for a conceptual model arising from the policy sciences, was the claim that the stages model was not particularly scientific. The basis of any scientific theory is the production of empirically falsifiable hypotheses. What are the hypotheses that come from the stages model? What hypothesis can we test about how a problem reaches the government agenda? What hypothesis can we test about the alternative that will be selected for implementation? What hypothesis can we test about policy evaluation? These questions point to the fundamental flaw in the stages model as a theory of public policy—it is not really a theory at all. It is a descriptive classification of the policy process; it says what happens without saying anything about why it happens. Paul Sabatier (1991a, 145) has written that the stages model "is not really a causal theory at all . . . [with] no coherent assumptions about what forces are driving the process from stage to stage and very few falsifiable hypotheses." In fact, Sabatier (1991b, 147) refers to the stages approach as the "stages heuristic." A scientific study of public policy should allow for hypothesis testing about relationships between variables in the policy process. This is *the* central failing for many policy scholars: because the stages model does not really generate any hypotheses to test, it renders the whole framework little more than a useful example of what a bad theory of policy looks like. But does this warrant complete rejection of the model? Does the stages model contribute nothing to our understanding of the policy process?

The stages heuristic or stages model is useful for its simplicity and direction. It provides policy researchers with a broad and generalizable outline of the policy process as well as a way of organizing policy research. Good policy theory should be generalizable and broad in scope (Sabatier 2007a). The stages model fits these criteria. Because of the stages approach, we also know what makes up what Peter deLeon (1999b, 28) referred to as the "parts" of the policy process. In fact, within the field of academic policy research, scholarly interest tends to break down along the stages model. There is a definitive research agenda that focuses on problem definition and how a policy problem reaches the decision-making and government agenda, often referred to as the agenda-setting literature (Cobb and Elder 1983; Nelson 1984; Baumgartner and Jones 1993/2009; Kingdon 1995; Stone 2002). Another research agenda focuses on policy implementation and evaluation (Fischer 1995). For this group of scholars, the key question is: What should we do? A third group of researchers is more broadly interested in how policies change over time and what causes significant breaks from existing policies (Carmines and Stimson 1989; Baumgartner and Jones 1993/2009; Jones and Baumgartner 2005). And still another group is interested in the effects of policy design on citizen attitudes and behavior (Schneider and Ingram 1997).

The burgeoning literature in each of these stages has no doubt contributed immensely to our understanding of various aspects of the policy process. In fact Paul Sabatier, a prominent critic of the utility of the stages model for studying public policy (see Jenkins-Smith and Sabatier 1993; Sabatier 2007a), has credited the work of Nelson (1984) and Kingdon (1995) as evidence of theory testing within public policy (Sabatier 1991a, 145). In other words, there are useful theories within each stage of the stages approach (see also Chapter 1, Table 1.1). Although the stages approach may lack falsifiability, it continues to provide *a* (perhaps *the*) major conceptualization of the scope of public policy studies and a handy means of organizing and dividing labor in the field. We venture to guess that most introductory graduate seminars in public policy include Baumgartner and Jones (1993/2009), Jenkins-Smith and Sabatier (1993), Kingdon (1995), Schneider and Ingram (1997), and Stone (2002), as well as some readings in policy evaluation and analysis. In short, the stages heuristic has organized the discipline for researchers and students and continues to do so.

From a Kuhnian perspective, the stages model remains viable. As Kuhn (1970) has argued, "paradigms" are not completely rejected until a new replacement paradigm is presented. A universal replacement theory of the policy process is still lacking. Completely discarding the stages model ignores the organizational benefits it has provided. The various stages frameworks shown in Table 2.1 have helped to clarify the "how" of Lasswell's emphasis on "how policies are made and put into effect." Although the nominal conception of the stages of the model varies ever so slightly among researchers, there is a great deal of substantive commonality. Moreover, most process scholars agree that the stages model is a useful analytical tool for studying the policy process, even if they differ over the labeling of the stages. Given such widespread agreement, any new model of the policy process will most likely retain some aspects of the stages approach.

The Lasswellian approach placed a strong emphasis on developing complex models capable of explaining the policy process, and the stages model represents one of the first comprehensive conceptual frameworks constructed with that goal in mind. Although critics argue that the stages approach provides little in terms of testable hypotheses, it does provide an organizing function for the study of public policy. The stages model has rationally divided labor within the field of public policy. Because of the stages approach, policy scholars know what to look for in the policy process, where it starts, and where it ends (at least temporarily). The "policy sciences" were first and foremost about bringing the scientific process into the study of public policy. Good theories simplify the phenomena they seek to explain. The policy process consists of numerous actors at various levels of government from different disciplinary backgrounds with different training and levels of knowledge on any given policy. These actors converge throughout the process, making decisions that affect future policy analyses. Yet despite such overwhelming complexity, the stages model provides a way for policy researchers to conceptualize the process of policymaking.

Thinking back to McCool's elements of good theory, the stages model actually does quite well. It is economical, provides an organizing function, is a heuristic, is useful, is reliable, is objective, and is powerful both in the sense of guiding the study of the policy process and in the effect it has had on the field of public policy. What the researcher must decide is where simplification actually inhibits testability and predictability and whether to discard the theory or to make adjustments. To date, the scholarly record suggests the stages model has been discarded without any adjustments or a replacement.

Another "Theory" of Public Policy: Policy Typologies

The stages model conceives of public policy as the product of the linear progression of political events. Problems are put on the agenda, there is debate over potential solutions, legislatures adopt alternatives on the basis of practical or partisan favor, bureaucracies implement them, and some impact is felt on the real world. The stages model says nothing about what types of policies are being produced by this process and what their differences might mean for politics.

Theodore Lowi, a political scientist, was interested in examining what types of policies were being produced by the policy process and what effect those policies had on politics. For Lowi, the questions were: What is the output of the policy process, and what does that tell us about politics? Lowi was frustrated by what he perceived to be an inability or lack of interest among policy scholars in distinguishing between types of outputs. Prior to Lowi's work, policy outputs were treated uniformly as an outcome of the political system. No attempt was made to determine if the process changed for different types of policies, let alone whether the types of policies determined specific political patterns. A single model of public policymaking was assumed to apply to all types of policy (Lowi 1970). Such overgeneralizations, argued Lowi, led to incomplete inferences about the policy process and more broadly, about the relationship between public policy and politics.

Prior to Lowi's work, the relationship between politics and policy was assumed to be linear and causal; politics determine policies. Lowi (1972, 299), however, argued for the reverse, that "policies determine politics." At a very basic level, public policy is an attempt to influence individual behavior; in short, "government coerces" (Lowi 1972, 299). When classified into general categories, such coercion allows for testable predictions about political behavior. By identifying the type of coercion, it is possible to predict the type of politics that would follow. Lowi developed a 2 x 2 matrix of government coercion based on its target (individual versus environment) and likelihood of actually being employed (immediate versus remote) (1972, 300). Where the coercion is applicable to the individual, politics will be more decentralized; where coercion is applicable to the environment, politics will be more centralized. Where the likelihood of coercion is immediate, politics will be more conflictual, with high levels of bargaining. Where the likelihood of coercion is more remote, politics will be less conflictual, with high levels of logrolling. As Lowi (1970, 320) observed, "each kind of coercion may very well be associated with a quite distinctive political process."

Lowi used his matrix to create a typology that put all policies into one of four categories: distributive policy, regulative policy, redistributive policy, and constituent policy. Table 2.2 provides an adapted model of Lowi's (1972, 300) policy typology framework. The policies and resulting politics in Table 2.2 are based on Lowi's observations about federal-level policies from the 1930s through the 1950s. Looking across the rows in Table 2.2, one can see that each policy provides a set of expectations about politics. Each policy category, Lowi (1972) argued, amounted to an "arena of power," and he saw policies as the predictable outcome of a regular subsystem of actors. Thus if one knows the policy type, it is possible to predict the nature of political interactions between actors in the subsystem. The expectations that policy actors have about policies determine the type of political relationships between actors (Lowi 1964). Lowi described his "scheme" in the following way:

1. The types of relationships to be found among people are determined by their expectations.
2. In politics, expectations are determined by governmental outputs or policies.
3. Therefore, a political relationship is determined by the type of policy at stake, so that for every policy there is likely to be a distinctive type of political relationship. (Lowi 1964, 688)

TABLE 2.2 Lowi's Policy Typologies and Resulting Politics

Policy Type	Likelihood/ Applicability of Coercion	Type of Politics	Congress	President
Distributive	Remote/ Individual	Consensual Stable Logrolling	Strong Little floor activity	Weak
Redistributive	Immediate/ Environment	Stable Bargaining	Moderate Moderate floor activity	Strong
Regulatory	Immediate/ Individual	Conflictual Unstable Bargaining	Strong High floor activity	Moderate
Constituent	Remote/ Environment	Consensual Stable Logrolling	N/A	N/A

Lowi's basic argument was that if one could identify the type of policy under consideration—in other words, if one could classify a policy into a particular cell in his 2 x 2 table—one could predict the type of politics likely to follow. As others have argued (see Kellow 1988), Lowi's model is theoretically similar to the work of E. E. Schattschneider (1965). For Schattschneider, policy and politics are interrelated. How a policy is defined has the potential to "expand the scope of conflict," bringing more groups of people into the policy process, thus shaping politics. Lowi observed that certain types of policy tend to mobilize political actors in predictable patterns. The utility of the typology framework is the ease with which it allows for hypothesis testing. Policies are assumed to fit neatly within one of four boxes of coercion, each generating distinct predictions about the type of politics.

Table 2.2 shows that distributive policies are characterized by an ability to distribute benefits and costs on an individual basis. For such policies, "the indulged and deprived, the loser and the recipient, need never come into direct confrontation" (Lowi 1964, 690). Lowi cites tariffs, patronage policies, and traditional "pork barrel" programs as primary examples of distributive policy. Because coercion is more remote with distributive policies, the politics tends to be relatively consensual. The costs of such policies are spread evenly across the population and as such lead to logrolling and agreement between the president and Congress. Congress tends to dominate the process, with the president often playing a relatively passive role.

Redistributive policies target a much broader group of people. These policies, such as welfare, social security, Medicare, Medicaid, and even income tax, determine the "haves and have-nots" (Lowi 1964, 691). The politics of redistributive policies tend to be more active than distributive policies, because the likelihood of coercion is immediate, resulting in more floor activity, with the president taking a slightly stronger role than Congress. Redistributive politics are also characterized by a high level of bargaining between large groups of people. Although such bargaining is relatively consensual, because it takes place between larger groups of people than with distributive policies, there is a greater potential for conflict.

Regulatory policies are aimed at directly influencing the behavior of a specific individual or group of individuals through the use of sanctions or incentives. The purpose of regulatory policies is to increase the costs of violating public laws. Examples are policies regulating market competition, prohibiting unfair labor practices, and ensuring workplace safety (Lowi 1972, 300). Regulatory policies, because the likelihood of coercion is more immediate and applicable to the individual, tend to result in more conflictual politics than either distributive or redistributive policies. These policies also tend to be characterized by a high level of bargaining and floor activity, often leading to numerous amendments (Lowi 1972, 306). As would be expected, groups tend to argue over who should be the target and incur the costs of government coercion. The result is "unstable" or more combative and divisive politics than is typically observed with distributive or redistributive policies. Commenting on the history of public policy in the United States, Lowi argued that these classifications follow a linear pattern: distributive policies dominated the nineteenth and early twentieth centuries, followed by an increase in regulatory policies as a result of the rise in business and labor, followed by an increase in redistributive policies as a result of the Great Depression and the inability of state governments to cope with national crises.

Lowi's fourth category, constituent policy, is arguably less clear than the others. It was not considered at all in his original typology formulation (1964), but is included in subsequent work to fill in the empty fourth cell (Lowi 1970, 1972). Lowi provides no empirical evidence regarding the role of Congress and the president in debating constituent policy. Therefore, we have left these boxes blank in Table 2.2. However, from the examples Lowi (1972, 300) uses (reapportionment, setting up a new agency, and propaganda), and the applicability and likelihood of coercion, we are left to assume that such policies are low salience and result in consensual politics. Little has been done to clarify constituent policies; they seem to be a miscellaneous category that includes everything not in the original three classifications.

Following Lowi, James Q. Wilson constructed his own typology framework using a similar assumption about the relationship between policy and politics. The political atmosphere is defined by people's expectations about the costs and benefits of a policy; "the perceived costs and benefits shape *the way* politics is carried on" (Wilson 1983, 419). Wilson's classification matrix, a 2 x 2 structure based on whether costs and benefits are broadly distributed or concentrated, defines four categories of *politics*, rather than policy: majoritarian, entrepreneurial, client, and interest group. Majoritarian politics, in which costs and benefits of a policy are perceived to be distributed, are best represented by social security policy. Entrepreneurial politics arise when perceived benefits of a policy are distributed but the costs are concentrated, such as antipollution policies and safety regulations for automobiles (Wilson 1983). "Since the incentive is strong to organize for opposition of the policy," an entrepreneur, or salient political actor, is required to squelch such opposition achieve policy passage (Wilson 1980, 370). Client politics occur when the perceived benefits are concentrated and the costs distributed, as in politics surrounding farm subsidies and "pork barrel" projects (Wilson 1983, 421). Finally, interest group politics are most likely to occur when both the perceived benefits and costs of a policy are concentrated. Such policies lead to a high level of bargaining and conflict between interest groups (Wilson 1983).

The typology framework was an attempt to redefine how policy and political scientists conceptualize the process of policymaking. Moreover, it was a bold attempt to put the discipline of public policy at the forefront of the study of politics. The framework posited that politics can only really be understood from the perspective of public policy. Lowi was frustrated by what he perceived as two general problems with existing research: 1) that the study of public policy to that point had treated policy outputs uniformly, with no effort to distinguish between types of policy; and 2) a general acceptance among policy and political scientists that the president dominated the political process. The typology framework suggests otherwise on both fronts. In fact, it is only in redistributive policies that the president tends to have a stronger role than the Congress; Lowi further argued that the role of the president is conditional on whether the president is "strong" or "weak" (1972, 308).

Lowi's typology framework was also a departure from the Lasswellian approach to public policy. In fact, the notion that "policies determine politics" turns the "policy sciences for democracy" argument on its head. Instead of studying public policy to improve the political system, public policy should be studied because it will help to predict the type of politics displayed in the political system. The normative aspect in the Lasswellian approach, however, is not completely absent. Rather, Lowi argued that the ability to predict the type of politics from a particular policy should give policy and political scientists a framework for determining what type of policies will succeed and what type will fail. Such a framework "reaches to the very foundation of democratic politics and the public interest" (Lowi 1972, 308). Thus we can say that the typologies contribute to the policy sciences by providing an additional method for improving public policy.

Typologies as Non-Mutually Exclusive Categories

If politics is a function of policy type, then classifying policies is crucial for making accurate inferences about politics. For any classification to be useful, the categories must be inclusive and mutually exclusive (McCool 1995b, 174–175). If policies can be objectively classified in such a fashion, then Lowi's notion of policy typologies becomes a testable theory of politics. And if it is correct, then specific patterns of political behavior and predictable power relationships should be observed to vary systematically across different policy types. This turns out to be the big weakness of the typology framework: the key independent variable (policy type) needs to be clearly operationalized to have a useful and predictive model of politics. For Lowi, policy classification was easy. If a policy distributes costs broadly, with controllable benefits, it is most likely distributive. If coercion is directed at specific individuals, it is regulative. If it distributes benefits broadly across social groups, it is redistributive. Most policies, however, do not fit neatly within a single category. This critique has plagued the typology framework since its inception.

Because Lowi gave scant attention to the actual classification of each policy type, scholars argue that his framework was doomed from the start. Take, for example, a bill proposing to increase the sales tax on cigarettes. At face value, this is clearly a regulatory policy. But if the added revenue from the tax goes toward health care or public education, then it becomes a redistributive policy. A higher tax on cigarettes is also meant to reduce the number of smokers in the general population as well as the effects of secondhand smoke. From this perspective, the bill is a public health issue and would most likely result in relatively consensual politics—the type associated with distributive and constituent policies. This is not an exceptional case; most policies can be reasonably argued to fit into more than one category. Yet from Lowi's framework, we see widely varying predictions regarding the type of politics surrounding such a bill. This creates a fundamental problem for formulating falsifiable hypotheses. What type of politics we can expect from a (fill in the blank) bill depends on whom you ask. In the example provided here, Lowi's model gives us three outcomes.

The point is that without a clear set of criteria for identifying policies, the typology framework is of little use (see Kjellberg 1977). If policy actors come to different conclusions about the type of policy under consideration, predicting politics becomes difficult if not impossible. Greenberg and colleagues (1977) provide the most systematic and sharpest critique of the typology framework, calling for a more diverse and non-positivist approach to public policy. For this group of authors, Lowi's model is too simplistic; it ignores the complexity of the policy process, namely that multiple actors will tend to view a particular policy through multiple lenses. Policy scholars should view public policy as a continuous process with multiple outputs; predicting politics depends on what output is being studied.

Policy should be broken down into smaller units or key decisions, what Greenberg and colleagues label "points of first significant controversy" and "points of last significant controversy" (1977, 1542). Both provide focal points for policy researchers, and the latter are useful for classifying policy type.

Steinberger (1980) agrees with Greenberg and colleagues (1977) about the need for accounting for multiple participants, but takes the argument a step further by suggesting that positivist methodology is simply inadequate to deal with the subjectivity of the policy process. Instead, a phenomenological approach is required. Policy actors attach different meanings to policy proposals according to their own beliefs, values, norms, and life experiences. To account for such variation requires a more intersubjective or constructivist approach to the study of public policy. This requires accounting for the multiple dimensions of policy, namely substantive impact, political impact, scope of impact, exhaustibility, and tangibility (Steinberger 1980). Presumably such dimensions are regularly assessed by policy analysts. But at the heart of the phenomenological approach is the notion that each person has a different set of values. Complicating Steinberger's argument is the expansion of policy types from three in Lowi's original model to eleven. Policies can fall into one or more categories with crosscutting dimensions. Although this expands the realm of classification, it does little to provide a parsimonious model of policy classification; indeed, it moves the whole typology project out of the rationalist framework and pushes it into post-positivist territory, where subjective perception takes precedence over a single objective reality.[1] In fact, Steinberger admits that "the range of possibilities is obviously enormous" (193). This also means prediction becomes a post hoc exercise, possible only when we know how specific actors subjectively classify a particular policy proposal.

That policy actors potentially view the same bill differently presents a serious problem for the typology framework. Whereas Greenberg and colleagues and Steinberger are right to argue that multiple actors will tend to have varying expectations about a single proposal, their solutions muddy the waters of analysis. In addition to assessing the substantive, cost-benefit impact of public policy, analysts would now also play the role of policy psychologist. Not only does this present a problem in terms of identifying the key independent variable in Lowi's model, but it also raises doubts about whether objective empirical research on policy classification is even possible.

Concern about the utility of Lowi's model came to a head in the late 1980s. A series of articles published in *Policy Studies Journal* demonstrated the enormity of this debate. Working within Lowi's framework, Spitzer (1987) saw a way out of the problems documented by Greenberg and colleagues and others. Rather than adding typologies, Spitzer revised existing ones. Like others, Spitzer recognized that many policies do not fit neatly within one of Lowi's four categories. To accommodate such cases, Spitzer placed a diagonal line through each policy typology to distinguish between "pure" and "mixed" cases. Pure cases were those that fit clearly within Lowi's original framework, whereas mixed cases were those that generally followed the pattern described by Lowi but also shared characteristics of other types of policy. The result was ten categories of public policy.[2]

Spitzer's article provoked a sharp reply from Kellow (1988). For him, the distinguishing trait of good theory is simplicity. Spitzer's model added unneeded complexity to Lowi's original framework. As Kellow noted, "the simpler and more powerful the theory the better" (1988, 714). Rather than adding categories, Kellow revised Lowi's model in accordance with the work by James Q. Wilson (1983, 1980, 1973b, Chapter 16) discussed previously. Rather than defining policy types according to the likelihood and applicability of coercion, they were defined according to the distribution of costs and benefits. Regulatory policy was divided into public and private interest regulatory policy, and constituent policy was dropped in Kellow's revisions.[3] Simplification was critical to preventing "an infinite parade of subcategories" (Kellow 1988, 722).

The problems with Lowi's original typology are numerous and have been well documented: it is not testable, it is not predictive, it is too simplistic (the categories are not mutually exclusive), it is post hoc, it does not provide causal explanation, and it does not account for the dynamic aspect of the policy process. The differences among Greenberg and colleagues, Steinberger, Spitzer, and others who question Lowi's typology (see Kjellberg 1977; Kellow 1988) tend to revolve around the inclusiveness of Lowi's model. Is the model too simplistic? Should future researchers work around or within the original four typologies? Sharp disagreement over these questions also prompted an important exchange between Kellow and Spitzer. Rather than continuing to press the criteria for classification, however, the debate appears to have settled on the question of epistemology. Spitzer (1989) advocates a Kuhnian and inductive approach to policy studies. The "tough" cases ignored by Kellow are critical to the theory-building process (532). Spitzer (1989) further criticizes Kellow on the grounds that his theory is not a theory at all but rather a tautological attempt to preserve Lowi's original framework. If, as Kellow observed, policy proposals determine politics, but political actors can manipulate the expectations surrounding those proposals, then does it not follow that policy proposals determine politics, which determine policy proposals? For Kellow (1989) the tough cases cited by Spitzer and others as creating problems for models of policy classification do not warrant a revision of the theory. In fact, Kellow is skeptical of the inductive and behavioralist approach attributed to Spitzer. Lowi's model provides a theory, a frame of reference for looking for supporting observations. Cases that do not fit neatly within one of Lowi's four categories simply represent limitations of the model; they do not warrant a paradigm shift.

This leaves policy studies in a bit of a dilemma. Did Lowi give policy studies a new paradigm from which to view the relationship between policy and politics? Or, because his model fails the classic Popperian test of falsifiability, is the typology framework useless? Many have come to the latter conclusion, consigning policy typologies to the same category as the stages model. It is a handy way to impose order on a complex topic, a good heuristic for compactly conveying information in the classroom and on the page, but it's not really an explanatory framework that is going to advance the field. Yet the typology framework does contain some attributes of good policy theory.

Public policy is often criticized for being devoid of generalizable and "ambitious" theory (Hill 1997). It is difficult to make that claim for the typology framework, which was nothing if not bold. The proposition that "policies determine politics" essentially renders the study of politics a subfield of public policy. In many ways, the typology framework is a victim of its own ambition. On the one hand, it was an attempt to redefine the relationship between politics and policy. On the other hand, it was an attempt to introduce an important but overlooked independent variable in the study of public policy. Lowi's typology framework also fits with Lasswell's emphasis on developing testable "models." The typology framework essentially gives us four different models about the relationship between policy and politics. By Lowi's (1972, 299) own admission, "Finding different manifestations or types of a given phenomena is the beginning of orderly control and prediction." Policy typologies give us a distinct set of "variables" for testing theories about the policy process (Lowi 1972, 299). Given a type of policy, we can make predictions about the type of politics that is likely to ensue. If such predictions do not hold up to rigorous testing, that is a cue that a paradigm shift is warranted or at least can be expected. A null hypothesis that fails to be disproven still contributes to scientific knowledge.

Ultimately, if the methodological issues surrounding policy classification are resolved—and we recognize that this is a big "if"—the generalizability of the framework is still possible. Lowi's framework did not fail because its first principles did not fit together logically or because it was empirically falsified; it has been kept in suspended animation because no one has figured out how to objectively and empirically classify policies into types. If that problem can be overcome, the framework may yet prove to be a new paradigm for understanding politics. Most are rightly skeptical about objective classification, though there are still periodic attempts to do this, and they have been met with at least some success (Smith 2002). The typology framework is still subject to robust empirical testing, suggesting there is still potential for progress in this area.

Where Do We Go from Here?

Valid theoretical frameworks are "subject to a fair amount of empirical testing" (Sabatier 2007a, 8). The stages model would seem to fail this test. The last major evolution of the model occurred with Ripley in 1985. The typology framework fares only slightly better. Scholars continue to utilize the typology framework as a model for explaining how policy affects politics (see Cook 2010; Mondou and Montpetit 2010), but such developments have left unresolved the classification dilemma. Indeed, more journal space has been devoted to criticizing the typology framework; the last major attempt at revision involved a sharp exchange between Spitzer and Kellow in 1989, and Smith (2002) has called for a shift to a taxonomic (as opposed to typological) approach to policy classification. The emphasis on policy classification, though justified, has slowed theory development. Brian Cook notes that "the focus should instead be on how policy ideas shape policymaker expectations and the patterns of politics that result, especially which types of political actors are empowered" (2010, 483).

The typology framework and stages model both provide a way of organizing the field (one regarding policy process, the other regarding policy outputs), but not without serious shortcomings in causality, testability, falsifiability, and predictability. The real dilemma for policy theory is whether it should be held to the same standards as theory in the natural or hard sciences. Paul Sabatier has written extensively on the need for "better theories" of public policy. For him, the path to better theories is most likely to be characterized by a mix of inductive and deductive approaches (Sabatier 2007b). Policy theories should be broad in scope and attempt to develop causal relationships. Most policy theories, including Lowi's typologies and the stages heuristic, fall short of scientific theory or are inadequate in ways that prevent systematic testing (Sabatier 2007b). For the typology framework, the problem lies with the operationalization of the key independent variable. The problem with the stages heuristic is that it presents an untestable and non-falsifiable model. Greenberg and colleagues (1977, 1543) conclude that policy theory "should be parsimonious to be sure, but not oversimplified." Both the stages heuristic and policy typologies appear to have fallen into the trap of oversimplifying the policy process at the expense of rigorous scientific theory. The stages approach ignores institutions and critical individual actors such as policy specialists and advocacy groups, as well as systemic characteristics such as political feasibility, all of which can affect the policy process in varying ways. All are assumed to be static in the stages model. Policy typologies ignore the complexity of policy content as well as the fact that the causal arrow can flow in both directions. That is, political actors may attempt to shape the content of public policy as a way to shape the ensuing political debate. Both the stages model and policy typologies also fall short of the Lasswellian call for improving the quality of public policy. The stages model is simply a descriptive model of the policy process, and despite Lowi's claim, the typology framework does not give us any sense of how to improve policy outputs. Good policy research includes substantive policy information that can potentially be used by policy practitioners (Sabatier 1991b). Neither the stages model nor the typology framework does this.

Does the field of public policy have a unifying theoretical framework? The answer is no. Has the field attempted to create such unifying frameworks? The answer is yes. The stages model and policy typologies, for all their inherent flaws, do provide a broad conceptualization of public policy and what public policy scholars should be doing. The paradox of the stages model is that while most scholars argue it lacks testable hypotheses, they also agree on the basic framework: problems must come to the attention of government before they can be addressed, alternatives are debated, and the best option is selected and then implemented, with the implemented policy being subject to evaluation and revision. The same holds for the typology framework. Whereas critics of Lowi argue that most policies do not fit neatly within one of his three (or four) categories, they agree that most policies share such characteristics. Moreover, policies that are "pure" cases do tend to be characterized by the politics predicted in Lowi's original model (Spitzer 1987). Lowi (1988, 725) himself wrote that the original typology framework outlined in his 1964 book review should be seen "not for what it accomplished but for what it started." The complexity of the policy process as well as policy content most likely means that any theory of public policy will continually be subject to revision. This is not meant to detract from the quality of such theories; it is simply recognition of the nature of the unit of analysis. The utility of the stages model and typology framework is that they both show what not to do while also contributing to the field of policy studies. The number of books and journal pages devoted to both topics are a testament to their effect on the field. In the final analysis, most policy scholars view these frameworks more as historical artifacts than as theoretical tools to guide research, and with some justification.

Notes

1. This sort of post-positivist approach has been used to construct some useful alternate typologies of politics and public policy. See, for example, Schneider and Ingram 1997, 109.

2. Ten rather than eight, because regulatory policy is further subdivided between economic and social regulation, resulting in four types of regulative policy.

3. Policy with widely distributed costs and benefits was labeled redistributive policy; policy with widely dispersed costs and narrow benefits was labeled distributive; policy with narrow costs and widely dispersed benefits was labeled public interest regulatory; and policy with narrow costs and narrow benefits was labeled private interest regulatory (Kellow 1988, 718).

CHAPTER 3

Who Makes Decisions? How Do They Make Decisions? Actors and Institutions

At a fundamental level, public policy is the study of decision making. Public policies, after all, represent choices backed by the coercive powers of the state. Who makes these decisions and why they make the decisions they do have always been important research questions for policy scholars.

How are decisions explained by policy scholars? Broadly speaking, policy studies has borrowed heavily from rational choice theory to explain decision making. In the ideal rationalist world, policy choices would be made objectively and efficiently. Policymakers would identify a problem; search though all possible alternatives for addressing the problem, weighing the pros and cons of each; and select the most efficient and effective solution. Most policy scholars, though, recognize such a model of decision making is wildly unrealistic, falling short of the rational ideal for at least two reasons, one political and one practical. On the political dimension, citizens tend to want immediate solutions to policy dilemmas. This compresses the time horizons of policymakers, limiting not just the time but also their ability to marshal the other resources needed (labor, information, etc.) to make fully rational decisions. On the practical dimension, the sheer complexity of most policy issues and the limited cognitive capacity of humans makes fully rational decision making virtually impossible. This does not mean that policy decisions are irrational. Many policy scholars agree that policymakers at least intend to be rational; that is, their decision making is goal oriented, and they make choices with the intent of achieving those goals (be they personal, political, practical, or some combination thereof).

The assumption of at least intended rationality fits well with the Lasswellian notion of the problem orientation of public policy. If the purpose of policy is to solve problems, then the rational choice framework, with its focus on systematically linking means to desired ends, is an attractive model to help explain public policy decision making. As rational choice theory is predicated on the notion of methodological individualism, it sets up the study of decision making in public policy as the study of how individuals make choices. Yet individuals do not make choices, especially choices about public policy, in a vacuum wherein self-interest is allowed free rein. There are strong expectations that public policy will be made to advance the public interest, not just the individual interests of the decision maker. What might cause policymakers to ignore their own self-interest in favor of producing better public policy? For some the answer rests with institutions. Institutional rules shape policy decisions and can solve collective-action dilemmas that emerge from a rational choice framework. By changing institutional arrangements, such as rules and norms, it is possible to change individual behavior (see, for example, Ostrom, Gardner, and Walker 1994). If public organizations are producing inefficient or ineffective policy, then one solution is to redesign the institution. In the end, it is not the individual policy actor or the institution that shapes public policy; both dictate decision making in the public policy process.

Bounded Rationality and Incrementalism

Herbert Simon's seminal work *Administrative Behavior* (1947) has for more than sixty years provided a foundation for understanding how policy choices are made. At the core of Simon's theory is the notion that people are not completely rational actors, but instead are limited by cognitive and environmental constraints. Policy actors do not operate with complete information or engage in exhaustive cost-benefit analyses when making policy decisions. Instead, they make compromises, adapting to the situation at hand.

For Simon, complete rationality is unattainable for three reasons:

1. Rationality requires a complete knowledge and anticipation of the consequences that will follow each choice. In fact, knowledge of consequences is always temporary.
2. Because these consequences lie in the future, imagination must supply the lack of experienced feeling in attaching value to them. But values can be only imperfectly anticipated.
3. Rationality requires a choice among all possible alternative behaviors. In actual behavior, only a very few of these ever come to mind. (Simon 1997, 93–94).

In short, "it is impossible for the behavior of a single, isolated individual to reach any high degree of rationality" (Simon 1997, 92). Organizational constraints, time constraints, and cognitive limitations all prevent decision makers from making fully rational decisions.

If decision makers are limited by their cognitive abilities, then how do they go about making decisions? For Simon, decision making is best characterized by what is known as "bounded rationality." The basic tenet of bounded rationality is that humans intended to be rational but are prevented from behaving in a fully rational manner by cognitive limitations. Memory, attention span, information-processing capabilities, and so forth all limit a person's ability to achieve complete rationality. Instead, the information search is incomplete, and people choose among options that are not completely optimal but are good enough for the situation (Simon 1947). Such behavior Simon has labeled "satisficing." According to Simon, satisficing allows policymakers to make decisions that, although not completely rational, are capable of solving the issue at hand. In other words, policymakers make the best decision given the situation. Importantly, this allows policymakers to make "good enough" public policy decisions.

Simon (1985) contrasted the debate between complete and bounded rationality as one between "substantive" and "procedural" rationality. Substantive rationality assumes the tenets of complete rationality as conceived in economics: people have complete information before making a decision, weighing the costs and benefits of all alternatives. Bounded rationality, by contrast, is best characterized as "procedural" rationality, most closely associated with the field of cognitive psychology (Simon 1985, 295; see also Jones 2001). People are limited in their mental abilities to process incoming information. This in turn limits their ability to conduct comprehensive informational searches when considering policy alternatives or the goals of a particular policy. Procedural rationality implies that policymakers rely on mental shortcuts when processing incoming information. Instead of starting fresh with each new problem, policymakers relate new problems to existing ones, drawing on existing solutions rather than starting from scratch. More recently, the field of behavioral economics has documented how tendencies to depart from complete rationality follow predictable patterns (Ariely 2009; Kahneman 2011), a topic we discuss more extensively in Chapters 9 and 10.

That people are bounded when making decisions, however, does not imply an absence of intention. From an economic perspective, irrationality is defined as a lack of consistent preferences. Simon was explicit about the fact that "bounded rationality is not irrationality" (see Simon 1985, 297). Bounded rationality, unlike what Simon described as irrationality, consists of goal-oriented behavior. People "usually have reasons for what they do" (Simon 1985, 297). Decision makers strive for and achieve rationality; it is just a degree that falls short of "substantive" rationality. So, although policymakers may not be what most people picture as the ideal decision makers, they are still capable of making rational decisions. That is, they are still capable of making good policy decisions. Shortly after Simon's groundbreaking work on bounded rationality (1947, 1955), Charles Lindblom (1959) applied these concepts directly to the study of public policymaking. According to Lindblom, rather than engaging in a rational and comprehensive updating of specific policies, policymakers "muddle through," making policy decisions based on small changes from existing policies. In other words, policymakers address each new policy problem from the perspective of what has been done in the past. Lindblom argued that both cognitive and situational constraints prevent policymakers from articulating clearly defined goals and conducting a wide and comprehensive search for alternatives. Rather, the policymaking process is best characterized by small, incremental adjustments, a model of policymaking that became known as "incrementalism."

Incremental decision making allows policymakers to process incoming information more quickly and deal with the complexity of many policy issues. As for Simon, decision making for Lindblom is governed by cognitive and environmental constraints—policymakers do not consider the full range of alternatives prior to making a decision, instead relying on heuristics that limit the information search. "Incrementalism," as conceptualized by Lindblom, is simply "satisficing" in practice. Like Simon, Lindblom saw a disconnect between the assumptions of substantive rationality, or the rational-comprehensive model of decision making, and the reality of decision making. Policymakers lack the temporal, financial, and mental resources to explore all policy alternatives. Because it is impossible to know all the viable policy options and their consequences, policymakers tend to seek agreement where it can be found. In most cases, this occurs when policymakers make incremental, as opposed to comprehensive, changes to existing policies.

Lindblom clarified this difference by distinguishing between the "root" and "branch" methods of policy decision making (1959, 81). The rational-comprehensive approach, because it treats each decision as an isolated event, is characterized by root decision making, whereas incrementalism, because it is based on small changes building off previous decisions, is based on branching. Policy decisions are not based on a new process for each decision; instead, they branch off from previous decisions. For Lindblom, the root method requires a separation of the means and ends. Policymakers first decide what the desired outcome of a particular policy is, then proceed by deciding the best means to achieve such an outcome. The branch method, by contrast, combines the means and ends. Policy decisions are a process of "successive limited comparisons," with each decision building off previous decisions (81). Lindblom confessed that the disadvantages of such an approach include overlooking optimal means and ends. However, the branch method is a more realistic depiction of how policymakers actually make decisions.

Just as a boundedly rational decision maker can still be rational, so too can policymakers employing the branch method make rational, or "good," policy decisions (Lindblom 1959, 83). Decision making based on successive limited comparisons is the most efficient way to achieve policy agreement. It is unlikely, Lindblom has argued, that policymakers employing the root approach will ever agree on the end goal of "old age insurance" or "agricultural economic policy," nor do policymakers have the time or mental resources to comprehend all possible consequences of such complex policies (1959, 83–84). They can, however, agree on small changes to existing policies.

Although the concept of satisficing was originally developed within the context of organizational decision making—specifically decision making in public bureaucracies—Simon was more interested in applying to it all human decision making. Lindblom's "muddling through" can be viewed as an extension of "satisficing" applied to the field of public policy. The only way for policymakers to agree and move forward with a policy is through successive limited comparisons. The end result, Lindblom argued, is a process of "mutual adjustment" (1959, 85). Policymakers, recognizing their individual and institutional limitations, agree on small adjustments as a way to improve policy. Such adjustments may not be optimal, but they keep the process moving forward. And for policymakers, this is the most efficient way of pleasing a demanding public.

Lindblom's seminal work was purely a theoretical exercise in the application of satisficing to the study of public policy. Despite his well-articulated argument about policy decision making, the empirical evidence to support such a claim was lacking. Moreover, incrementalism seemed to actually move us further away from the notion of the rational decision maker. That is, though it was difficult to comprehend how a boundedly rational decision maker could make sound policy decisions, the idea of an incremental decision maker making such decisions seemed even more unrealistic.

Davis, Dempster, and Wildavsky (1966) were the first to systematically test Lindblom's notion of incrementalism as a way of conceptualizing public budgetary processes. Despite the complexity of the federal budget, budgetary decisions are based on a relatively simple formula: agency requests and congressional appropriations tend to be predicted by small deviations from the previous year's request or appropriation. Though Davis, Dempster, and Wildavsky have admitted that their work is largely descriptive, it does provide empirical backing to Simon's and Lindblom's claims that decision making is primarily bounded and incremental. These authors found that policymakers, rather than reviewing each program anew prior to the beginning of a new fiscal year, make adjustments based on the previous year's allotment. As Davis, Dempster, and Wildavsky argue, attempting to engage in a rational and comprehensive updating of the federal budget would simply overwhelm policymakers with information and prevent the policy process from ever moving forward. Simply put, the complexity of budgetary decisions forces the policymaker's hand to accept small, incremental changes, resulting in agency requests and congressional appropriations deviating only slightly from the previous year's decision. Gradual, incremental adjustments in policy best explain how policy actors make budgetary decisions—a process of decision making that is predicted by the tenets of bounded rationality.

At face value, incrementalism appears to be a useful explanatory framework for answering the question: Why do policymakers make the decisions that they do? The answer: because they are boundedly rational. Policymakers do not start from scratch with each new policy problem. Limitations in their ability to consider all possible policy goals or alternatives lead to a heavy and necessary reliance on past decisions, mental heuristics, and institutional rules. Some scholars, however, have argued that incrementalism offers little in the way of testable predictions. These critics have questioned its predictability and suggested that its tenets are little more than a descriptive model of policymaking. Wanat (1974, 1221) notes that incrementalism "infrequently meets the canons of academic and scientific explanation." As Wanat explains, existing models of budget incrementalism are descriptive rather than explanatory. Using the Davis, Dempster, and Wildavsky model, Wanat demonstrates that political factors, such as the size of the request made by Congress, provide the explanation of why incremental changes occur. More recent work by Jones, Baumgartner, and True (1998; see also True, Jones, and Baumgartner 1999) suggests incrementalism may be even less prevalent than originally indicated by Lindblom and Davis, Dempster, and Wildavsky. As we discuss more extensively in Chapter 4, policy scholars have found that policy decisions are subject to relatively frequent "punctuations," or nonincremental changes in policy.

Simon's research remains fundamental to policy decision theory because most policy scholars realize that policy actors are not completely rational. Few policy scholars question whether policymakers make decisions with incomplete information. Bounded rationality is based on the notion of individuals being limited in their information-processing capabilities. Incrementalism is a product of this framework and explains why policies seem to exhibit relatively little change from year to year. However, the degree of incremental change that takes place and how much change is considered incremental remains a theoretical and empirical question. For example, what explains significant policy change? What explains why a problem that received no money in the previous year's budget suddenly receives significant attention and a substantial amount of money? Nor does incrementalism explain rapid change in a policy. Until such questions are answered, incrementalism and bounded rationality will remain useful and powerful explanatory frameworks, but their predictive abilities will remain in question.

To be fair, incrementalism is a realistic and often descriptively accurate appraisal of the decision-making process. This tendency to place heavy emphasis on past decisions is far from a unique feature of public policymaking; it is a universal human trait. Dan Ariely (2009) describes numerous experiments with undergraduates in which information given to experimental subjects prior to a treatment "anchored" future decisions (identification of the tendency to anchor is credited to the work of Tversky and Kahneman 1974). When given a price for an object and then later asked how valuable the object is, subjects tended to use the initial price as a benchmark. Ariely describes this as "arbitrary coherence" because there is no rational reason to consider the initial price when making value judgments (2009, 28).[1] What does this tell us about incrementalism? For one thing, policy actors may not be making decisions based on a rational evaluation of new facts and figures. Incremental adjustments could, in theory, be rational if small incremental adjustments are all that is required to meet public demand. The tendency toward "anchoring," however, tells a different story. A past decision, such as the previous year's budget allocation, will significantly affect future budgetary decisions independent of any new "rational" information (i.e., changes in the economic climate, public demand, etc.) brought to the table.

Public Choice and the Tiebout Model

One of the inherent contradictions in the Lasswellian notion of policy studies is the paradox of an elitist technocrat, a policy scientist, playing a central role in democratic decision making. As we shall see throughout this book, one of the issues that consistently divides the rationalist project from its post-positivist critics is the desire to make public policy more bottom-up and participatory. Neither the study nor the practice of policymaking can be democratic, the argument goes, if it is driven by the policy science elites.

The study of policy decision making, with its roots in classical economics and its heavy reliance on rational choice theory, is typically thought of as squarely in the rationalist tradition. Yet drawn from this perspective is perhaps the most participatory, systematic theory of who should make policy decisions and how they should be made. Public choice is essentially the application of neoclassical economic ideas to the public sector; the basic idea is to transfer the logic and theory of how markets work and apply it to politics. Public choice claims normative and objective status (i.e., it claims to be how the world *does* work and also how the world *should* work). From a public choice perspective, governments should supply public programs and services in a similar fashion to private sector businesses; in other words, they should respond to demand from their "customers." Customers, that is, citizens, should be given choices in the public programs and services they consume (and the associated costs of providing them); driven by these quasi-market forces, governments will supply the demanded services efficiently.

One of the earliest public choice frameworks was proposed by Charles Tiebout (1956). In his short essay on public service delivery, he describes the ideal structure for local governance. The primary objective of any community is to serve its citizens by providing services. Certain services, such as water, garbage removal, police protection, fire protection, and so forth, take the form of a public good. According to Tiebout, centralized or consolidated communities are ineffi-cient in delivering such goods and unresponsive to the demands of individual citizens. Such inefficiency, he argues, stems from the nature of public goods. Be-cause public goods, by definition, are indivisible, the provision of such goods is traditionally left to a centralized governmental structure. Centralized structures have a monopoly over the provision of such goods and therefore have little in-centive to respond to citizen preferences. As a result, public goods are ineffi-ciently produced.

Local jurisdictions, like large, centralized bureaucracies, are prevented from distributing public goods. But what localities can do is offer service that is com-paratively superior to that of surrounding localities. For example, localities do have control over the quality of water, garbage removal, education, and most im-portant, tax burden they offer to citizens. By varying the level of service, localities are in effect offering citizens a choice about where to live. This choice is the hall-mark of the Tiebout model. Citizens expressing their preferences for certain lo-calities over others change the monopolistic relationship prevalent in centralized jurisdictions. Municipalities must respond to citizen demands or risk losing their tax base. When citizens are choosing communities based on the quality of ser-vices provided, and communities are responding to such choices, the market model takes hold. Thus, for Tiebout, citizen choice is the key to improving orga-nizational efficiency, and this choice manifests itself in the form of fragmented local government.

Two key assumptions rest at the heart of the Tiebout model: perfect informa-tion and perfect mobility. First, citizens are assumed to be rational decision mak-ers with perfect information about the services provided by surrounding communities. Second, they are assumed to have the financial means to pick up and move at any time to a more satisfactory community. Other factors, such as employment opportunities, are considered irrelevant (Tiebout 1956, 419). That is, if people are presented with an "exit" option that offers superior services, they will choose the community that best represents their interests. Because people choose which community to reside in based on the quality of services provided, communities will be composed of people of similar interests. This has important policy implications. Organizations and policymakers in such communities will be more responsive to citizen demands. And responsiveness breeds satisfaction; citizens will be more informed and more satisfied in a community in which they chose to reside.

That citizens, or what Tiebout labeled "consumer-voters," act on their preferences is fundamental to the Tiebout model. "The act of moving or failing to move is crucial. Moving or failing to move replaces the usual market test of willingness to buy a good and reveals the consumer-voter's demand for public goods" (Tiebout 1956, 420). For the Tiebout model to hold, citizens must be willing to move when they become dissatisfied with the services being provided. Without their acting on such choices, competition between jurisdictions becomes nonexistent, and there will be an inefficient production of public goods.

The Tiebout model is one of the most influential applications of public choice to public service delivery, and its intellectual heirs continue to shape policy debates in areas ranging from school vouchers to tradable pollution permits. The policy prescription from the model is interesting because it requires devolving sovereignty over local-level policymaking to the level of the individual citizen; policymakers either respond to citizen preferences, or the citizens "vote with their feet"[2] and, in effect, put that "brand" of public program or service out of business. Centralized governments are inefficient in the delivery of public goods because they have no incentive to respond to their primary clientele. Multijurisdiction communities should in theory be more efficient than single-jurisdiction communities. When citizens vote with their feet, they are making a statement about the current state of public policy. To be competitive, policymakers must respond, and in doing so, they improve the quality of services being provided.

This citizen-as-policymaker perspective offered by the Tiebout model was purely a theoretical exercise aimed at solving the dilemma of inefficient provision of a public good. Because of its emphasis on giving individual citizens influence over what programs and services are provided by government, public choice frameworks such as the Tiebout model have been championed as a means to resolve the democratic dilemma of the policy sciences. From this perspective, public choice represents much of the positive of the Lasswellian vision, a systematic theory generated by academic technocrats, one that is rigorously examined across disciplines and aimed at setting up an institutional mechanism to guide policy solutions to social problems (essentially a public sector equivalent of the "invisible hand" of the marketplace).

Two major objections stand in the way of public choice achieving the status of the Lasswellian ideal. First, on a theoretical level it equates democracy with free markets, and they are not synonymous. Democracy makes no guarantee that you get what you want—the customer is not always right—it simply guarantees you have a voice in the public space. Public choice basically eliminates public space; everyone is sovereign, and his or her civic duties extend no further than narrow self-interest. For such reasons, post-positivists reject public choice as the democratic white knight of the rationalist project. On the contrary, they see public choice and its market-based institutional prescriptions as atomizing public policy preferences rather than effectively aggregating citizen preference. Democracy institutionalizes voice, not exit. Second, and perhaps more damning from the rationalist project's point of view, is that it is not at all clear that public choice works as well in practice as it does in theory. Empirical support for the model has been mixed at best.

Citizens as Efficient Policymakers?

The Tiebout model rests on the assumption that citizens will choose municipalities that offer the best service. Scholars have picked up on this assumption, testing whether multijurisdiction (fragmented) or single-jurisdiction (centralized) government is better for increasing citizen satisfaction. Such work tends to center around the basis of choice for individual citizens. If citizens choose jurisdictions based on concerns other than service quality (say, for example, on the basis of racial segregation), the Tiebout model breaks down empirically, and its normative claims in terms of democratic principles also start to appear suspect. Similarly, if people living in fragmented communities lack perfect information about surrounding jurisdictions, or people living in consolidated communities are equally satisfied as those living in fragmented communities, the Tiebout model becomes problematic. Finally, the Tiebout model posits that people have perfect mobility, that citizens are capable of "exiting" a community if services become unsatisfactory. For Tiebout, these mobility decisions should not be affected by external considerations. As Tiebout puts it, "restrictions due to employment opportunities are not considered" (1956, 419). In other words, people should not be constrained in their ability to change communities. Like other assumptions in Tiebout's model, these assumptions have been challenged by scholars as unrealistic and deserving of empirical scrutiny.

Lyons, Lowery, and DeHoog (1992) offer one of the most comprehensive and systematic empirical tests of the Tiebout model. They draw on data obtained in a survey of citizen attitudes in a fragmented community and a centralized community. The data are based on a matched sample in both communities. The Tiebout model rests on the assumption that citizens make their decisions about which community to reside in the same way they do decisions in the marketplace; citizens will shop around for the community that delivers the best-quality services, explaining why Tiebout uses the phrase "consumer-voter" rather than citizens. As a consequence of such behavior, Tiebout argues, a clear set of testable hypotheses emerges: citizens should be more informed, more satisfied, and more aware of alternative jurisdictions in fragmented communities than those in single-jurisdiction or centralized communities. The results of the Lyons, Lowery, and DeHoog (1992) study cast considerable doubt on these assumptions.

Reviewing citizen responses to surveys in polycentric (fragmented) and monocentric (centralized) jurisdictions, Lyons, Lowery, and DeHoog find little support for Tiebout's model. Specifically, citizens in polycentric jurisdictions tend to be *less* informed about surrounding jurisdictions and *less* informed about what services are provided by their own local government (1992, 98–99). Moreover, there was no statistical difference in the level of satisfaction with the services provided between citizens in polycentric communities and citizens in monocentric communities (1992, 101). Finally, despite Tiebout's assumption that people "vote with their feet," there was relatively little difference in the use of the exit option between the two communities. In short, citizens in centralized communities tend to be happy about the quality of services being provided and have little desire to exit.

The disagreement between Tiebout and the findings presented by Lyons, Lowery, and DeHoog is critical to understanding how and why policymakers make the decisions they do. If the evidence presented by Lyons, Lowery, and DeHoog is correct, then citizens and policymakers are making inefficient public policy. From a purely democratic point of view, this is not a problem; democracy, as scholars like Stone (2002) have taken some pains to point out, is not particularly efficient and makes no claim to be so. For public choice, however, the empirical claim that more market-like arrangements do not increase efficiency in public policy is fairly devastating. Unlike democracy, efficiency *is* the central normative value of economic theory, and efficiency is the central normative justification for public choice. If policymaking remains inefficient under a public choice framework, then public choice does not provide a solution to the problem originally proposed by Tiebout—that all centralized communities are producing inefficient public goods. Are citizens actually staying in communities in which public service delivery is inefficient? Probably, but it does not seem to bother them that much, at least if one looks at levels of service satisfaction in studies like those by Lyons, Lowery, and DeHoog. So do citizens really not care about inefficient service? This also seems questionable, given the level of knowledge citizens in centralized communities have about services being provided relative to citizens in fragmented communities. In an attempt to resolve this dilemma, Paul Teske and his colleagues further examined the Tiebout model.

Teske and colleagues (1993) began with the assumption that not all citizens are fully informed. Like Herbert Simon, they see citizens as making decisions appropriate for the situation. The situation, for most citizens, rarely involves decisions about tax-service packages or the quality of garbage removal in a community. As such, the average citizen is unaware, or has no incentive to be aware, of the difference in services between jurisdictions.

Teske and colleagues challenge Lyons, Lowery, and DeHoog on the notion that for Tiebout's model to be correct, all citizens must be fully informed. Rather, the authors contend that for markets to function efficiently, only a "subset" of actors must make fully informed decisions. This "subset" most likely consists of people who have the most to gain from being fully informed, specifically those who are actually moving between jurisdictions. Teske and colleagues tested this proposition by surveying "established" residents and movers in a single county in New York about school district expenditures and taxes. They hypothesized that movers, because they have an incentive to obtain information about tax-service packages, are more likely to be informed and therefore are more likely to fit the assumptions of Tiebout's model.

The results of the survey by Teske and his colleagues do provide some empirical support for their hypothesis. Examining citizen perceptions about school district expenditures and taxes, they found that a small group of citizen consumers were well-informed about educational policy in their district as well as surrounding districts. Importantly, however, this group of "marginal consumers" did not consist of general movers, as originally proposed by the authors. Instead, high-income movers were most well-informed about school district taxes. The utility of this finding, according to Teske and colleagues, is that it resolves the problem presented by Lyons, Lowery, and DeHoog: How can having relatively uninformed citizens make for efficient public policy? The findings suggest that local governments can be competitive and efficient simply by responding to a small group of citizen-consumers. High-income, mobile citizens tend to be the most well-informed because they are the ones "shopping" around for a new community and are most likely to have the time and resources to do so. And, as Teske and colleagues (1993, 709) point out, it is this group that "communities have the strongest incentive to attract."

This work provides a lifeboat for the Tiebout hypothesis and presents an important revision to the conclusions of Lyons, Lowery, and DeHoog (1992).

However, it also undercuts a key normative claim of public choice and brings back the paradox inherent in the policy sciences of democracy. Rather than all citizens actively participating in the policy process, only a small minority will drive the marketplace for public goods and services. These citizens are not technocrats, but they are an elite minority, and there is no guarantee that they are representative of the preferences of others. In other words, this vision of public choice ends up being more elitist than egalitarian; it simply switches the elitist policy technocrat for an almost certainly socioeconomically distinct minority. To post-positivist critics, and perhaps many others, that tradeoff is unlikely to provide a satisfactory squaring of the democratic circle.

There are also some empirical objections to the reformulation of public choice provided by Teske and colleagues. Lowery, Lyons, and DeHoog (1995) challenged the key findings in two ways. First, Teske and colleagues focused on education policy, which Lowery, Lyons, and DeHoog describe as "atypical" and highly salient, particularly for the county from which the sample was derived (1995, 705). A less salient policy, such as water or garbage service, would be more appropriate. Second, Teske and colleagues' measure of "informed" citizens was rather simplistic, asking respondents whether the school district's expenditures were average, above average, or below average for the area. As Lowery, Lyons, and DeHoog point out, given the "absurdly unchallenging level" of being informed, that high-income movers perform better on this question does not necessarily imply a great deal of depth to their knowledge of school expenditures. Thus, we seem to be back to the original dilemma. Citizens are not behaving as proposed by Tiebout, but they are not any less satisfied with the services being provided, nor are they any less informed. So what explains public service delivery in local governments, and how are policy decisions being made?

Some scholars argue that the Tiebout model, applied narrowly, provides a means for constructing a more efficient system of delivering public goods (Chubb and Moe 1988, 1990). Applied more broadly, however, as evidenced by the debate between Lyons, Lowery, and DeHoog and Teske and colleagues, the Tiebout model receives mixed support. One way to interpret the findings of Lyons, Lowery, and DeHoog is that polycentric communities do not increase the efficiency of public service delivery. This of course assumes people are making decisions based on the quality of services provided. An alternative explanation is that people actually make decisions based on factors other than the services being provided. The quality of water service or garbage removal being provided may have no effect on people's level of satisfaction or their desire to exit. Acknowledging the relatively low level of knowledge citizens have about local government service provision, Lyons, Lowery, and DeHoog (1992, 103) speculated that "local factors are probably more important in determining satisfaction and responses to dissatisfaction than the kinds of institutional factors addressed by both the Tiebout exiting hypothesis and traditional civic reformers." The questions then become: What are these local factors, and how do they affect how policy decisions are being made?

Policy scholars have struggled to determine exactly how citizens make mobility decisions. Even though "marginal consumers" may make fully informed decisions, how do nonmarginal consumers make decisions? The Tiebout model, by the admission of its author, is an "extreme" one (Tiebout 1956, 419). If local factors are important, the range of possible alternatives is potentially endless. To narrow the search, scholars have revisited educational policy, specifically the issue of school choice. School choice provides a good example because it assumes people make decisions on the basis of a specific policy outcome: academic performance.

Mark Schneider, Paul Teske, and others (Schneider et al. 1998) asked the question: What factors drive school choice? The voucher system is based on the assumption that parents are choosing schools on the basis of academic performance. If, however, other factors are driving such choice, this has important policy implications. What Schneider and colleagues found is that parents tend to pick schools based on their own individual preferences, but those preferences are not always related to academic performance. Parents who are marginal consumers, who tend to be high-income parents, are more informed about schools' academic outcomes. Schneider and colleagues argue that these parents are enough to induce competitive pressures on the school to improve academic performance. However, for nonmarginal parents, school choice decisions are more complex. Although parents tend to have erroneous assumptions about school characteristics, they are able to match their preferences about schools. These preferences, however, are based on the demographic characteristics of the school and the reported number of violent incidents at the school. Citizens are making public policy decisions, but the basis of such decisions varies widely. Like Teske and colleagues, Schneider and colleagues found that high-income citizens with a vested interest in the policy do make "rational" decisions. However, for the vast majority of citizens, policy decisions are being made in a way that violates the underlying assumptions of the existing policy.

Mark Schneider and Jack Buckley (2002) picked up on this notion of "local factors" or non-outcome factors as dictating school choice and mobility decisions.

To understand how parents make school choice decisions, Schneider and Buckley monitored Internet usage on a Web site providing school district information for Washington, D.C., schools. Their purpose was to monitor the search behavior of parents to determine what factors are important when making school choice decisions. What they found was that although parents are initially interested in academic performance factors (test scores and programs offered), the most prominent school attributes parents access in the initial search process are racial diversity and school location. In other words, non-outcome factors are much more prevalent in the search process than would be assumed by the Tiebout model. Such findings put a serious dent in the policy prescriptions offered by school choice advocates and public choice more generally. Perhaps even more revealing from the Schneider and Buckley article is that the demographic attributes are prevalent in the search process of college educated and non–college educated parents and that such attributes tend to dictate the entire search process. "Local" factors pervade policy choice decisions and create an environment ripe for racial disparity.

The findings of Schneider and Buckley (2002) present policymakers with a serious dilemma. Should they respond to citizen preferences, whatever those preferences may be? Or should they make decisions based on what they believe is the best outcome? School choice, or the voucher system, is a direct application of Tiebout's exit model. However, as the findings by Schneider and colleagues and Schneider and Buckley suggest, parents are not making educational decisions based on academic performance, but rather on factors unrelated to education, with potentially undemocratic results.

Institutional Rational Choice

Using public choice theory as the basis for understanding how policy decisions are made has important implications, because it provides prescriptions regarding public service delivery (Frederickson et al. 2012, 195). Those prescriptions, however, have a mixed empirical record. The exchange between Lyons, Lowery, and DeHoog (1992) and Teske and colleagues (1993) demonstrates that citizens can make policy, but that mobility decisions are much more complex than originally proposed by Tiebout. Some citizens may in fact "vote with their feet," but such decisions are not nearly as widespread or as simple as suggested by Tiebout. Subsequent work by policy scholars has also confirmed the potential disadvantages of designing jurisdictions in accordance with the Tiebout model. If left to their own devices, citizens will make decisions that have the potential to further racial and economic disparities. Summarizing research in the fifty years since the Tiebout model, Howell-Moroney (2008) notes that though the Tiebout model preserves efficiency and economy, it ignores equity. Left to their own devices, citizens produce, if not wholly irrational policies, then certainly suboptimal policies (i.e., policy that is not particularly efficient and is potentially inequitable). Does this mean policymaking authority should be removed from the hands of the individual citizen?

Some scholars have argued that rules or institutions can be employed to improve the rationality of individual decision making, thereby improving the overall quality of policymaking. The rational actor model, for this group of scholars, presents a shortsighted and incomplete view of human decision making. Policymakers, citizens, and other human beings make decisions in the context of institutional rules. These rules, in turn, shape individual preferences. Labeled "institutional rational choice," this approach to policy decision making was most prominently advanced by the late Nobel laureate Elinor Ostrom. At the heart of this framework is an interest in "how institutions affect the incentives confronting individuals and their resultant behavior" (Ostrom 2007, 21). Quoting evolutionary psychologists Leda Cosmides and John Tooby, Ostrom (1998, 6) contends that institutions allow individuals to make "better than rational" decisions. The belief among institutional rational choice scholars is that institutions can be designed to solve collective-action problems. Contrary to decision-making models discussed in the previous sections, the independent variable of interest in this framework is the institution or institutional rule.

Institutionalism and School Choice

A good example of institutional rational choice applied to a practical policy problem is John Chubb and Terry Moe's widely cited work on school choice (1990, 1988). They began with the assumption that public schools, because they have a monopoly on the service being provided (public education), have no incentive to respond to their consumers (parents). As a result, the public school system fosters an unresponsive environment. The Tiebout model is based on citizens having an "exit" option. For parents in public school systems, the exit option does not exist. The institution (public school) has no incentive to respond to parents' demands. Instead, as Chubb and Moe argued, public schools respond to other actors, namely the elected officials who provide financial support for the school. In public schools, school administrators become so focused on satisfying the demands of these elected officials that they rarely respond to the demands of teachers and parents, the primary users of the service provided by the school. Chubb and Moe view this dilemma as an institutional design flaw, with the solution being a redesign of the institution such that it has an incentive to respond to its primary clientele (i.e., parents and teachers).

Coming from a neo-institutionalist perspective, Chubb and Moe have argued that public choice presents opportunities for major reforms in public education. Their argument is based primarily on the assumption that policymakers behave as rational, self-interested agents (see Niskanen 1971). Applied to education policy, this means that public schools are top-heavy agencies governed by self-interested administrators. This has serious and negative consequences for public schools. Rather than listening to teachers and parents who utilize the service being provided by the school, administrators are more focused on obtaining resources. As a result, academic performance suffers. The policy prescription put forth by Chubb and Moe is rooted in institutional theory: redesign the incentives for the primary policymakers (i.e., school administrators) within the institution. To do so, Chubb and Moe argued for removing policy delivery mechanisms from democratic control. As Chubb and Moe state, "Democratic control normally produces ineffective schools" (1990, 227). Remove the connection between administrators and elected officials and give parents a choice about their children's schools. Doing so will force administrators to respond to parents' and teachers' demands to maintain sufficient funding. Chubb and Moe, in short, have argued that democratic control creates a perverse set of top-down incentives, and that policy effectiveness would increase by replacing this institutional arrangement with a market-based framework in which incentives are produced from the bottom up.

The market model of public education put forth by Chubb and Moe (1990) is often cited by school choice advocates. The policy prescriptions from this model were designed to maximize the collective good by providing an exit option with competing alternatives. Public education institutions should be reformed by decentralizing, allowing parents to choose which school their children attend. There is, however, disagreement about the underlying assumptions of Chubb and Moe's neo-institutionalist approach, specifically the direction of the relationship between school administrators and school performance. Kevin Smith and Kenneth Meier (1995) ask the question: Is it really that school bureaucracy causes negative performance, or is it that school bureaucracy is a response to negative performance? They find in favor of the latter, that the causal arrow presented by Chubb and Moe is actually reversed—bureaucracies are top-heavy because of the needs of the school. In other words, school bureaucracies are a response to demands by parents and teachers, not elected officials (see also Meier, Polinard, and Wrinkle 2000). As schools are required to meet the demands of a more diverse student body, the number of administrators working on behalf of the schools is likely to increase. Previous test scores, not the size of the bureaucracy, tend to be a stronger predictor of school performance. And where school choice policies are in place, there is a greater risk of educational segregation (Smith and Meier 1995, 55–58). That citizens are making choices based on non-outcome factors, and that school bureaucracies are responding to the needs of the school as opposed to elected officials, create two significant and fundamental problems for Chubb and Moe's neo-institutionalist framework.

Chubb and Moe proceeded primarily from a rational choice perspective. Policymakers are viewed as acting in their own self-interest, and by doing so they create inefficient public institutions. From a rational choice perspective, collective-action problems or social dilemmas present a significant problem. Rational choice, as originally understood, is based on the following assumptions: 1) behavior is best explained at the level of the individual; and 2) people are self-interested utility maximizers (see Downs 1957 and Buchanan and Tullock 1962).³ By definition, the role of public policymakers is to make decisions that are in the public's best interest. If, however, rational choice theory is correct, then policymakers are incapable of making public decisions. The neo-institutionalist framework put forth by Chubb and Moe does little to resolve this dilemma.

Collective-Action Dilemmas:
Ostrom's IAD and the Logic of Appropriateness

Despite the mixed success of the institutionalist approach with regard to education policy, scholars continue to recognize that institutions do matter. Like Herbert Simon, Elinor Ostrom viewed human decision making as bounded by cognitive constraints. Ostrom, however, put forth two additional propositions. First, institutions can shape individual preferences. Second, people will use institutional rules to solve collective-action problems. Out of the institutional rational choice perspective, Ostrom and her colleagues developed an entire research agenda, known as "institutional analysis and development," or IAD, focused on the application of institutionalist theory to solving common-pool resource dilemmas. Ostrom (2011,

2007) argued that the IAD framework is useful for policy analysts in explaining and predicting how people will respond to institutional rules. Using it, however, requires conceptualization of what is known as the "action situation" (Ostrom 2011, 11),[4] which is described as "the social spaces where individuals interact, exchange goods and services, solve problems, dominate one another, or fight (among the many things that individuals do in action situations)" (Ostrom 2011, 11).

In Ostrom's IAD framework, the action situation is influenced by a set of external variables: biophysical conditions, attributes of community, and rules-in-use (see Ostrom 2007, 27 or 2011, 10). The action situation in turn affects interactions and outcomes, the latter of which is affected by "evaluative criteria." Outcomes also serve a feedback function, affecting external variables and the action situation (see Ostrom 2011, 10 for an overview of the framework and details on the "action situation"). McGinnis describes the action situation as the "core component of the IAD framework," given its focus on individual behavior (2011, 173). The purpose of the IAD framework is to describe and explain outcomes resulting from human interaction in the context of existing institutions. As Blomquist and deLeon note, "the IAD framework assists us in clarifying what to think about when we are observing a phenomenon having to do with people's resources and (literal) lives in the workaday world" (2011, 2).

One of the more intriguing findings from this research agenda comes from earlier work by Ostrom, Walker, and Gardner (1992). Rational choice and noncooperative game theory suggest that the only way to solve collective-action problems in a one-shot dilemma is through the use of external sanctions. These theoretical predictions are then used to justify the allocation of punishment power to the state. To ensure cooperation, there has to be the threat of punishment. Ostrom, Walker, and Gardner challenge this assumption, citing evidence that communication can solve collective-action problems, even in one-shot encounters. Using an experimental design, the authors invited subjects to play a common-pool resource game. In this game subjects were endowed with tokens at the beginning of the game and had a choice about whether to contribute to one of two public-good markets. The first market gave a fixed return based on the amount contributed by the individual. The second market gave a return that was based on the number of tokens invested by other players. In the second market, the game-theoretic prediction was for individual players to free ride off others' contributions, because investing in this market was both costly and risky.

In the baseline condition, in which no sanction and no communication were possible, players tended to conform to game-theoretic predictions. However, in additional treatments, when communication and sanction were introduced, contribution levels changed. In one-shot and repeated communication treatments, subjects yielded more efficient outcomes (higher payoffs) than did treatments in which subjects were allowed to sanction others, but without communication. In cases where subjects were allowed to communicate and sanction, they were able to negotiate a sanctioning mechanism that achieved near-optimal results. In other words, subjects were able to achieve an efficient policy outcome in the absence of an external enforcer.

From an institutionalist perspective, the findings of Ostrom, Walker, and Gardner make perfect sense. A change in rule should lead to a change in behavior. Allowing communication and self-sanctioning increases the ability of policymakers (subjects) to achieve better and more efficient policy outcomes. Since this initial publication, Ostrom and her colleagues have further demonstrated that communication and other institutional rules can increase the efficiency of policy outcomes (Ostrom, Gardner, and Walker 1994; see also Ostrom 2007). For policymakers, this implies that institutional rules may hold the key to producing better public policy. If certain rules allow individuals to coordinate their behavior to achieve more efficient outcomes, then institutions should be designed accordingly. If Ostrom, Walker, and Gardner (1992) are correct, there may be situations in which policymakers are able to remove the need and cost for policy oversight.

IAD scholars focus on common-pool resources for two reasons: 1) common-pool resource dilemmas tend to lack any sort of formal institutional rules; and 2) if people are able to solve such dilemmas in the absence of an external authority, it would provide insight into how best to solve other collective-action dilemmas. Despite progress in this area, however, the IAD is enormously complex. McGinnis's (2011) overview of the IAD framework identifies sixteen key sections while defining more than one hundred key terms and phrases critical to understanding the framework's operations. If anything, the IAD seems to move us closer to the rational-comprehensive model of decision making or Simon's substantive rationality. This may in fact encompass how people make policy decisions, but it hardly presents a parsimonious model of decision making. Ostrom admits that "strong inferences" about decision making are most likely possible in "tightly constrained, one-shot action situations under conditions of complete information, where participants are motivated to select particular strategies or chains of action that jointly lead to stable equilibria" (2007, 32).

Despite such complexity, the IAD framework retains much utility. The IAD has had an enormous impact on the policy field, like other frameworks, providing a valuable organizing function for policy scholars. It is arguably the best representation of the reality, complexity, and confusing nature of the policy process in its entirety. As scholars have noted, the IAD framework allows for great flexibility in terms of adapting to different units of analysis (Schlager 2007, 314) and, unlike other theories of the policy process, places a strong emphasis on institutions (Nowlin 2011, 44). This flexibility, though, comes at a significant cost, namely parsimony.

A more simplistic model of decision making is presented by James March (1994), whose "logic of appropriateness" states: "Action, policy making included, is seen as driven by rules of appropriate or exemplary behavior, organized into institutions" (March and Olsen 2006, 689). Put simply, people will do what is appropriate given the situation. In any given situation, the logic of appropriateness suggests that people will ask: What kind of situation is this? What kind of person am I? What does a person like me do in a situation such as this? (March and Olsen 2006, 690). People tend to adapt to the situation at hand and to make the decision that will best satisfy their preferences given the current set of rules and norms, as well as their past experiences and expectations of their position within the organization.

The logic of appropriateness, like bounded rationality, is a departure from models of pure rationality. "Appropriate" goes beyond standard operating procedures to include informal rules and norms within an organization, thus helping to explain extreme decisions such as organizational protests and defiance of authority (March and Olsen 2006, 692). Like Ostrom's IAD framework, the logic of appropriateness relies on institutional rules to solve collective-action dilemmas. What is appropriate seems to be an intuitive understanding among policymakers. We venture to guess that most policymakers can recall when a colleague acted inappropriately and probably can recall even more vividly when their own actions violated the "logic of appropriateness." Like the IAD framework, the logic of appropriateness enhances the explanatory power of models of policy decision making, but with greater parsimony.

Despite this intuitive appeal, questions still linger. For example, who or what defines what is "appropriate?" How do changes in what is appropriate occur? If "appropriate" is defined only after someone is working within an organization, how are we able to predict policy decisions? Without answers to these questions, it is difficult to make predictions with any degree of certainty about how people will respond to changes in institutional rules.[5] Even March and Olsen (2006, 695) have admitted that "rules, laws, identities, and institutions provide parameters for action" rather than exact predictions about what decisions will be made. As policymakers take on more roles and identities within an organization, determining what is appropriate in any given situation becomes ever more important to understanding how people make policy decisions.

There seem to be two glaring problems with the institutionalist framework. First is that when it is applied to real-world policy problems, empirical and theoretical support tends to be lacking. The causality of Chubb and Moe's neo-institutionalist approach has been questioned extensively. Although the Tiebout model is based on assumptions about citizen choice, the policy prescriptions clearly fit within the same institutionalist framework. In the more than fifty years since its publication, scholars have struggled to find sustained empirical support for its key assumptions (see Howell-Moroney 2008). Second is that where empirical support does exist, as in the area of common-pool resources demonstrated by Ostrom and her colleagues (see Ostrom 2007, 46–51), there is little theoretical backing for why certain rules, such as face-to-face communication, are so important for coordinating behavior. Ostrom (1998) speculated that such mechanisms allow for "better than rational" decisions, and although her more recent work (see Ostrom 2005) was devoted to theoretically modeling such mechanisms, it has yet to be fully tested. Theoretical insight is critical to identifying the conditions under which communication in common-pool resource dilemmas and other collective-action problems will fail. The complexity of the IAD framework makes it difficult to make predictions about when institutional rules will work. Ostrom (2007, 22) noted that the effects of rules at any one level of decision making are likely to be affected by rules made at other levels. Yes, institutions matter. Most scholars agree on this point. But when? The interactions between rules and norms and between policymakers of varying levels of authority makes it difficult to assess the exact effect of institutions on individual decision making. Thus, in their current form, institutional rational choice and IAD remain powerful explanatory frameworks, with uncertain predictive qualities.

Conclusion

What do we know about how policy actors make decisions? First and foremost, policy actors are not fully rational. They do not make decisions with complete information, nor do they weigh the pros and cons of all possible alternatives prior to making a decision. As Herbert Simon established more than sixty years ago, policy actors, whether they are top-level officials or ordinary citizens, are bounded in their degree of rationality. Policymakers rely on cues, heuristics, in-stitutional context, and what is "appropriate" when making decisions. Simon's (1947, 1955) early work on bounded rationality spawned an entire subfield of public policy based on incrementalism (Lindblom 1959, 1979; Davis, Dempster, and Wildavsky 1966; see also Goodin 1999, 72) that provides a glimpse into how policymakers deal with complex policy problems. Second, if left to the decisions of ordinary citizens, public policy would potentially create an inequitable social environment. Citizens do not make choices based on the quality of service pro-vided or what would be the most efficient public policy. Instead, they are more interested in demographic factors. This raises questions about whether bound-edly rational citizens are capable of making good policy decisions. So, where does this leave us?

Institutionalist scholars argue that the problem rests not with individual pol-icymakers or citizens; when it comes to making choices, humans are what they are. Instead, the problem lies with the design of public institutions, which could be better constructed to channel individual self-interest toward choices that result in more effective and efficient policy outcomes. If certain policies are delivering inefficient or inequitable outcomes, then there must be a design flaw in existing institutions. Although some important policy prescriptions have emerged from this framework, particularly regarding behavior in a public goods setting or a collective-action dilemma (see Ostrom, Gardner, and Walker 1994 for an appli-cation to common-pool resources), others have not been so successful (see Chubb and Moe's 1990 neo-institutionalist approach to school choice and Tiebout's 1956 model on public service delivery).

Common to both the individual and institutionalist framework is a desire to understand and ultimately predict the choices of policy actors. Unfortunately, research on decision making in public policy seems unable to get away from its rational choice/public choice roots. Most policy scholars now seem to accept the bounded rationality view of human decision making, and most seem to accept that institutions matter. What is missing is a theoretical framework that explains the origins of our boundedly rational preferences. Why does face-to-face com-munication increase cooperation so dramatically? Why are people extremely sensitive to violations of fairness norms in group settings such as common-pool resource dilemmas? From an institutionalist perspective, answers to such ques-tions are desirable because they present an opportunity for the implementation of a new set of rules. The current state of policy research, however, seems rela-tively uninterested in answering these and other questions about preference formation, instead taking bounded rationality as a given. The result has been a series of policy decision-making models with a high degree of explanatory power but little predictive ability. This descriptive framework is useful, but the lack of predictive power forces policymakers into a largely trial-and-error approach to policymaking. Thus, we are left with policy decisions being made by boundedly rational actors who may or may not change depending on the situation and existing institutional rules.

Notes

1. Ariely (2009, 31n.) notes that the tendency toward anchoring is not confined to undergraduates.

2. Although Tiebout did not use this phrase explicitly, scholars routinely use it when describing the policy implications of the Tiebout model.

3. Since the work of Downs and Buchanan and Tullock, many scholars have questioned the feasibility of rational choice assumptions. See Green and Shapiro (1994) for an exhaustive critique of the assumptions of rational choice theory, with a response by Friedman (1996).

4. Ostrom notes that in previous work the "action area" and "action situation" were considered separately but often led to confusion (2011, 9).

5. For a review of what is "appropriate" in social dilemmas of varying characteristics, see Weber, Kopelman, and Messick (2004).

CHAPTER 4

Where Does Policy Come From?
The Policy Process

Foundational to the notion of the policy sciences is problem orientation, the assumption that public policy is a solution-oriented response to major social problems. Although this assumption can be (and has been) challenged, it fits intuitive notions and generally accepted definitions of what public policy is and what it is supposed to do: A deliberative action (or nonaction) undertaken by government to achieve some desired end. Accepting problem orientation, however, raises a series of complex questions. What problems should government pay attention to? Who decides what a problem is and whether it merits government attention and action? When and why do policies change? Is it because the problem is solved, is it because the problem is redefined, or is it something else?

These sorts of questions are at the heart of the study of policy process, which can be thought of as the study of how public policy is made. This includes the means by which problems are identified and brought to the attention of governments as well as how solutions are formulated and decided upon. The primary objective of this broad research literature is to try to understand where policy comes from and how and why it changes. Policymakers are inundated with pressure for action from constituents, issue interest groups, think tanks, the media, and numerous other information sources. And more often than not, such groups tend to disagree over what the most pressing issues are. So what determines whether government will pay attention to an issue and take some purposive action to address it? For example, why did child care suddenly become a problem meriting intensive government attention in the 1960s and 1970s (see Nelson 1984)? Why did special education become such a high-profile policy issue during the same period (see Cremins 1983; Turnbull 1986)? Certainly such issues were prevalent long before legislation was enacted to address these concerns, and certainly lawmakers were aware of them. So why did policymakers decide to act when they did? How did these issues move from relative obscurity to the government agenda? Agenda setting is "the process by which information is prioritized for action, and attention allocated to some problems rather than others" (Jones and Baumgartner 2005, ix). It is frequently assumed that this process is logical and rational; in reality, the process is as much political as it is logical, and some theorists have claimed that it is more rationalized than rational (e.g., Kingdon 1995).

Process and Power

Policy process is frustratingly complex and difficult to understand, but this has not stopped scholars—particularly political scientists—from trying to identify and understand systematic causal relationships. The special attraction for political science is not hard to fathom: the study of policy process is ultimately the study of political power. Think of political power as relative influence over policy outcomes, that is, the decisions and actions that are backed by the coercive powers of the state. What are effective ways to wield such influence? Students of the policy process readily affirm that an effective means to wield such power is to play a role in determining the list of problems and proposed solutions government is actively paying attention to.

The power associated with agenda setting, or the process of bringing certain topics to the attention of decision makers to make policy, has long been recognized by scholars (Cobb and Elder 1983; Majone 2006; Page 2006). Accordingly, policy process scholars are intensely interested in how problems gain government attention and who gets to define those problems and suggest solutions. This has particularly important implications for democratic systems, because policy scholars quickly established that whatever the intricacies of the process of policymaking, they frequently did not conform to the notions of a pluralist democracy. The ability to decide what is to be decided upon is often referred to as *indirect power*; it has long been recognized that such power is more influential in determining policy outcomes than direct power, or the ability to actually make policy decisions (Bachrach and Baratz 1962). The actors who wield true political power within a given system are ultimately those who can influence or control the problems and policy alternatives that are placed on the government agenda. Theories of the policy process are in part devoted to understanding who these actors are and how they wield this influence. More generally, these theories seek to explain why policy changes, which is largely a question of how policymakers and citizens process information.

Policy Subsystems and Issue Networks

So who does get to decide what topics are important enough for the government to address? How do they go about making such decisions? Is this process democratic, or is it dominated by elites? The pluralist theoretical tradition in political science suggests that the policy process is mainly a competition among organized groups that account for all interests, each vying to get the government to pay attention to its problems or concerns and to take particular actions (Truman 1951). Policy process scholars—and certainly some influential theories of the policy process—are highly skeptical of this pluralist framework. Early on, iron triangle theorists argued that Congress, the bureaucracy, and special interest groups formed an unbreakable triad, offering ideas and policy solutions with narrow benefits accrued to themselves at the expense of the public interest.

The power of iron triangles to control policy agendas, however, has also come under fire. In the late 1970s and early 1980s, scholars revised the notion of the iron triangle. These scholars argued that policy process, rather than being dominated by a select group of actors, was more open. In what came to be known as subsystems theory, they emphasized the role of public and private organizations, including think tanks, research institutes, interest groups, and ordinary citizens. The main premise of subsystems theory was that rather than the clear, separable, and semipermanent sides of iron triangles, the policy process was increasingly decentralized, fragmented, and characterized by informal and shifting alliances.

Freeman (1965) was the first to discuss the existence of policy subsystems, but Hugh Heclo (1977, 1978) is generally credited with developing the first significant subsystems conceptual framework that really helped explain agenda setting and policy change. Heclo argued that existing studies based on the iron triangle framework were incomplete because they were unable to account for decentralization and change in the policy process. If the iron triangle is the only source of public policy, how do new policy proposals emerge? How can the iron triangle explain rapid change in public policy? Examining the policy landscape system in the 1970s, Heclo did not see a rigid and impenetrable structure, as suggested by iron triangle scholars. Rather, he observed a tremendous increase in intergovernmental lobbies coupled with a rise in the role of state governments in public policymaking. The political system was highly fragmented and much more dynamic than suggested by iron triangle scholars.

Heclo's research (1978) coined two important terms relevant to agenda-setting scholars: "issue networks" and "technopols." Rather than tight-knit policy groups within government acting as the sole administrators of public policy, Heclo saw this function being carried out by informal alliances among interest groups, public and private organizations, and ordinary citizens. Such groups tended to coalesce around certain issues to form autonomous policy subunits that exerted considerable influence on the policymaking process. Because of their mutual interest in a particular policy arena, Heclo labeled these groups "issue networks."

Issue networks "overlay" rather than replace existing alliances and differ from "shared-attention, shared-action, or shared-belief" groups (Heclo 1978, 103–105). Instead, issue networks tend to consist of politically active individuals with specialized policy knowledge who are drawn to the group for noneconomic benefits. Heclo (1978, 116) described the rise of issue networks as having three important advantages for the policy process: 1) issue networks tend to reflect the general sentiment of citizens who are less constrained by party identification and who tend to engage in issue-based politics; 2) they provide more policymaking options to members of Congress and the executive branch; and 3) political actors in the legislative and executive branch are less constrained in their policymaking decisions than would be expected in an iron triangle. Put simply, issue networks tend to be highly fluid groups, expanding or contracting depending on the level of attention surrounding a particular issue, and provide governing bodies with more alternatives in the policymaking process.[1]

Using issue networks to conceptualize and understand the policy process suggests a pluralist response to the iron triangle model. Yet whereas issue networks suggest open points of influence within government, the increasing complexity of public policy has further disconnected citizens from the policymaking process. Within issue networks, those with specialized, technical knowledge of the policy at hand tend to wield the most power. Heclo refers to such individuals as "technopols" and maintains that the process of policymaking occurs at the level of policy specialists. Because technopols are located well below high-level political appointees, they operate under the radar and are often disconnected from ordinary citizens. Yet they wield considerable power, because elected officials rarely have the time and resources to obtain complete information about a particular issue. Instead, they rely on technopols. Consider, for example, congressional hearings on a complex issue such as air pollution. An expert (the "technopol") from the Environmental Protection Agency (EPA) provides testimony relaying specialized information about the topic. Subsystems theory suggests that the expert, and the EPA more generally, are part of a larger coalition advocating on behalf of environmental policy. As we discuss in the next section, policy scholars view such coalitions as key to understanding policy change.

The emergence of issue networks run by technopols splinters the connection between policymakers and citizens. According to Heclo, the dependence on specialized experts has created a push-pull effect in the political system. While responsibility for public policy is being pushed away from the federal government and iron triangle politics, the overreliance on technopols pulls the policymaking process further away from ordinary citizens. This highlights one of the drawbacks of Heclo's subsystems theory for democratic politics. Even though the policy process may be susceptible to influence from a multiplicity of groups, technopols maintain a strong grip on policymaking. Issue networks and technopols thus present a dilemma for Heclo. On the one hand, he argued that the rise of issue networks had created a situation in which "no one, as far as one can tell, is in control of the policy process" (1978, 102). On the other hand, policy experts within these issue networks have a distinct informational advantage over other participants.

Following Heclo, agenda-setting scholars embraced subsystems theory, but not without important revisions. Keith Hamm (1983) was the first to systematically apply Heclo's research to the study of federal policymaking. Like Heclo, Hamm perceived the policy process as highly decentralized, consisting of numerous and complex subgovernments. Hamm's research, however, also highlighted the tight-knit nature of policy subsystems. Focusing on the relationships among congressional committees, interest groups, and federal agencies, Hamm's research indicates that these groups work closely together in the formation of public policy, often to the benefit of their own self-interest. While the policy process has become more decentralized, Hamm's work suggests specialized subunits still play a central role.

The emergence of policy subsystems theory, in short, does little to narrow the gap between ordinary citizens and actual policymakers. Issue networks and the policy subsystems frameworks have displaced the notion of a fairly narrow and inaccessible group of actors who exercise primary influence over what problems are or are not addressed. Yet these frameworks do not necessarily support a pluralist model of the policy process. Rather, elites—the technopols, to use Heclo's term, or committee staff as suggested by Hamm—as well as well-organized and well-funded groups—still exercise a disproportionate share of indirect power.

Advocacy Coalitions: Theory or Framework?

While the work of Hugh Heclo provided a solid theoretical basis for subsystems theory, later work by Hamm showed that these policy subsystems were in fact more similar to the iron triangle than originally suggested. This left subsystems theorists at an impasse. Was agenda setting controlled by elites? Or were policy subsystems permeable and accessible? If the latter, how were they permeable, and who could gain access? One of the best known conceptual frameworks of the policy process, the advocacy coalitions framework, or ACF, was developed to address these sorts of questions. ACF originated in work by Paul Sabatier (1988), who, following Heclo, argued that the iron triangles of politics are in reality highly permeable and often unpredictable. Multiple participants are able to wield power throughout the policy process. Again, this stands in direct contrast to traditional iron triangle scholars as well as Easton's (1965) stages model, which describes the policy process as a predictable and repeated pattern among a select group of actors. For Sabatier, the answer to the question, "Where do policy proposals come from?" is similar to Heclo's answer and much broader than suggested by iron triangle scholars. It was to try to impose order on this complex and dynamic process that Sabatier (1988) and Sabatier and Jenkins-Smith (1999) developed ACF. Sabatier and Jenkins-Smith (1999, 118) contend that there are five "premises" to this framework, though implicit in all of them is the basic assumption that the policy process is dynamic.

Advocacy coalitions, like issue networks, represent groups with shared beliefs that coordinate activity following the emergence of a particular policy on the governmental agenda (Sabatier and Jenkins-Smith 1999). These coalitions consist of legislators, interest groups, public agencies, policy researchers, journalists, and many other subnational actors who wield influence in the policy process (Sabatier and Jenkins-Smith 1999, 119). Although these coalitions may disagree on the details of a particular policy, or "secondary beliefs," there is widespread agreement on the fundamental, or "policy core," beliefs of the group. Advocacy coalitions differ from Heclo's issue networks in that the former are usually organized around core policy beliefs, whereas the latter tend to be organized around technical expertise and ideology (Sabatier 1988). ACF posits that policy actors are foremost motivated toward advancing the beliefs of their policy domain or subsystem. As such, they are less prone to free riding than other types of coalitions (Sabatier and Jenkins-Smith 1999). This emphasis on core beliefs means that coalitions are expected to be long-term alliances; indeed, so long-term that Sabatier recommends a minimum time frame of ten years for analyzing coalition behavior.

The ACF helps explain change in the policy process by arguing that advocacy coalitions engage in what Sabatier (1988) described as "policy-oriented learning." These groups are continually adapting to changes in the political and socioeconomic environment and revising their preferences for policy design and even specific policy goals in response to new information (May 1992, 336). Like issue networks, the size and strength of advocacy coalitions are affected by the reframing of an issue and the ebbs and flows in attention on a particular issue.

This framework is an important contribution to helping us understand the policy process, for several reasons. First, it provides a theoretical basis for explaining both stability and rapid change in the policy process (Sabatier and Jenkins-Smith 1999). As public agencies, interest groups, or issue networks develop relationships, their ability to coordinate activity on a particular issue increases. Such reinforcement allows for the development of long-term and stable policy alliances. Rapid change, according to Sabatier, is most likely when dissatisfaction with existing policies creates an atmosphere ripe for the emergence of new coalitions. Second, the ACF moves scholars away from the notion of the policy process as a linear progression of predictable events as originally suggested by Easton (1965). It also moves scholars away from a conception of policymaking as a rational process based purely on economic benefits. The ACF does not even dictate that core policy belief systems operate on purely instrumental terms. To paraphrase Paul Sabatier and Hank Jenkins-Smith, at the heart of ACF are core beliefs, how coalitions organize around such beliefs, and how these belief systems coordinate activity among coalition members to seek policy change. Put another way, the ACF is "collections of actors sharing similar beliefs and coordinating their actions to achieve political goals" (Matti and Sanstrom 2011, 386).

The ACF has been used to successfully frame studies of policy subsystems across multiple policy arenas as well as cross-culturally. It does, however, have some limitations. For example, it has no standard methodology for operationalizing the underlying conceptual framework; ACF-based studies have been collectively criticized for having an "unspecified" methodology (Weible, Sabatier, and McQueen 2009, 127). By its very nature, the ACF creates some important challenges for scholars. Sabatier and Jenkins-Smith's call for a ten-year window through which to test for policy change (1999) creates practical problems of data collection and/or observation for a single issue area, let alone a comparative sample of issue areas.

Yet scholars are clearly willing to invest the resources to overcome those problems in pursuit of a framework for policy process theory that is both "helpful" and "grand" (Weimer 2008, 493). One review of publications from 1987 to 2006 revealed that more than eighty articles adopted the advocacy coalition framework in one form or another (Weible, Sabatier, and McQueen 2009). Since the publication of the first edition of this text, the *Policy Studies Journal* has devoted an entire issue to revisiting the utility of the ACF and directions for future research.[2] Elsewhere, scholars continue to expand the framework to include the effects of "significant perturbations external to the subsystem" (Weible, Sabatier, and McQueen 2009, 129), as well as applying the framework across multiple policy areas and geographic locations (Weible, Sabatier, and McQueen 2009, 126–127). Empirical evidence increasingly supports the ACF's claim that policy subsystem coalitions are highly stable; this stability has been found across both time and space (Pierce 2011; Weible et al. 2011; Weible, Sabatier, and McQueen 2009). In short, the ACF continues to encourage policy scholarship to be both helpful (e.g., explaining policy change, the structure of coalitions, and how such coalitions learn) and grand (with applications across policy types and varied by location).

Finally, there is reason to expect an increasing interdisciplinary element to ACF scholarship. For example, recent survey data indicate coalitions on both sides of an issue tend to filter information in a way that places disproportionate weight on evidence that fits within their existing belief systems (Henry 2011). Coalitions contract or expand according to "systematic cognitive biases" in the way in which members process information (Henry 2011, 378). And in some cases, coalitions form not based on influence or power (as would be suggested by rational models of policy change), but because of agreement on core beliefs (Matti and Sanstrom 2011). As we discuss in Chapter 9, this fits with evidence emerging from behavioral economics and social psychology about how people process political information and how they go about socializing in the political world. These advances in other disciplines may find fruitful application in future refinements of the ACF.

The bottom line is that the ACF is a robust framework that many scholars employ to examine policy change, notably change that does not comply with the assumptions of incrementalism. Although ACF's ability to accumulate generalizable knowledge is limited by its lack of a standardized methodology and some of the practical issues of data collection, it remains a useful framework for imposing order on the policy process and generating empirically testable hypotheses.

Punctuated Equilibrium: A Descriptive Framework for Policy Change

We now have some sense of where policy proposals come from: they originate in issue-centric subsystems characterized by one or more advocacy coalitions. But how and why do policies change, if they change at all?

For decades the mainstream answer to this question was centered on the concept of incrementalism. According to Charles Lindblom (1959), time constraints and/or political limitations prevent policymakers from articulating clearly defined goals and conducting a wide and comprehensive search for alternatives, weighing the costs and benefits of each. Instead, policymakers rely on previous policy decisions, resulting in a policy process that is characterized by small, incremental adjustments. In effect, incrementalism is the notion that policymakers start from an existing baseline and make adjustments to that baseline based on pressures from the current task environment (Lindblom 1959, 1979; Wildavsky 1964; see also Davis, Dempster, and Wildavsky 1966 for an application of incrementalism to federal budgeting).[3] Incrementalism is largely bounded rationality applied to policymaking, and for many years the incrementalist framework was the primary model for explaining stability in the policy process. However, it has an obvious flaw: policymaking is not always incremental. The framework of boundedly rational actors in policy subsystems producing incremental change struggles to explain why public policy periodically undergoes radical change.

Baumgartner and Jones (1993/2009) accepted that the policy process is complex and dynamic, following Heclo and Sabatier, but crucially drew attention to the fact that the pace of change is not always constant or linear. Based on a longitudinal analysis of the tone of media coverage and congressional activity on a number of policy issues, they concluded that an important and often overlooked aspect of the policy process was the "long-run fragility" of policy subsystems (1993/2009, 3). Drawing from the work of biologist Stephen Jay Gould, Baumgartner and Jones suggested that although there are periods of stability in the process—periods compatible with an incremental view of the policy process—there are also periods of rapid and significant change. Borrowing a term from Gould and his colleague Niles Eldredge, Baumgartner and Jones labeled these periods of rapid change "punctuated equilibria." Significant change to a policy subsystem—a policy punctuation—may result in a radical shift in policy and a new point of equilibrium. In effect, these punctuations cause the political system to "shift from one point of stability to another" (Baumgartner and Jones 1993/2009, 17). For Baumgartner and Jones, periods of relative stability are characterized by the theory of incrementalism, but periods of change are better captured by the concept of punctuated equilibrium.

The big question, of course, is what punctuates equilibria? What forces disrupt the process of incremental policy change and precipitate a radical shift in policymaking? Baumgartner and Jones argue that underlying these shifts is the breakdown of a traditional policy subsystem(s), or "policy monopoly," defined as a set of structural arrangements that keep policymaking in the hands of a relatively small group of interested policy actors. What Baumgartner and Jones recognize is that, for a variety of reasons, these policy monopolies periodically come under extreme stress. At these points, other actors penetrate these subsystems, creating instability in the policy process and the opportunity for significant shifts in policymaking.

The driving force for the theory of punctuated equilibrium, and by default the driving force for stability and instability in the policy process, is issue definition. As long as issue definition does not change, it is unlikely the underlying policy subsystem will. However, changes in the tone of an issue can lead to changes in the level of attention it receives, fostering a change in image and in the institutional venue in which the issue is considered. In short, changes in issue definition can alter the structural arrangements of a policy subsystem, breaking the policy monopoly and paving the way for radical shifts in policymaking. Baumgartner and Jones use the rise and fall of the nuclear power industry to make their point. In the 1950s the image of nuclear power was positive—a clean and cheap source of energy—and the policy monopoly built around the regulation and expansion of the nuclear power industry benefited from this image. The incident at Three Mile Island in 1979, however, produced a radical shift in this image; suddenly nuclear power was the focus of intense questioning and was viewed as dangerous, a threat to the safety of millions. The intensity of attention and the change in issue definition brought different government decision-making bodies into the policy monopoly—this is what Baumgartner and Jones characterize as a change in venues—that shattered the policy monopoly. The result was a significant change in policy from regular endorsement of nuclear power to a sudden withdrawal of funding for such power. In short, the nuclear power policy subsystem collapsed. A similar story emerges when looking at the tobacco industry. Both the nuclear power and tobacco industry subsystems were rendered obsolete following a shift in image that forced attention on the public safety/health aspect of the issue. Reflecting on the tobacco industry following the 1998 settlement with the states, Baumgartner and Jones wrote, "we think there is little doubt that the subsystem was destroyed" (1993/2009, 280).

Important to the theory of punctuated equilibrium is the notion of positive and negative feedback. Lindblom, drawing from Downs (1957), argued that increased attention in the policy process often fails to result in any institutional adjustments. Public interest in an issue declines following a wave of enthusiasm as the cost of change becomes apparent, resulting in a process of negative feedback. The theory of punctuated equilibrium, however, posits that as issues emerge on the formal agenda, they leave behind an "institutional legacy" (Baumgartner and Jones 1993/2009, 37), resulting in a *positive* feedback system. Positive feedback is the process by which a change in policy image based on criticism results in a new point of stability. Positive feedback is "anti-Downs," because increased attention does not necessarily result in a favoring of the status quo but potentially the opposite (Baumgartner and Jones 1993/2009, 64). This process of relative stability, followed by rapid change, followed by a new point of stability, creates as an "S-shaped diffusion curve." This is an important distinction from Lindblom's work on incrementalism. A change in image can produce a change in venue and thus a change in the institutional structures addressing the issue. Policy entrepreneurs, issue networks, and advocacy coalitions are well aware of this fact and tend to engage in what Baumgartner and Jones described as "venue shopping." Policy actors will continue to redefine an issue until it reaches a favorable venue, thus ensuring a favorable governmental response.[4] When this occurs, the policy process is subject to rapid change. As was the case with the tobacco industry, rapid change can mean policy extinction if the supporting venue is no longer available.

As would be expected, the media are influential actors in shaping public opinion about an issue. How the media define an issue ultimately shapes who will be involved in the public debate. Drawing on Schattschneider (1965), Baumgartner and Jones argued that the "losers" in the policy debate have an incentive to manipulate the image of an issue to increase political receptivity and the likelihood of finding a favorable venue. Redefining an issue has the potential to motivate previously uninterested groups of society into taking action, destabilizing a once-stable policy process. Baumgartner and Jones have referred to such cases as the "mobilization of the apathetic" (1993/2009, 21). Policymakers thus have an incentive to preserve the status quo, to preserve existing policy monopolies by limiting or discouraging debate.

Baumgartner and Jones have cited attempts by those in the nuclear power industry to control the image of nuclear power by highlighting only the cost-savings and energy-efficient aspects of nuclear power. With the disaster at Three Mile Island as well as dissension among top nuclear scientists regarding safety concerns, the public image began to change, resulting in more groups emerging against nuclear power. The rapid rejection of nuclear power as a cheap and clean source of energy resulted in a significant shift in policy, such that the new policy equilibrium was one in which nuclear power was viewed with skepticism. The nuclear power industry, once a dominant policy subsystem, immediately collapsed due to a change in how the issue of nuclear power was defined. Policy monopolies, then, are simply policy subsystems that contend to offer the best solution with a single, positive policy image. This means they can either be created or destroyed depending upon how an issue is defined (Baumgartner and Jones 1993/2009, 161). Stability in the policy process is thus deceptive, because it can be disrupted very quickly through issue redefinition and mobilization of those previously uninvolved in the policymaking process.

How an issue is defined ultimately determines the institutional response and whether the policy process is characterized by stability or instability. A change in the image associated with a particular issue will tend to lead to a change in venue in which the issue is advanced. Stability in the policy process is contingent upon two factors: 1) existing structure of the institutions and 2) definition of issues processed by the institutions. As Baumgartner and Jones (1993/2009) argued, the former is a source of stability or "friction" given the anemic pace at which institutional rules tend to change (see also Jones and Baumgartner 2005), while the latter is the first to change and represents the source of rapid shifts in the policy process. Political entrepreneurs seek to maintain that stability if they are part of a policy monopoly perceived favorably by existing institutional structures. Baumgartner and Jones describe such a stalemate in the policy process as "structure-induced equilibrium." Because images are inherently tied to venues, those on the opposing side of policy monopolies seek to manipulate the image of a certain policy to reach an alternative institutional venue. Institutional structures are contingent upon the attention and intensity of citizen preferences. The mobilization of the apathetic represents a destabilizing force in the policy process. Thus, the answer to the question "Why do policies change?" is that as issues are redefined, preferences change, which leads to political instability. Political and policy actors that were either uninterested or unmotivated are brought into the policy process through policy definition and/or redefinition.

One of the implications of punctuated equilibrium is that policy decisions or changes in a given issue area will follow a distinct leptokurtic distribution (a large number of data points near the center and in the tails of the distribution) as opposed to the normal distribution that would be expected if the process were completely random (True, Jones, and Baumgartner 1999, 109–110). Government budgets are a classic example of such distributions; mostly these tend to reflect incremental changes—small, incremental annual increases or decreases. Every once in a while, though, this relative equilibrium is disturbed by a shock to the system (e.g., war, economic depression) that overcomes institutional friction or inertia and results in dramatic budget increases or decreases. Such patterns of change are referred to as the "power law," exhibiting high levels of kurtosis or "peakedness" (Baumgartner and Jones 1993/2009, xxii), and have been shown to apply across political systems (Jones et al. 2009), at the subnational level (Breunig and Koski 2012), and over time (Jones and Baumgartner 2005). Jones, Sulkin, and Larsen (2003) expanded on this notion of a leptokurtic distribution of policy change and found that bargaining and information-gathering costs contribute to the size of the policy punctuation. Highly complex organizations with a large number of participants tend to have more institutional friction (Jones, Sulkin, and Larsen 2003, 155). This is important, because it appears that higher levels of friction result in a higher probability of punctuation and a higher likelihood that policy change is leptokurtic rather than normal. Following in the footsteps of Jones, Sulkin, and Larsen (2003), Scott Robinson and his colleagues also found evidence linking institutional structures to the likelihood of policy punctuation. Analyzing budgetary data from school districts, Robinson and colleagues found that highly centralized school districts are more susceptible to "nonincremental changes" (2007, 147). Centralizing districts tends to increase the probability of large policy changes, whereas increases in organizational size decrease such probability. That such punctuations have been empirically verified across time and space is critical to building a systematic and reliable framework for studying policy change.

Recent empirical studies continue to refine and expand the punctuated equilibrium framework. For example, Breunig and Koski (2012) demonstrated that functional spending categories within state budgets tend to be less stable and smaller over time following a budget punctuation; in other words, punctuations have been found to affect future policy outcomes. John and Bevan (2012) argued that there are different types of policy punctuations and classified these in a typology based on nearly one hundred years of policies enacted by the British parliament. If the purpose of studying policy change is to uncover what factors predict policy change, then such contributions are significant.

Despite its continuing development as a mainstream framework for understanding the policy process, punctuated equilibrium does have some important limitations. Notably, it is a descriptive rather than a predictive framework. Its lack of predictive power is largely rooted in its acceptance of bounded rationality, that is, its assumption that cognitive limitations prevent humans from being classically rational decision makers (Simon 1947, 1985). Descriptively, this is not a problem. There is abundant evidence that humans are not classically rational decision makers and have all sorts of cognitive biases (e.g. Kahneman and Tversky 1978; Dawes and Thaler 1988; Druckman 2004; Ariely 2009). The problem is that classical rational actor models are predictive—they provide explicit and testable hypotheses about how humans will make decisions—whereas models anchored in bounded rationality are not. The latter may be more descriptively accurate, but they are constructed to explain why people deviate from rationality, not to produce testable hypotheses about future decision making. The theory of punctuated equilibrium imports this limitation along with bounded rationality; in short, it does little to help us predict policy change. It provides a superior descriptive account of why rapid changes in policy occur, but fails to offer any forecasts of when such changes will occur. The predictive limitations of punctuated equilibrium may also be traced to its antecedents. Punctuated equilibrium, as originally formulated in biology, was a "mechanical model"; it said nothing at all about individual choice (Prindle 2012, 37; see Jones 2003 for an opposing argument).

To be fair, Baumgartner and Jones are wholly up front about the inability of punctuated equilibrium to serve as a forecasting model for policy change: "a complete model will not be locally predictable, since we cannot predict the timing or outcomes of the punctuations" (True, Jones, and Baumgartner 1999, 111).

Predicting policy stability (what Baumgartner and Jones consider the norm of the policy process) and rapid change remains difficult, largely for three reasons. First, a period of relative stability will often shift to one of rapid change (i.e., a policy punctuation) because of events external to the subsystem. These events—acts of terrorism, nuclear accidents, the bursting of stock market bubbles—are inherently unpredictable. Second, policy change does not flow in a single direction; punctuations can go both ways. A drastically new policy, for example, might be overturned by a Supreme Court ruling. Third, there is a psychological element that is critical to the punctuated equilibrium framework, and human psychology is, to put it mildly, imperfectly understood.

Despite some limitations, the work of Baumgartner and Jones has undoubtedly improved our understanding of the policy process in many ways. First, and perhaps most important, it recognizes that significant change in the policy process can and often does occur. This addresses a major gap left unexplained in incrementalist frameworks. In fact, one of the main objectives of Baumgartner and Jones's work is to explain why policy monopolies, such as the nuclear power industry or the tobacco industry, fail. Punctuated equilibrium is also evidence that the policy process is not rational or incremental. Rather than progressing through a series of stages (Ripley 1985), the arguments presented by Baumgartner and Jones suggest the policy process is susceptible to rapid change.

Second, punctuated equilibrium recognizes that changes in institutional design occur following the emergence of an issue on the government agenda, moving policy scholars away from the Downs (1972) model of negative policy feedback. This has important implications for policy entrepreneurs. The key to disrupting policy equilibrium is finding the appropriate policy image that mobilizes citizens previously disengaged from the political process. No one group controls the policy process, and no one issue fits neatly into a particular venue or subsystem. Jones and Jenkins-Smith (2009) make the case for a "policy topography" that includes how subsystems are linked through macro-level factors such as public opinion. This "trans-subsystem" framework recognizes how subsystems may interact due to sudden external events (Jones and Jenkins-Smith 2009, 41). Labeled "salience disruption," such shocks to the system force previously independent subsystems to cooperate and coordinate activity (Jones and Jenkins-Smith 2009, 42). As an example of salience disruption, Jones and Jenkins-Smith use shifting views on immigration policy, from an economic development issue to one based on national security following the terrorist attacks on September 11, 2001. Policy entrepreneurs, utilizing the media and other political actors, can continually redefine their policy image until it finds a receptive audience, setting the stage for rapid policy change.

In their updated version of *Agendas and Instability in American Politics*, Baumgartner and Jones made the case for a more comprehensive model based on "disruptive dynamics" (2009, 285). This is rooted in a recognition that periods of relative stability punctuated by rapid change are not limited to particular policy subsystems but can occur throughout the political system. A more comprehensive view, argued Baumgartner and Jones, will allow for an examination of how rapid change in the political system (i.e., through elections) can affect policy change. Others similarly argue for a more expansive view of subsystem politics, suggesting that "information flows in the policymaking system" (rather than the policy subsystem itself) are more important (Workman, Jones, and Jochim 2009, 76; see also Jones and Baumgartner 2012). Understanding how policy change fits into a larger system of political change would no doubt be useful. However, this only adds to the methodological and operationalization burden faced by policy process scholars.

Finally, Baumgartner and Jones's original research has spawned numerous attempts to improve the generalizability of punctuated equilibrium theory, creating fruitful areas for new research (Jones and Baumgartner 2012, 1). In the nearly twenty years since its original introduction, policy scholars have significantly refined and expanded the punctuated equilibrium framework (see Pump 2011; Nowlin 2011 for reviews). Punctuated equilibrium fits with the general Lasswellian notion of the policy sciences in that it is methodologically sophisticated, interdisciplinary, and generalizable. The Policy Agendas Project started by Baumgartner and Jones allows any researcher to freely track changes in national policy since 1946, across multiple policy areas, using numerous indicators of attention or change. Other work by Jones and Baumgartner (2005) tracks budgetary changes in the U.S. federal budget over fifty years across multiple spending categories. We question whether any policy framework (or even any framework in political science) is so comprehensive and open to replication.

Garbage Cans and Policy Windows: A Multiple Streams Approach to Policy Change

Whereas Baumgartner and Jones provide an explanatory framework for why the policy process is subject to stability as well as change, this framework is not predictive. Thus, we are still left with the question: Why do policies change? Why are some policies more successful than others in terms of garnering public support? And similarly, why does the government pay attention to some policies but not others?

Like Baumgartner and Jones, John Kingdon (1995) has argued that the best way to understand the policy process is by examining policy image. In fact, Baumgartner and Jones's analyses are in part based in Kingdon's original research on agenda setting. This work suggests that how a policy is defined and how it is perceived by the public and policymakers ultimately determine whether the policy will receive positive or negative feedback. Policy change is best understood through these sorts of subsystem dynamics, focusing on internal actors and events, as well as changes in the external political world.

Kingdon constructs a simple and parsimonious model of the policy process. It begins with the question (1995, 1), "What makes people in and around government attend, at any given time, to some subjects and not to others?" For Kingdon, the level of analysis is the government agenda and the items government pays attention to, and the unit of analysis is "predecisions," or decisions that affect whether an issue reaches the government agenda. Rather than focus on policy stability, Kingdon is interested in explaining the process by which issues reach the government agenda and allow significant policy change to take place. To do this, he examined health and transportation policy in the late 1970s, focusing on successful cases of policy initiation as well as cases in which initiation seemed likely but never occurred.

For Kingdon, the agenda-setting process and alternative selection are best viewed through the "garbage can model" presented by Cohen, March, and Olsen (1972). This model is centered on the concept of "organized anarchies" (Kingdon 1995, 84), or organizations that share three general characteristics: problematic preferences, fluid participation, and unclear technology. In an organized anarchy, people routinely move in and out of organizations or organizational subunits and thus rarely understand the organization's purpose or their role within it. Various participants work autonomously to provide independent solutions to similar problems. In the process, ideas are jumbled together, with solutions actually searching for problems, rather than the reverse, as would be suggested by the stages model or the rational-comprehensive model of decision making (Kingdon 1995, 85). Policy entrepreneurs learn by trial and error regarding alternative selection. The end result is that both problems and solutions are "dumped" into the proverbial policymaking garbage can. The policy process here is not linear, nor does it always move in incremental stages. Rather, it is best described as relative chaos among competing policy communities. Kingdon revised the garbage can model to include three separate "streams": problems, policies, and politics. Each stream contributes to our understanding of why government pays attention to some problems more than others; this is more generally thought of as the "multiple streams" approach.

First is the problem stream. For policy change to take place, policy actors must first recognize that there is an existing problem. The most obvious way for a problem to capture the attention of the public or government is through a "focusing event." For example, the disaster at Three Mile Island in 1979 was a focusing event for the nuclear power industry, ultimately shifting the focus away from energy efficiency to health and safety concerns. "Indicators" such as regularly conducted surveys or published reports can also raise awareness of an existing condition. For example, the regular release of the "nation's report card" from the National Assessment of Educational Progress (NAEP), showing the relatively static performance of U.S. students over time in science and math, tends to capture the attention of the public and election officials for a brief time. Focusing events, however, tend to be more effective. The media also play an important role in shaping the saliency of a particular issue.

Policy is the second of Kingdon's streams. It is here that policy alternatives are generated to address emerging problems. Participants in the policy stream are represented by both a "visible" and a "hidden" cluster of actors (Kingdon 1995, 199). The former represents prominent policy actors such as the president and members of Congress; the latter tends to be composed of policy specialists, operating deep within federal or state agencies, who set the available alternatives upon which policy decisions are made. The policy stream consists of a "policy primordial soup" in which multiple ideas are just "floating around," waiting to be scooped up by prominent government actors (Kingdon 1995, 116). Both problems and solutions get dumped into the same policy can, resulting in an unpredictable process of policy change. It is in the policy stream that we see the role of the policy entrepreneur as critical to creating significant policy change, capable of determining policy outcomes by manipulating and narrowing the number of policy alternatives. The visible cluster of participants, who serve an important role in the problem stream as the movers and shakers of public opinion, are relegated to the sidelines in the policy stream (Kingdon 1995, 30).

The process of selecting policy alternatives is not random, however. Kingdon has argued that within the policy stream are two important aspects for understanding how alternatives move from the primordial soup to being a viable policy option: 1) through "softening up" and 2) through "coupling" (1995, 200–201). Policy specialists, interest groups, and even academics and researchers in the hidden cluster can help to soften up the agenda to ensure favorable political receptivity. This process is critical in terms of determining whether a policy actually reaches the government agenda. Coupling is the ability to link alternatives with problems. For elected officials, policy alternatives must be justified in terms of costs and benefits, with particular attention to core constituencies, and must also be workable solutions to the problem. Although many good ideas may be floating around among policy specialists, without a specific problem, they are unlikely to reach the government agenda.

The third and final stream is the political stream. Here it is best to think of Baumgartner and Jones's notion of venue shopping or "political learning" (May 1992). A significant shift in the national political ideology and/or a realigning election can cause a significant shift in the type of policies that reach the attention of elected officials. In short, politics (e.g., election results, the national mood, etc.) determine whether a problem will find a receptive venue. Existing conditions that were previously not considered problems can suddenly move onto the government agenda. The political stream is characterized by bargaining among elected officials, constituents, and organized political forces. Even though hidden participants are important within their own agency, Kingdon (1995, 30) argued that such experts tend to be less influential outside their agency and thus less effective in the political stream. Instead, more visible participants within the executive branch are critical to raising national awareness of a policy and to transforming a condition into a problem to be addressed by the government.

The convergence of the three streams creates what Kingdon referred to as a "policy window," or the opportunity for rapid policy change. The problem and political streams open the window. For significant change to take place, however, the savvy policy entrepreneur operating in the policy stream must be capable of recognizing the opportunity the window presents. The role of the policy entrepreneur is to "couple" the three streams before the window closes, which, according to Kingdon, can occur quickly and without notice: "Once a window opens, it does not stay open long" (Kingdon 1995, 169). Thus, on the one hand policy entrepreneurs and policy communities are limited by the political stream. Without a receptive political venue and/or receptive national mood, coupling of the policy and political streams is unlikely. On the other hand, the problem and political streams depend on existing policy communities. Cases of "partial coupling," in which one or two streams are joined without the remaining stream(s), rarely lead to policy change (Kingdon 1995, 200–201).

The importance of predecisions, or what others refer to as nondecisions, in the policymaking process can be traced back to the work of Bachrach and Baratz (1962). It is helpful to think of the first two streams of Kingdon's model as directly linked to the issue of nondecisions. Problem definition and the alternative development (problem stream and policy stream) are critical in determining the nature of the final policy outcome. These nondecisions determine whether a policy window will be useful in achieving policy change. Thus, policy entrepreneurs, according to Kingdon, are potentially more important than individuals considered responsible for the original creation of the policy. This of course raises issues with normative democratic theory about preserving an open and transparent government, as well as concerns about who actually controls the policy process: Elites? Technopols? Policy specialists? Or citizens?

The multiple streams framework is not without its critics. Zahariadis (2007, 79–83) identifies three main weaknesses: a lack of use in models of change, an inability to distinguish clear lines of separation between streams, and an absence of empirically falsifiable hypotheses. These present significant challenges for policy scholars trying to apply this framework. For example, as suggested by Zahariadis, it seems to be extremely difficult to empirically isolate and analyze streams independently. Using survey data from school board superintendents, Robinson and Eller (2010, 209) were able to demonstrate that the probability of participating in the "problem stream" increased significantly if the participants were identified as participating in the solution stream. In other words, actors in the solution stream and problem stream were not operating independently of one another.

On the other two points, scholars are working to utilize and empirically test the tenets of the multiple streams model. Liu and others (2010) conducted 271 interviews with local policy stakeholders across three states and found that local government actors were more concerned with how a particular policy fit with existing state and federal statutes than with its political feasibility (81). There is, however, evidence that advocacy groups do strategically adjust the attention devoted to certain issues depending on the salience of such issues in the national media. Boscarino (2009), for example, found empirical support for "problem surfing" by the Wilderness Society and the Sierra Club. Both groups shifted the attention they gave to a particular issue (e.g., climate change, wildlife, water quality, etc.) according to its prominence in the *New York Times*.

Whether an issue reaches the decision-making agenda ultimately depends on how it is defined. Not only do nondecisions have the potential to determine who is involved in the policy process, they significantly affect the nature of political debate throughout the policymaking process. However, although nondecisions remain critical to explaining the policy process as well as policy outcomes, they remain difficult to study systematically. What is a nondecision? Are different types of nondecisions more important than others? Extending the "garbage can model," Kingdon (1995) simply asserted that the policy process is complex and that nondecisions are influential in determining policy outcomes. However, describing the policy process as complex does not move us closer to a comprehensive theory of policy change.

Thus, some of the same limitations of punctuated equilibrium also apply to multiple streams, especially issues related to predictive power. Do certain indicators increase the probability of conditions turning into problems? Why do some policy images lead to more public receptivity than others? Nonetheless, like Baumgartner and Jones's seminal work, Kingdon laid the groundwork for systematically studying the policy process and provided us with a powerful explanatory framework for policy incrementalism and rapid policy change.

Conclusion

In this chapter we have reviewed three dominant frameworks for explaining where policy comes from, or what is commonly referred to as agenda setting: the advocacy coalition framework, punctuated equilibrium, and the multiple streams approach, or policy windows. Criticism has been leveled at all three for their inability to rule out alternative explanations. But we have also shown that each framework is capable of generating testable hypotheses about policy change: How stable are coalitions over time? What is the pace at which policy changes, as measured by levels of kurtosis? Do policy specialists shop around ideas waiting for the right political window to appear? Or, put another way, do policy specialists change what solution is advanced following elections in which partisan control changes?

To be sure, other explanations exist regarding how an issue moves from being a problem to capturing the attention of government. Notably absent in our chapter is a discussion of policy diffusion. Policy, particularly state-level policy, is significantly impacted by what other states are doing (Walker 1969). If one state adopts a lottery, states within close geographic proximity are more likely to do the same (Berry and Berry 1990). States "learn" from one another, and such learning transcends policy typologies, even when controlling for "internal determinants" of state policy (Berry and Berry 1990; Shipan and Volden 2008). Recent work has even attempted to apply the characteristics of the punctuated equilibrium model to identifying types of diffusion (Boushey 2012).

The core research questions of policy process scholarship are: Where do policy proposals come from? Why do policies change? Why does the government pay attention to some policies and not to others? Where does the process of policy-making actually take place? The research literature on subsystems and agenda setting has provided systematic responses to all of these questions, though it is fair to say that none has provided definitive answers.

From Heclo, Sabatier, Weible, and others, we know that policy proposals tend to emerge from large, informal alliances comprised of highly diverse policy actors. Indeed, Sabatier and Jenkins-Smith's (1988) original work on advocacy coalitions has spawned nearly one hundred articles that use the ACF as the basis for theorizing about subsystem politics and policy change (Weible, Sabatier, and McQueen 2009). What we do not know, however, is what type of alliances are the most successful in terms of pushing an issue onto the government agenda. What is success for a policy subsystem? Is it simply raising awareness of an issue, or is it actually causing significant policy change? Heclo's work frequently mentions policy change, but how much change is required for an issue network to be successful? Sabatier and Jenkins-Smith (1999, 147) distinguished between "major" and "minor" policy change, but readily admitted that the type of change depends on the subsystem.[5] To empirically assess the role of advocacy coalitions and issue networks in the policy process, these questions need to be answered (see also Sabatier 1991b).

From the existing literature, we also know that how policies reach the government agenda is a mystery. Baumgartner and Jones's (1993/2009) punctuated equilibrium is less a theoretical framework for predicting policy change and more of a descriptive analysis of the policy landscape. Without a theory explaining why the particular frame of an issue is more receptive than another frame, punctuated equilibrium fails to offer a predictive account of when "losers" will be successful in reframing the debate and thereby successful in causing a major disruption in the policy process. By depicting policymakers as decision makers guided by bounded rationality, Baumgartner and Jones were less interested in predicting why policymakers make the decisions they do than in explaining how policymakers respond to the task environment. The punctuated equilibrium framework has arguably been subjected to the most systematic empirical testing to date and remained largely intact. Yet it is limited, because policy change can occur simply because of changes in how people view a particular issue. To more fully grasp how such changes can occur requires a heavy dose of psychology, social psychology, and even neuroscience. Chapters 8 and 9 discuss patterns in the acceptability of certain policy narratives.

There are also limitations to Kingdon's work. For the three streams framework to apply to the study of policy change, policy actors must first recognize that a problem exists. Kingdon argued that focusing events are the first of the three streams necessary for triggering a policy window. But what constitutes a focusing event? Can we really predict a focusing event, or even if a focusing event occurs, whether it will ignite significant policy change? These questions are left unaddressed by Kingdon's analyses (see also Zahariadis 2007).

The study of policy process has important implications for the study of interest representation. If elites or policy experts are able to wield control of the policy process, often through indirect and unobservable decisions, then the potential exists for the abrogation of citizen interests. Subsystems scholars shifted the focus away from iron triangle politics to a more open and complex policymaking process (see Bardach 2006). Policy outcomes are not the final say in the policy-making process. Rather, multiple actors within and outside of government are constantly seeking to influence the government agenda, resulting in a highly dynamic and highly complex process. The policy process is not rational, but it is also not random. Policy entrepreneurs seek to find receptive policy venues by adjusting the policy image and policy definition according to changes in the political environment. Punctuated equilibrium and "policy windows" frameworks also move us away from an overreliance on incrementalism and recognition that rapid policy change is possible and in need of constant examination.

Though the subsystems and agenda-setting literatures have their fair share of critics, both literatures are moving forward. The trend in subsystems and agenda-setting research seems to be expansion of the unit of analysis (see Nowlin 2011, 54). Jones and Jenkins-Smith's (2009) policy topography is one such example, but others are the work of Jochim and May (2010) on "policy regimes" as well as Baumgartner and Jones's (2009) "disruptive dynamics." Still others have called for subsystems analysis that allows for a prominent role of the bureaucracy (Ellison and Newmark 2010; Pump 2011). Such expansion no doubt improves the reliability, robustness, and explanatory power of these frameworks, even if they do continue to lack predictive capabilities. Expanding the concept of what constitutes a subsystem capable of achieving policy change also creates new problems. For the past decade public administration scholars have noted the blurring of the line between the public and private sectors in the delivery of public goods (see Frederickson et al. 2012). Governing is increasingly characterized by public-private partnerships, raising concerns about accountability (Koppell 2010), but also issues for process scholars attempting to measure influence in the policy arena. How do we measure the role of a private organization in public policymaking? Policy process scholars will be forced to be creative when pulling from their methodological tool kit to address such concerns. On the other hand, if the subsystem no longer refers to the policy subsystem, a more expansive view of how institutions process information will lead to more reliable theories about change in the political system, perhaps moving us one step closer to a generalizable theory about policy change.

Agenda-setting studies are based on how policymakers and the public respond to policy images and issue definitions. Emerging work in experimental economics, social psychology, and even neuroeconomics on how the human mind processes incoming information are already being incorporated into this agenda (see Leach and Sabatier 2005). Still, punctuated equilibrium and multiple streams face a monumental task if prediction is to be a goal (and it is not at all clear that prediction *is* a goal of these frameworks). The unit of analysis, policy change, is so complex and encompassing that establishing causal order is difficult if not impossible. Evolutionary theory is heavily present in both, and for this reason John (2003) calls for paying more attention to the development and use of evolution as a guiding framework for the development of general theory of policy change. In the previous edition of this text we attempted to do just that by focusing on how evolutionary theory applies to individual decision making and the patterns we observe in what captures the attention of citizens and lawmakers. We believe this is a promising approach for the agenda-setting literature and return more generally to this topic in Chapter 9. In short, the future is bright for policy process scholars. Predictability will continue to remain an elusive goal, but the explanatory power and generalizability of such work is commendable indeed.

Notes

1. See Gormley (1986) for an examination of how issue networks operate concerning regulatory policy.

2. In a recent special issue of *Policy Studies Journal* (volume 39, number 3) devoted to the ACF, four of the six articles using the ACF were about the structure of advocacy coalitions, while the other two examined policy change (Weible et al. 2011, 352).

3. We discuss the tenets of incrementalism and its pros and cons more fully in Chapter 3.

4. "Venue shopping" is akin to what May (1992) described as "political learning," wherein policy elites "learn" how to adapt their proposals to garner the most political support.

5. Sabatier and Jenkins-Smith (1999, 153) also identify a number of limitations to the advocacy coalition framework, including lack of knowledge about the conditions for coalition formation and the need for more longitudinal studies on how subsystems and belief systems change over time.

CHAPTER 5

What Should We Do?
The Field of Policy Analysis

Government has a finite ability to address the infinite claims made on it. It is asked to address a virtually unlimited set of issues and problems within an all too limited set of political, financial, institutional, personnel, legal, temporal, and informational constraints. Say a particular issue or problem—educational performance, a budget deficit, or whatever—has made its way onto the institutional agenda. The government now has to decide what action (if any) to take to address that problem. Pay teachers more? Increase test standards? Cut spending? Raise taxes? Something else? Whenever policymakers seek to address a pressing issue or problem, the starting point boils down to a single question: What should we do? (Rose 1993, 19). The fundamental task of policy analysis is to seek an answer to this question.

There is considerable disagreement over how to approach this question. On the one hand are those who believe the question charges the analyst with an obligation to provide a reasonably objective, single response; an answer that, in effect, says *this* particular policy alternative is *the* best choice. On the other hand are those who view the idea of expert policy analysts being society's problem-solvers as naive, or even worse, dangerous. They argue that the question raises a normative problem, not a series of technical or instrumental problems. When a government faces the question "What should we do?" it is like confronting a clash of values. Liberals want one thing, conservatives another; particular policy responses to a problem create winners and losers; and the various stakeholders in this process compete noisily over whose preferences will gain the favor of government. This is the reality of politics, and the job of the analyst is better conceived as a task of interpretation and facilitation: understanding the different perspectives that create the conflict of values and judging them on their own terms. "What should we do?" is a question best answered by reflective deliberation and discourse among these various perspectives, not by a causal theory or a regression coefficient.

These views reflect a continuum rather than completely independent camps, and later in this chapter we examine recent attempts to reconcile and merge various elements of these perspectives. For now it is useful to roughly divide the field into two generic approaches to answering its central research question. So although a number of frameworks have been formulated to structure the search for answers to the question "What should we do?" we will frame our discussion, at least initially, in terms of the rationalist approach and the post-positivist approach. The rationalist approach views policy analysis as a linear problem-solving process, "as a tool for choosing among alternatives in an effort to solve problems" (Shulock 1997, 227). Proponents of this orientation to policy analysis favor deploying the theoretical and methodological tool kit of social science to generate a reasonably objective and neutral ranking of policy alternatives. Post-positivists argue that it is impossible for policy analysis to inoculate itself against the normative nature of answering the key question. The conceptual framework of science and the sophisticated methodological firepower wielded by the rationalists are propped up by their own value systems (Fischer 2003). Post-positivists seek to put other values and perspectives on an equal footing with science in the process of deciding what should be done.

As traditionally and currently practiced, policy analysis is dominated by the rationalist approach. In general, this means policy analysis has a strong bias toward quantitative methods and conceptual frameworks taken from the positivist traditions in social science (economic theory, especially, is used to structure many analyses). Post-positivists, drawing on decidedly less positivist theoretical foundations like discourse and critical theory, have leveled some important criticisms at the rationalist approach. Post-positivist policy analysis, however, has struggled to establish a practical set of methodological alternatives to those employed by the rationalists and conceptually has yet to convince the mainstream of the field that it is not leading a charge into the swamp of relativism. The rationalist approach at least produces an answer to the fundamental question of the field. According to its critics, post-positivism produces as many answers as there are opinions and perspectives, all given equal value and validity. That, the rationalists argue, is no answer at all, just an amplification of the confusion in politics. Still, evolution of rationalist methods and conceptual models increasingly reflects a reaction to, and an attempt to account for, many post-positivist criticisms.

In this chapter we examine these two approaches to policy analysis and assess their ability to provide useful explanatory frameworks for answering the question, "What should we do?"

The Rationalist Approach

Joseph Priestly was a notable eighteenth-century scientist, philosopher, and theologian. His many accomplishments include discovering oxygen gas, authoring scholarly manuscripts on electricity, and helping to found the Christian denomination of Unitarianism. He also indirectly prompted an early expression of the rationalist approach to policy analysis. In the early 1790s Priestly was struggling with a decision over whether to leave the ministry and take up a more lucrative offer from the Earl of Shelburne, a well-known British statesman of the time. Priestly was struggling with the individual version of the public policy analyst's question, his being the dilemma "What should *I* do?" One of his friends, Benjamin Franklin, wrote Priestly a letter stating that he had devised a system of "prudential or moral algebra" to solve exactly this sort of dilemma. When unsure what course of action constituted the best response to a question, Franklin said he did the following:

1. Divided a sheet of paper in half and listed the pros of a decision or course of action on one side and the cons on the other.
2. Assigned weights to the pros and cons, i.e., assigned them numbers reflecting their importance or desirability.
3. Struck out equalities. If one pro carried equal weight as one con, he would strike them both out. If one pro carried the weight of three cons, he would strike those out. Eventually, the pro or con side would reveal itself to have more weight.
4. Used the information from these calculations to make the decision.[1]

Franklin's method of "moral algebra" succinctly captures the basic notion of the rationalist approach to policy analysis (indeed, it has been cited as an early form of cost-benefit analysis; see Boardman et al. 2001, 1). When faced with the question of what to do, the best approach is to employ a means of systematically ranking the various alternatives and choosing the one that ranks highest. More formally, policy analysis is traditionally defined as "an applied social science discipline which uses multiple methods of inquiry and argument to produce and transform policy-relevant information that may be utilized in political settings to resolve policy problems" (Dunn 1981/2011, 35).[2]

The rationalist approach to policy analysis clearly takes its cue from Lasswell's notion of the policy sciences. It takes an instrumental view of public policy: policies are viewed as means to address problems or achieve goals, and the central objective of policy analysis is to identify the most desirable means to achieve these ends. Identifying those means is a largely technocratic undertaking that draws on multiple disciplines, is heavily quantitative, and is keenly interested in assessing causal relationships. The rationalist approach follows this generic process for generating knowledge useful for answering questions about what should be done:

1. Define the problem. For a policy analyst, a "problem" typically implies some state of the world that is and will remain unsatisfactory or undesirable without government intervention (Mohr 1995, 14).
2. Identify alternative courses of action. This means generating a series of policy options that will have a desired impact on the problem. Linking alternatives to problems implies a causal link—if government does X, Y will happen. Rationalists draw heavily on social science theories to understand such causal links.
3. Estimate outcomes. This involves creating a set of criteria on which to judge various policy alternatives, then generating estimates of how each policy alternative is likely to perform on those criteria. For example, a policy analyst may wish to estimate the impact of various policy alternatives on the basis of costs, particular outcomes (say a reading program on test scores), and distribution (who bears the costs and who reaps the benefits). Importantly, this means dealing with uncertainty. None of these potential impacts is directly observed; they are future events that must be forecast.
4. Compare alternatives. This means ranking the different alternatives according to their forecast performance on the various criteria from step 3.

5. Choose the most preferred alternative. The alternative that scores the highest, or is judged most likely to achieve a desired objective or fulfill a desired value, is the alternative forwarded as the best option to translate into government action, that is, to become a public policy.[3]

The rationalist approach, in other words, is an updated version of Franklin's moral algebra. The theoretical and methodological horsepower employed in modern rationalist approaches has increased considerably since Franklin's time, but the underlying concept remains the same. Resolving questions of what to do is best approached as a systematic, problem-solving exercise.

In its modern Lasswell-like form, the original idea behind the field of policy analysis was to put teams of experts into the highest reaches of government who would employ social science theory and methods to put this problem-solving process into action (Dror 1968). The hope (since proven naive) was that policy analysts would deal in facts more than values; they would produce relatively objective assessments of what would and what would not work for a given problem.[4] Policymakers would take the role of clients, meaning they would come to the analysts with the problems, specify the desired outcomes, and set values that would serve to rank policy alternatives. The analyst's job was to develop and supply the technical know-how and employ the best social science theory and methods to identify the alternatives that addressed client needs.

Many aspects of this vision have become firmly entrenched as mainstream policy analysis. For example, graduate courses in policy analysis typically train students to view policy analysis as a linear problem-solving paradigm whose main objective is to advise a client on the best policy alternative for a given problem (Shulock 1997, 228; Weimer and Vining 2005, 1; Bardach 2005/2011). This is often accomplished using sophisticated quantitative methods; just about everything in the statisticians', econometricians', and game theorists' tool kit has been adapted to serve the needs of policy analysis (for a comprehensive introduction to the range of quantitative policy analysis methods, see Gupta 2001; Dunn 1981/2011). The increasing sophistication of methods, however, has not yet addressed a fundamental conceptual problem the rationalist project has struggled with since its modern inception.

If the underlying purpose of the rationalist project is to come up with some ranking of policy alternatives, it needs a measure with which to rank them. On what grounds does rational policy analysis judge a particular policy alternative "best?" In Franklin's system of moral algebra this was a comparatively easy question to answer. Because the problems the system was designed to solve were individual, the subjective judgments of the individual were enough to attach weights to the pros and cons of various choices. The rationalist does not have it so easy; the subjective values of the analyst are not a valid yardstick to judge the worth of public policies that represent collective interests. But if rationalists are not going to incorporate the individualistic values employed in Franklin's moral algebra to operationalize their problem-solving process, what should they use? Answering this question has proven to be a central challenge for the rationalist project.

Following the generic problem-solving process listed above requires having a clear definition of the problem to be addressed and accurate forecasts of how differing policy options will address that problem. Unfortunately, in practice the problems public policies are called upon to solve rarely have a universally agreed upon, precisely defined, easily measurable, single goal. Educational performance, for example, is a pretty vague goal. How do we measure this? Test scores? Graduation rates? Even if those questions can be answered comprehensively (a tall order in and of itself), we still face the problem of figuring out how different policy options might increase test scores or graduation rates. In practice what this means is forecasting the likely impact of policy alternatives on these measures; that means dealing with the uncertainty of the future. Even if we can manage to do that (an even taller order), a policy analysis is still likely to get pretty messy. Our analysis may show that the program forecast to increase test scores the most—tougher academic standards, say—lowers graduation rates. The policy that increases graduation rates the most is forecast to lower test scores. Which option should we choose? What if the policy deemed best by our analysis of expected impact on educational performance is very expensive? Upsets the teachers' unions? Results in clear losers as well as clear winners? The issues raised in this brief example arise in frustratingly complex ways in virtually any attempt to apply the rationalist framework to questions of what should be done. Again, the fundamental problem is normative: What do we use to judge what's best? Identifying and rank ordering policy alternatives inescapably means identifying and ranking values (Anderson 1979, 711). Public policy, most agree, should promote social welfare; it should represent decisions and actions that further the public interest. That, however, simply redefines the problem. How does one measure social welfare or the public interest? Anyone with even a passing comprehension of politics recognizes that what best serves the greater good is often in the eye of the beholder.

Rationalists have formulated a number of ways to deal with this key normative issue, ranging from the dismissive (ignore the problem altogether) to the inclusive (keep the methods and theory, but use a range of values to judge the comparative worth of policy alternatives; see Smith 2003). Perhaps the most common approach to dealing with this question, however, is to judge policy alternatives on the basis of a particular value: efficiency. The rationalist approach takes a good deal of criticism for relying so heavily on efficiency to solve its key normative challenge. In particular, the use of efficiency—as opposed to more democratic values such as equity—is at the core of a number of post-positivist criticisms. Yet using efficiency as the basis for judging policy alternatives, that is, as the normative basis for operationalizing the rationalist approach, is not done without justification. In doing so, rationalist analysis draws heavily from welfare economics, a framework that has a well-founded argument for using efficiency as the basis for deciding what is best.

The Welfare Economics Paradigm

Welfare economics is the study of the normative properties of markets. In general terms, it is devoted to trying to assess what economic policy or regulation is "best" (Zeckhauser and Schaefer 1968; Just, Hueth, and Schmitz 2004). This objective has a clear parallel with the goal of rationalist policy analysis, which is different only in that it seeks to assess what public policy—economic or not—is best.

This similarity in objectives makes adapting the welfare economics framework to the general study of public policy highly attractive. The key question of policy analysis is essentially a question of social choice: What should we do? The government has limited resources, so how can it best allocate those resources in a way that maximizes the public interest? The conceptual tools of welfare economics are readily adaptable to such questions of social choice. In effect, the welfare economics paradigm offers a systematic framework to answer the critical normative question of what alternative is best.

Welfare economics rests on a foundation of methodological individualism. Individuals are viewed as rational actors, as the best judges of their wants and needs, who seek to satisfy those wants and needs in a way that maximizes their individual utility (Campen 1986, 28). Social welfare is seen simply as the aggregation of individual welfare. Policies that maximize the aggregate level of individual welfare are thus viewed as maximizing social welfare. Social welfare is in turn operationalized through the concept of efficiency.

The term "efficiency" comes with considerable baggage and prima facie is frequently viewed as an antidemocratic value (see Stone 2002). At least in a purely theoretical sense, however, efficiency from the view of welfare economics is simply a characteristic of a distribution of resources. Specifically, the most efficient distribution is one that maximizes social welfare. Efficiency from this perspective is defined by the Pareto criterion, which describes an allocation of resources such that "no alternative allocation can make at least one person better off without making anyone worse off" (Boardman et al. 2001, 26). It is easy to convey this concept visually.

Figure 5.1 shows a simple two-person society in which individual A has y resources, and individual B has x resources. Where the two lines labeled "x" and "y" intersect is the status quo. Any policy that shifts the distribution of wealth from this status quo point up and to the right would produce a Pareto superior outcome; at a minimum it increases the wealth of one individual while costing the other nothing. Any policy that shifts the distribution down and to the left is Pareto inferior; at least one individual is losing wealth under this distribution. Any policy that results in a move up and/or to the right of the status quo point, in other words, is efficient, and any that shifts down and to the left is inefficient. The Pareto principle strikes many as an intuitively appealing way to conceive of social welfare. It defines the best or most desirable policy as the one that generates the highest level of benefits while doing no harm to others.

In theory, perfectly functioning markets will allocate resources in such a way as to produce Pareto superior outcomes (Nas 1996, 19). Perfectly functioning markets, of course, are conceptual creatures of theory rather than part of our real-world experience. Still, for many private goods, markets do a remarkably good job of allocating resources efficiently in a more or less Pareto-like way (in any supermarket in the United States, what is taken for granted—an astonishing choice of foodstuffs at reasonable prices—is a rough-and-ready example). The problem with using the Pareto principle to operationalize the concept of efficiency, of course, is that even reasonably free markets are not much good at distributing public (as opposed to private) goods. Also, much of public policy is explicitly redistributional in nature, with some people bearing the costs while others enjoy the benefits. There is no reasonable approximation of a free and functioning market for providing national defense or universal social security for the elderly or free parking spaces. Most public policies do not fall into the clean categories of Pareto superior or Pareto inferior quadrants of the graph represented in Figure 5.1. They fall into the unlabeled upper-left and lower-right quadrants, where there are some winners and some losers. A shift into those quadrants pretty much describes what happens whenever the government purposively backs an action or inaction with its coercive powers.

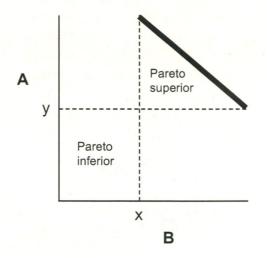

FIGURE 5.1 The Pareto Principle

To make the Pareto principle tractable in the real world, welfare economics uses what is known as the Kaldor-Hicks compensation principle (developed independently by two British economists in the 1930s; see Hicks 1939; Kaldor 1939). The Kaldor-Hicks principle is simple in notion, if controversial in practice, and serves to make the concept of efficiency a practical means to judge the relative social worth of public policies. Basically Kaldor-Hicks states that if those who gain from a policy could, in theory, make a set of side payments to those who lose from the policy, such that the losers become indifferent, that policy is *potentially* a Pareto superior outcome. This translates in practical terms as, "if the benefits outweigh the costs, the policy is efficient."

The reasoning here is still intuitive: if a decision or an action results in more benefits than costs, or more pros than cons, it is preferable to any decision or action that has the opposite outcomes. The basic notion is not unique to welfare economics—Franklin's moral algebra is, more or less, just the individual version of the same concept. Nor does it necessarily require the inputs and outcomes of a policy to be translated into monetary terms (though this is a requirement for certain analytic methods such as cost-benefit analysis). What is useful from the policy analyst's perspective is that it offers a well-defined and operationalizable concept of social welfare, a means to measure the comparative worth of policy alternatives. This concept of social welfare is essentially utilitarian in nature; it judges the policy that generates the most overall benefits as "best." Utilitarianism as expressed through the Kaldor-Hicks efficiency criterion is certainly not the only means to conceive of social welfare, but it is a systematically and normatively defensible way to practically judge the relative worth of public policies (Weimer and Vining 2005, 133–138).

A simple example shows how this concept of social welfare can be used to quantitatively estimate the impact of a public policy or program on social welfare. Imagine a municipality considering building a new public garage to address a critical shortage of downtown parking spaces. To estimate the impact of the garage on social welfare, the welfare economics approach would seek to construct a demand curve for parking spaces. Such a graph is depicted in Figure 5.2. The graph plots the demand for parking spaces, in terms of average daily parking use, against parking fees. The demand curve (labeled "D") that slopes down and to the right shows that as parking fees decrease, use of public parking facilities increases. A $1.00 fee results in an average of one thousand motorists using the public parking garage. A $5.00 fee drops demand to zero—this is the point where the demand curve crosses the y axis.

This simple demand curve contains several pieces of important information relative to the pros and cons of the project, as well as its impact on social welfare. The rectangle defined by the points $1, a, 1,000, and 0 represents the average daily revenue generated by the garage. The triangle defined by the points a, D, and 1,000 represents what economists call a "deadweight loss." This represents unmet demand for parking spaces, those that motorists want but are not willing to pay a dollar for. Of most interest to the policy analyst, however, is the triangle defined by the points $1, a, and $5. This area represents what economists term "consumer surplus"; it represents the difference between what consumers are willing to pay for a good or service and what they actually pay for a good or service. Consumer surplus can be thought of as a measure of the project's impact on social welfare—it represents in monetary terms the net benefits society receives from the parking garage.[5] This amount is calculated by simply computing the area of the triangle, easily done using the Pythagorean theorem: height multiplied by width divided by 2. In this example, then, the net social benefit of the parking garage is $4 x 1,000/2 = $2,000. Using this approach, the net benefit of the garage can be calculated even if parking is free. If no parking fees are charged, the consumer surplus is simply the area of the triangle 0, D, $5. This conceptual approach, in other words, has no problem estimating the social value of public services and goods as long as the relevant demand curve can be reasonably estimated. The same general conceptual approach can be employed to compare projects; the project that best maximizes social welfare is the one that produces the most benefits as measured by social surplus.

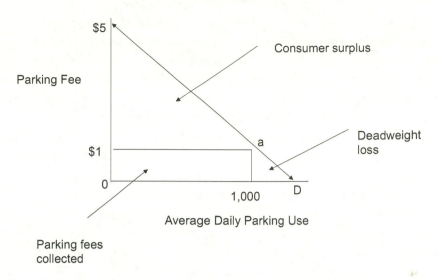

FIGURE 5.2 Hypothetical Demand Curve for Parking Spaces

In short, the welfare economics paradigm offers a rigorous conceptual frame-work to deal with problems of social choice. It has a clear notion of what is best; the policy that maximizes social welfare. Social welfare is operationalized using the concept of efficiency and can be quantified and directly measured using the standard conceptual and analytic tool kit of economics as seen in Figure 5.2. Actually doing policy analysis within this framework presents considerable technical difficulties, not the least of which is the problem of estimating reasonably accurate demand curves for public goods and services. If the actual demand curve in Figure 5.2 has a different slope or is nonlinear, our estimates of consumer surplus are obviously going to be inaccurate.

Rationalist Successes and Failures

Drawing on theoretical frameworks such as welfare economics makes rationalist approaches tractable, allowing the basic conceptual framework to be translated into real-world practice. Building on such foundations, rationalist analysis can generate enormous quantities of information of potential use to policy decision making. Such policy analyses rank alternatives not just in terms of efficiency but also in terms of anticipated impacts and expected payoffs, and systematically catalog the trade-offs inherent in different policy choices. Indeed, that's exactly what rationalist analysis has been doing for four or five decades: generating mountains of information from whose peaks it is presumably easier to see solutions to policy problems. As the field has matured, its methods have become more sophisticated: cost analysis, econometric forecasting, decision theory, and many other tools taken from the social science tool kit have been adapted and refined to make the process of linear problem-solving ever more rigorous and accurate.[6]

Nonetheless, there remain serious questions about the development, direction, and payoffs of rationalist policy analysis. Although even its critics acknowledge the primacy of the rationalist approach in policy analysis, they are quick to point out that rationalist analysis never lived up to its original vision (see Radin 1997, 2000). Most obviously, rationalist policy analysis is not confined to the high levels of public agencies, but rather takes place at all levels of government and in many places outside of government (academia, think tanks, interest groups). Policy analysts are often addressing the same problem with their rationalist methods and often come to very different conclusions about what constitutes the best solution. This means that rationalist policy analysis often gives policymakers very different—even completely contradictory—answers to the question, "What should we do?" The contradictions occur in part because of the explicit client orientation that has long been a central feature of rationalist policy analysis (see Meltsner 1976). An agency head, a legislature, a single-interest issue group, a government watchdog organization, and an academic may all be interested in a particular problem and may seek policy analyses following the generic rationalist approach. Because they start from different perspectives and are addressing different audiences with different desired outcomes, the results of such policy analyses may end up with very different recommendations.

It is not just that policy analysts have different clients and thus focus on different elements and alternatives to particular policy problems. More generally, it is clear that a gap exists between knowledge generated by policy analysts and the policymakers who are targeted as the primary consumers of such knowledge. Policy analysts in the rationalist tradition have sought to be data- rather than value-driven. Yet political decision making, which is to say policy decision making, is often unavoidably value-driven. Any analysis, regardless of its theory, methods, or results, attains a normative dimension as soon as it enters the political arena—it will support somebody's preferences while opposing others. No analysis can avoid this inevitable political fate, even if an analyst is a genuinely value-free logical positivist. An analysis that is purely data-driven cannot avoid being championed or opposed on the basis of its comfort to a particular ideology or value system.

The bottom line is that political decision makers, the very people policy analysis is supposed to inform, are often explicitly value-driven and not interested in policy analyses that do not support their preferred values. Rationalist policy analysis is instrumental; it seeks a technical solution to a well-defined problem. In the political arena, solutions are championed not just because of their technical efficacy but also based on how well their conclusions support preconceived political agendas. Thus, connecting the knowledge generated by rationalist analyses to the values that drive the political world, at least in a fashion that does not relegate policy analysis to just another manufacturer of partisan ammunition, has proven to be maddeningly difficult to achieve. Much to the frustration of policy analysis professionals, policymakers have a tendency to cherry-pick their research to suit preexisting preferences or, even worse, to ignore it altogether (Smith 2005).

This has led to considerable hand-wringing among policy analysts (especially academic policy analysts). Though policy analysis in the rationalist mode exploded in the last quarter of the twentieth century, a wide range of studies examining the impact of these studies came to two sobering conclusions: 1) rationalist policy analysis often produced very bad advice, or at least advice that did not result in government actions achieving desired objectives; and 2) even when policy analysis produced, by virtually any criteria, good advice, it was often ignored by policymakers (see deLeon 2006, 42–47). In short, these studies show that rationalist policy analysis rarely functions as the central problem-solving tool it was designed to be; indeed, many studies conclude that it has relatively little impact on policy outputs or outcomes (e.g., Jones 1976; Mooney 1991; Rich 2001). Some scholars have argued that at some point this checkered performance record will catch up with the rationalist project and doom it to quiet extinction. If policymakers and stakeholders favor whatever supports their position, then anecdote may trump systematic analysis, and passion may trump reason. The key players in the policymaking process will willfully ignore careful and reasoned policy analysis because its factual goring of valued political oxen is resented. The result is irrational public policies, or at least policies with lower probabilities of actually achieving a desired end. This will lead to the "end of policy analysis," at least in its rationalist variant (Kirp 1992).

Though gloomy forecasts for its future are issued periodically, rationalist policy analysis shows no signs of fading away. Still, the problem of practically and meaningfully connecting its positivist and quantitatively generated knowledge with the real, messy, and value-driven world of politics is real enough. And that gap between knowledge and politics is where post-positivist alternatives to the rationalist project thrive.

The Post-Positivist Approach

The rationalist approach, especially as practiced within the welfare economics paradigm, represents a distinct theory of public policy. Public policy is conceptualized as a solution to a problem, its central goal is efficiency, and the practice of policy analysis is theoretically and methodologically oriented to identifying the most efficient solution to a given problem. Post-positivists do not necessarily disagree with this as one approach to policy analysis; what they disagree with is any claim that the rationalist project is *the* approach to policy analysis.

Using its scientific basis to claim a privileged place in the hierarchy of policy knowledge, post-positivists argue, leads the rationalist project down a decidedly antidemocratic path. The main criticisms of the antidemocratic nature of the rationalist approach have been succinctly summarized by Dryzek (1989, 101). Rationalism conceives of politics in purely technocratic terms, seeing policy as a means for a political elite to manipulate causal systems to achieve a desired end. It treats ends simplistically, viewing them as being fixed in nature; it explicitly ignores political debate and conflict, instead imposing its own preferred values, such as efficiency. Rationalism falsely assumes that a general consensus supports these favored values; it promotes a form of policymaking wherein technocrats exercise central influence and leave little role for citizens. It ends up reinforcing bureaucratic and hierarchical power systems, and in doing so has a distinct bias toward the status quo. In other words, "the most widely practiced kind of policy analysis aspires to rationality, but this proves to be at the expense of democracy" (Dryzek 1989, 104). The field of public administration faces a similar dilemma, in which some focus on more practical solutions to a problem (i.e., the rationalist approach), while others are less concerned with practicality and more concerned with solutions that are more democratic or open to citizen participation (Frederickson et al. 2012).

While post-positivists object to the rationalist approach across a range of theoretical and methodological issues, the core of the post-positivist critique is value-based. It argues that the rationalist approach is predicated on the assumption that better—more comprehensive, more accurate—information will lead to better policies (Collingridge and Reeves 1986). Most analysts in the rationalist tradition are not likely to disagree with this claim. The problem from the post-positivist perspective is that policy belongs to the political realm and is not particularly likely to respond to empirical claims regardless of their technical sophistication or theoretical rigor. This inability to successfully bridge the gap between knowledge and politics is not news to rationalist scholars (e.g., Kirp 1992). Post-positivists argue that policy, like politics in general, is an interpretive exercise driven by values rather than data. The nature of a particular problem, its existence, extent, and the best policy alternative to address it, rest not on neutral and objective observation but on the social values used to interpret the world (Fischer 2003, 13). Post-positivists thus view public policy in expressive rather than instrumentalist terms (Yanow 2000, 22). Rather than judging public policy as an objective means to achieve a clearly defined end, post-positivists view policy as a means to communicate, implement, and enforce explicitly political values. The entire realm of public policy is suffused with values, and policy analysis has to account for these values if government actions are going to uphold the norms of liberal democracy and be granted legitimacy by citizens.

Post-positivists argue that the rationalist approach itself is value-based, and pretty ruthless about promoting its favored values. Post-positivists seek not necessarily to kill the rationalist project, but to highlight its value-laden, normative foundation. The idea is to unmask its presence as a player in the political realm, to expose it as an enthusiastic combatant in the arena where values clash. Underlying the supposedly neutral and objective social science foundation of the rationalist orientation is a set of "underlying and usually unspoken political and social assumptions," and it is these values that drive the methods, the theory, and ultimately the results of rationalist research (deLeon 1988, 70).

As an example, consider the oft-repeated claim that money makes no difference to the performance of schools. This claim has considerable support from a large body of empirical research carried out in the rationalist tradition (see Hanushek 1997). The vast majority of these studies are carried out in the education production framework. This is an analytical framework appropriated from the study of profit-making firms that typically uses regression models to provide point estimates of how the inputs of schooling (student characteristics, school resources, teaching experience, etc.) relate to the outputs of schooling (test scores, graduation rates, etc.). Such studies have been used repeatedly to support claims that "money does not matter," or more technically that there is no significant positive correlation between monetary inputs (usually measured as per student expenditures) and test scores or other education outputs. These studies are often technically very sophisticated and are presented as objective representations of the causal relationships that exist in the real world. As the data clearly indicate that money does not matter, the response to "What should we do about school performance?" should focus on alternatives such as institutional reform rather than on more resources (e.g., Chubb and Moe 1990; Moe 2001). Rather than objective policy analysis, post-positivists (and even some self-proclaimed rationalists; see Smith 2003, 50–57) argue that the conclusion that institutional reform and not more resources is the best solution to the problem of school performance is driven as much by values as by data.

Values are seen as driving such conclusions at virtually every stage of the rationalist analytic process. These begin with the values inherent in the scientific method. In testing causal claims, the standard scientific approach is to assume the research hypothesis (in this case, that money is positively related to school outputs) is false and requires overwhelming evidence to reject that assumption. In hypothesis testing, there is a distinct bias against making Type I errors (concluding something has an effect when in fact it does not). The consequences of a Type II error (concluding something has no effect when in fact it does have an effect) are considered less serious (e.g., Gravetter and Wallnau 2004, 243). This bias shapes how research results are interpreted. Consider Hanushek's (1997) review of 377 studies examining the link between resources and school or student performance, concluding that an extensive research record backs the claim that "money does not matter." Yet most of the studies cited in Hanushek's review actually show positive relationships between resources and outputs. A plurality show positive and statistically significant relationships. The conclusion that money does not matter rests not on overwhelming evidence of an absence of a relationship, but on statistically insignificant results in roughly a third of the studies (Verstegen and King 1998; Unnever, Kerckhoff, and Robinson 2000). That the latter finding was given so much credence, a post-positivist would argue, is because of the values used to interpret the results of research, not an independent and objective "truth." That so much rationalist-based education policy analysis ends up calling for the imposition of market values—school vouchers and the like—is not surprising from the post-positivist perspective. Market values (or at least economic theory supportive of such values), after all, are what frame the research, not democratic values.

The bottom line is that post-positivists charge the analytical frameworks and the methodological practices of the rationalist approach with carrying and promoting a particular set of values. The post-positivist critique does not seek to eliminate these values (indeed, it would argue that such an effort would be doomed to failure) as much as it seeks to make them explicit. Failure to take account of these values leads to the common perception that the rationalist approach is more neutral and objective than any alternative. This perception, post-positivists argue, is not only incorrect, but dangerous. Ceding policy analysis to technocrats leads to policy alternatives that promote consistently anti-democratic values. Democracy, after all, is supposed to be egalitarian, not efficient; its policies are supposed to uphold democratic values rather than market values.

One of the preeminent forms of rationalist policy analysis is cost-benefit analysis (CBA), a technique whose ultimate objective is to rank policy alternatives on a straightforward measure of allocative efficiency (typically a benefit-cost ratio, or net social benefits expressed in monetary terms). Efficiency in this case is, of course, defined by the Kaldor-Hicks compensation principle. Post-positivists lodge a raft of objections to cost-benefit analysis, ranging from the heroic assumptions often necessary to make the technique mathematically tractable to the perceived affront to democratic values inherent in its intellectual framework. For example, because CBA requires all costs and benefits to be monetized, it requires putting dollar values on things that strike many as beyond the ability of markets—even theoretical benchmark markets—to price. Clean air, human life, and freedom from sickness or disease, for example, have all been monetized by CBA studies (Boardman et al. 2001, 1–3). Such valuations are frequently challenged as inaccurate, misleading, or meaningless (Wolff and Haubrich 2006).

Kaldor-Hicks, unsurprisingly, comes in for particular criticism as anchoring policy analysis in a market framework that pays little attention to the distributional issues often at the heart of public policy. Remember that Kaldor-Hicks describes a *potential* Pareto, an outcome where the winners could conceivably compensate the losers to the point where they become indifferent to the policy. This is controversial, because the side payments are purely theoretical; there is no requirement for compensation to the losers. This raises immediate distributional concerns. Post-positivists are quite right to point out that political conflict is often about just such distributional concerns; that the winners gain more benefits than the costs incurred by the losers will not make that political conflict any less intense. Just because a policy is efficient under Kaldor-Hicks does not make a political decision any less political; it certainly does not stop the potential losers from expending their political capital to prevent the policy from being adopted.

The crux of the post-positivist critique is that the rationalist approach seeks to divorce policy analysis from politics, to set up policy analysis as a neutral and objective generator of knowledge that stands independent of politics. Post-positivists argue that the rationalist approach fails miserably on all counts. Its methods and theories promote a particular set of values (typically those of science and the market) while elevating technocrats and experts into privileged positions of policy influence. The end result is a form of policy analysis that promotes fundamentally undemocratic, or even antidemocratic, values. Efficiency trumps equity, and a technocratic elite has more weight in decision making than the citizen (see, for example, Dryzek and Torgerson 1993; deLeon 1997).

Post-Positivist Methods

If policy analysis is not undertaken in the rationalist framework, however, what's the alternative? Post-positivist policy analysis (like rationalist policy analysis) employs a wide range of conceptual frameworks and methods. Generally speaking, however, the post-positivist approach is distinguished by viewing public policy through the lens of deliberative democracy.

Roughly speaking, deliberative democracy is the (normative) notion that public decision making should be done through a process of informed reflection and dialogue among citizens, politicians, and stakeholders. As James Fishkin put it, deliberative democracy is about "how we might bring some of the favorable characteristics of small-group, face-to-face democracy to the large-scale nation-state" (1991, 1). More broadly, deliberative democracy draws on ideas taken from such theorists as John Rawls, Jurgen Habermas, and Amy Gutmann about how polities should deal with issues of social choice (for a good introduction to the basic concepts of deliberative democracy, see Fishkin and Laslett 2003). From this perspective, informed deliberation and consensus will provide the best answer to the question "What should we do?"

The main question, of course, is how to go about this. Post-positivist frameworks and theories require a radical epistemological shift from the rationalist approach. It means shifting from a focus on "discovering a set of universal laws about objective, sense-based fact to the human capacity for making and communicating meaning" (Yanow 2000, 5). Post-positivist policy analysis is premised on the assumption that the political world is socially constructed. How this world is interpreted depends on one's perspective, and there is no neutral, independent reality that exists outside of this perspective. Accordingly, post-positivist policy analysis rejects the linear, putatively objective, problem-solving approach in favor of discourse and interpretive analysis. The job of a policy analyst is to understand the various perspectives, why they lead to conflict, and how they might accommodate each other in the form of purposive government action or inaction. Post-positivist policy analysis seeks to translate the different stories or narratives of the political world into a coherent argument; it seeks to translate the stories of "what is" from different perspectives into a case for "what ought to be" (see Fischer 2003).

The post-positivist approach, then, views the policy analyst not as a lab-coated neutral analyzer of facts but instead as an interpreter, a mediator, and a facilitator. A post-positivist analyst is someone who not only understands different perspectives, why they exist, and why they conflict, but someone who understands different modes of communication and seeks to bring disparate views together. One way to go about doing this is through participatory policy analysis (PPA), a method that seeks to put the ideals of deliberative democracy into action and to create a new role for policy analysis. It has a number of variants and travels under slightly different guises in different disciplines, but "all reject positivism; view phenomenology or a variation of it, as a better way to interpret the nature of knowledge; and accept an interpretive or hermeneutic paradigm of inquiry" (Durning 1993, 300). In other words, PPA is predicated on the assumptions that the knowledge of the expert has no privileged position in deciding what to do, and that the best response to a given social-choice situation depends on one's point of view. It seeks to build consensus among these differing perspectives through informed deliberation.

The general idea behind PPA is to bring together ordinary citizens from different walks of life and with different perspectives, educate them on an issue or problem, and have them deliberate about what we should do. These participatory panels would meet for an extended period of time and deal with a single issue. Knowledge from expert policy analysts (analysts in the rationalist tradition) would be made available to the panels, and this information, combined with their own perspectives and experiences, would provide a basis for informed deliberation. Not designed to be just a negotiation among stakeholder groups, PPA is also meant to provide "a fair and impartial representation of all citizens' values and preferences, be they organized or not" (Renn et al. 1993, 206). There are a number of studies suggesting such panels can provide an important contribution to policymaking. Kathlene and Martin (1991), for example, found that a panel of roughly 150 citizens provided key input into the public transportation planning in Boulder, Colorado. The Danish Board of Technology has put something very much like PPA into practice in the form of the "consensus conference." The idea of the consensus conference is to weave together expert knowledge with the often clashing social, political, and economic perspectives that surround controversial policy issues, such as the use of nuclear power. A conference typically involves about twenty-five citizens, who spend several months on a single issue or topic, guided by a facilitator who is an expert in communication and cooperation techniques. The end result is a report (often presented in a high-profile media setting) to the Danish government, and these reports have had a not insignificant role in shaping policy decisions (Kluver 1995; Fischer 2003, 210–213). A similar PPA process that brings together differing stakeholders and policymakers has been proposed and at least partially adopted for setting policies on land use in the European Union (see Morris et al. 2011). Related experiments with citizen panels have been conducted across the globe through deliberative polling, which bears a strong resemblance to PPA in that it brings together a representative sample of citizens, provides them with expert information and a facilitator, and asks them to deliberate on important political issues. It differs mainly in that the panels meet for relatively brief periods and that there is no direct policy role for the panel (e.g., there is no official report presented to a legislature).[7] Postmodernists in public administration also call for a more open and participatory response to issues relating to governance (Bogason 2007).

However, PPA remains a sparsely employed technique for helping to decide questions about "what we should do." It tends to be labor intensive and is not designed to converge on a particular "best" option like rationalist analysis. More common are various forms of interpretive analysis (application of hermeneutics, phenomenology, discourse theory, and the like), though even these do not represent mainstream policy analysis (for examples see Yanow 2000; Schneider and Ingram 1997). Most policy analysts are trained in rationalist rather than post-positivist conceptual frameworks and research methodologies, so unsurprisingly, rationalist frameworks are more commonly applied in policy analysis (Etzioni 2006, 840–841).

An Emerging Middle Ground?

At first glance—and perhaps at second and third glances—the rationalist and post-positivist perspectives seem irreconcilable. Their underlying assumptions and treatment of values lead not just to different conceptual models and methods, but to very different ideas about how we should go about answering the question "What should we do?" Nonetheless, over the past decade or so there have been increasingly successful attempts to merge elements of these two philosophies of policy analysis. These attempts have been fueled by two movements. The first is an increasing recognition by rationalists that post-positivist critiques have at least some merit and must be addressed, or at least acknowledged, and rationalist analysis framed in such a way that it fits into a political (as opposed to a purely objective and empirical) context. Second is the emergence of a broad movement questioning the underlying assumptions of the welfare economics paradigm, especially assumptions of individual-level rationality. This latter movement comes mostly from within the rationalist camp rather than as a reaction to outside post-positivist critics—it is primarily a result of emergence of what is known as behavioral economics. As policy analysis absorbs the concepts of behavioral economics, however, it also begins to take on a decidedly post-positivist spin.

Rationalists have become increasingly cognizant of the need to account for the fractured and value-laden nature of the political arena (e.g., Radin 1997, 2000), and part of this accounting is coming from a shift in perspective or framing rather than from a shift in theory or methods. Rationalists increasingly recognize that their frustrations over the inability of policy analysis to shape policy directions may actually be misplaced. There are good reasons to believe that rationalist policy analysis is having an important impact in shaping public policy, ironically in a fashion that can be appreciated by post-positivists. Shulock (1997) asked why, if policy analysis is really so ignored, there is so much of it being produced. Her answer was that policy analysis is not being ignored and actually plays a critical role in the policymaking process, just not the role anticipated or intended by the rationalist project. Mainstream (i.e., rationalist) policy analysis was actually being used in a fashion that fit more with a post-positivist perspective. Specifically, policy analysis was used to provide substance to policy debates. Though rationalists often despair that the products of their efforts end up as just more partisan ammunition, Shulock argued that this is the wrong way to look at things. It is better to engage in disputes with information and ideology than with ignorance and ideology. Both sides lean on rationalist analysis to gain an edge in policy debates; both sides in other words prefer their position to be backed with empirical evidence and recognize that if their evidence is weak, so is their political argument. This makes rationalist analysis a critical part of political debates about what should be done. That rationalist analysis is shaping the value conflict rather than providing technical solutions to problems is not necessarily a bad thing. Indeed, it can be viewed as a central contribution to the political process. Research on how policy analysis is actually done and how it is typically interpreted and applied finds exactly this sort of role for rationalist studies, whether those studies are done by government bureaucrats, academics, or nonprofits (e.g., Howlett and Wellstead 2011; Smith 2005). Rather than being the ultimate arbiter of what we should do, in practice rationalist policy analysis is a primary means for differing sides and stakeholders to duke it out in the political arena; all camps press rationalist concepts and methods into service for their cause. The same is not necessarily true of post-positivist analysis, because the concepts and methods found here are messier, more labor intensive, and less likely to produce a clear answer to the underlying question of what we should do. Ironically, it is rationalist analysis that seems to be performing the political role envisioned for post-positivist analysis.

In a somewhat related vein, a serious and ongoing reevaluation of the core assumptions underlying the welfare economics paradigm is not just altering how people think of rationalist analysis and how it is used, but prompting an evolution of concepts and methods. This effort is mainly being driven by the emergence of behavioral economics. Welfare economics has traditionally been based on classic economic assumptions that humans are self-interested, rational utility-maximizers. Behavioral economics is more interested in why humans systematically deviate from this model and how those systematic deviations might be incorporated into better explanatory frameworks. For example, behavioral economists recognize that preferences about outcomes—critical to accurate estimation of the worth of different policy options—are dependent upon how they are framed. People tend to place a higher value on losses than they do on gains (see Kahneman and Tversky 1978), so the social worth of, say, a public parking garage may be worth more or less depending on how it is perceived. If it is seen as a loss of private property rights because the land was taken through the power of eminent domain, people may oppose it. Frame it as a gain of a valued resource (downtown parking spaces), and those same people may support it. By incorporating more psychology into economic theory, behavioral economics is increasingly helping rationalist policy analysis to address (if not entirely overcome) some post-positivist criticisms. For example, cost-benefit analyses are being rethought along behavioral economic lines that may allow such studies to be much more sensitive to varying preferences and perspectives and produce more realistic and accurate estimates of individual discount rates, willingness to pay, and other concepts critical to tallying the costs and benefits of differing policy options (for a good summary of these benefits, see Robinson and Hammit 2011; and Congdon, Kling, and Mullainathan 2009; for a more skeptical take on behavioral economics and cost-benefit analysis, see Smith and Moore 2010).

As an example of how behavioral economics has the potential to alter rationalist analysis, consider the development of reference class forecasting (RCF). A big criticism of rationalist policy analysis is that its inferences are critically dependent on accurate forecasting and, as discussed previously, post-positivists have been quick to point out that the track record of quantitative forecasting is highly checkered. One of the most notorious areas of inaccuracy in forecasting is in the costs of big ticket projects such as infrastructure (roads and bridges), defense contracts, and the like. The projected costs of such programs routinely underestimate—sometimes by multiples—the actual costs of these programs. RCF was developed to make such cost estimates more accurate, and it does so by incorporating the concepts of "the planning fallacy" from behavioral economics. The planning fallacy refers to the systematic tendency of people to underestimate costs and overestimate benefits; this is also known as "optimism bias," and has been repeatedly empirically demonstrated (Kahneman 1994; Kahneman and Tversky 1978). In other words, a systematic bias creeps into the estimates of rationalist methods like cost-benefit analysis, not necessarily because the analysts are consciously jiggering the numbers, but because they are all equipped with this basic human psychological mechanism. Developed by Bent Flyvbjerg, RCF seeks to account for this systematic bias by requiring an analyst to look to similar previous policies and their outcomes—this constitutes a "reference class." The cost-benefit over- or underestimates of the reference class can be used to create what amounts to a probability distribution that can be employed to adjust for optimism bias. RCF has been so successful in reducing inaccuracy in cost estimates that it is now employed as standard practice in certain big ticket infrastructure programs in Europe, and the American Planning Association has urged analysts to adopt its use in the United States (Flyvbjerg 2008). This new method is a potentially important contribution to the rationalist's tool kit, but note that it also addresses an important post-positivist critique about the realism (or lack thereof) of the assumptions anchoring rationalist analysis.

Conclusion

When considering a problem or matter of concern, the central objective of public authorities is to decide what action to take (or not to take). Public policy thus invariably begins as a question of social choice, and this universal scenario provides the field of policy analysis with its fundamental question: "What should we do?"

Within policy analysis there is a good deal of disagreement about how to structure the search for answers to this fundamental question. Whereas the preceding discussion has to some extent oversimplified this disagreement by splitting the entire field into rationalist and post-positivist camps, that division does serve to highlight the fundamental theoretical debate in the field. Basically what we have is two conceptual frameworks that in many ways seem to be mutually exclusive, forcing an analyst's loyalties toward one camp or the other. The rationalists cannot—and do not want to—fully release their grip on positivism. These positivist foundations prop up the causal frameworks that rationalists use to explain the world and make systematic sense of policy choices. The post-positivist cannot see those positivist foundations as anything more than one of any number of value systems, one that has no legitimate claim to hierarchy over any other. The rationalist looks at post-positivism and sees messy relativism, where knowledge cannot accumulate, and the information needed for good policymaking is reduced to equal status with the ideologically fueled opinions of the ignorant and uninformed. The post-positivist sees just such information produced repeatedly by rationalists, only to be ignored by politicians, and claims to know why this happens.

It is quite possible, however, that this debate is producing more heat than light. The post-positivist critique has clearly led the rationalist camp to think through some important issues, and as a result rationalist analysis is evolving and adapting. It is not abandoning its key roots—a mostly positivist perspective, quantitative methods, and privileging the values of science above all other values. Rationalists are, however, somewhat grudgingly accepting that its products provide the substance for political debate rather than the unassailable answers to end it. They are questioning the core assumption of rationality that underlies the welfare economics–based concepts and methods that define much of the rationalist enterprise. In the process they are responding to—and in some cases entirely absorbing—post-positivist concerns of perspective, distribution, and values other than efficiency. Matrix analysis, for example, is entirely capable of incorporating values such as "justice" or "democracy" into a comparative ranking of policy alternatives (e.g., Munger 2000).

Thus far, the field of policy analysis clearly has produced no universal theoretical platform for answering the question "What should we do?" In that sense, the post-positivists might be correct in arguing that rationalism has failed, or at the very least has not succeeded as originally advertised. Yet the rationalist approach has proved itself to be a remarkably adaptable and practical conceptual platform for systematically assessing choices among differing policy options. In that sense, the rationalist approach continues to be the dominant perspective and looks likely to be for the foreseeable future.

Notes

1. Franklin's original letter to Priestly is available from a number of Internet sites. One source is http://www.procon.org/franklinletter.htm.

2. Like public policy, policy analysis is formally defined in a variety of ways. A representative sampling of these definitions can be found in Weimer and Vining (2005, 24, n. 1).

3. The majority of policy analysis textbooks present some version of this generic process. See Bardach (2005/2011) and Levin and McEwan (2001) for representative examples.

4. In embracing the fact-value dichotomy, policy analysis followed the mainstream orientation of public administration, which through roughly the 1960s conceptually separated administration from politics. The fact-value dichotomy theoretically collapsed following the work of a number of public administration scholars, notably Dwight Waldo (1946), who convincingly demonstrated that decision making in public agencies was unavoidably political. In other words, facts could not be separated from values in public-sector decision making. This shattered the theoretical unity at the core of public administration, and the field has struggled to incorporate values into its conceptual frameworks ever since (see Frederickson and Smith 2003). The rise of post-positivist challenges to the rationalist approach shows that policy analysis as a field shares a similar intellectual challenge.

5. Technically, the measure used to assess relative efficiency is social surplus, or the combination of consumer and producer surplus (the latter being estimated in a similar fashion to consumer surplus, but using supply rather than demand curves). In practice, however, consumer surplus is typically used as the benchmark for assessing the relative worth of public policy alternatives (see Gupta 2001, 361–363; Weimer and Vining 2005, 57–70).

6. Numerous textbooks have been devoted exclusively to the ever-growing sophistication of the quantitative methods of policy analysis (e.g., Quade 1989; Gupta 2001; Weimer and Vining 2005).

7. Deliberative polling is primarily the brainchild of James Fishkin, who sought to use public opinion research to inform policy debate. A good overview of deliberative polling can be found at the Center for Deliberative Democracy Web site: http://cdd.stanford.edu/polls/docs/summary/.

CHAPTER 6

What Have We Done?
Impact Analysis and Program Evaluation

Sooner or later, the government is expected to answer the question "What should we do?" by actually doing something, enacting a public policy or program to address the problem or issue at hand. In response to concerns about educational performance, for example, curricular reforms may be adopted, more stringent teacher qualifications approved, or high-stakes systems of standardized testing required. Whether on the basis of efficiency as judged by a cost-benefit analysis or the joint agreement of various stakeholder groups as judged by a PPA, one of these policies, or some combination of them, might be adopted as the preferred answer.

Taking purposive action on the basis of a systematic policy analysis, however, is no guarantee that a policy will effectively address the targeted problem. Once implemented, a policy's consequences may lead stakeholders, policymakers, and policy analysts to reevaluate how the question of what we should do was answered. Even the best ex ante policy analysis is an exercise in crystal-ball gazing. It may be a systematic and informative form, but it is crystal-ball gazing nonetheless. Unforeseen events, unaccounted for consequences, and misunderstood causal relationships can result in a very different reality from the one projected in a policy analysis. The most careful cost-benefit projections, for example, may be undone by any number of factors that lower anticipated benefits or increase projected costs. The policy judged to provide maximum net social benefit in an ex ante analysis may prove to be a voracious consumer of public resources that produces few of the anticipated benefits.

Because of the uncertainty that policy analysis has to deal with, it is important to make judgments about the worth or benefit of a policy ex post as well as ex ante. Impact analysis (also known as quantitative program evaluation) is the field of policy studies devoted to systematically assessing what impact or effect a public policy has actually had on the real world, and as such is the ex post counterpart of ex ante policy analysis. The latter is the prospective, and often the prescriptive, assessment of how the coercive powers of the state can/should be used to address a problem or issue of concern. Impact analysis is the retrospective assessment of policies that have been adopted and implemented. If the fundamental question of policy analysis is "What should we do?" then the fundamental question motivating impact analysis is "What have we done?" More formally, impact analysis is defined as "determining the extent to which one set of directed human activities (X) affected the state of some objects or phenomena ($Y_1 \ldots Y_k$) and . . . determining why the effects were as small or large as they turned out to be" (Mohr 1995, 1). Using Mohr's definition, X represents a program or policy, and Y is the observed or intended outcome of the policy.

Generally speaking, it is not methodology, but the ex post nature of impact analysis, that conceptually distinguishes it from policy analysis as discussed in the previous chapter. Cost-benefit analyses, for example, can be conducted ex post. As described in Chapter 5 on policy analysis, CBA is a tool to systematically answer the question of what *should* be done. Conducted in the impact analysis framework, a CBA is an assessment of what *has* been done. Ex post, a CBA assesses whether X (a program or policy) has resulted in a particular outcome Y (in this case efficient allocation of resources). A CBA is arguably of less practical use in the latter case; it can assess whether a policy results in a net social benefit, but this information does not allow policymakers to revisit their decisions if the policy turns out to be inefficient. Ex post cost analyses, however, provide an important evaluative function and can inform decisions on whether to make changes in a program or policy. Providing this sort of practical, applied, and often narrowly targeted information is often what impact analyses are intended to do. These are the sorts of broader questions that motivate impact analysis: What is the policy actually doing? What outcomes is it affecting? Is it worth the money it costs? Should it be continued, expanded, cut back, changed, or abandoned (Weiss 1998, 6)?

Like policy analysis, impact analysis has struggled with the question of how to go about answering the questions that define it as a field of study. Impact analysis is squarely in the rationalist tradition, and the same post-positivist criticisms that are launched against policy analysis are also made against impact analysis. Yet while the clash between the rationalist project and its post-positivist critics rings at least as loud in impact analysis as it does in policy analysis, at some level impact analysis faces a more straightforward theoretical challenge than policy analysis. Policy analysis cannot proceed without coming to some accommodation with the normative justifications for government action. Whether it is efficiency, effectiveness, distributional concerns, or some other yardstick, policy analysis has to impose a normative yardstick to differentiate among policy options. An impact analysis also has to deal with a range of normative difficulties, but dealing with the consequences rather than the justifications of public policy puts a slightly different spin on these normative issues. The fact that a policy exists suggests that somebody at some point must have believed that it would achieve some goal that justified deploying the resources and coercive powers of the state. The central theoretical challenge of impact analysis, then, is not justifying the normative values used to rank policy alternatives. It is more about identifying those objectives and the actions taken to achieve those objectives, then understanding the causal beliefs that link the two. In other words, an impact analysis does not have to justify the normative values motivating a public policy; its purpose is to empirically test the causal claim between the means (the policy) and the end (the policy objective). This is a fairly clear contrast with the central problem of theory in policy analysis, which is providing some normative justification for deploying the resources and coercive powers of the state in the first place.

In practice, of course, these issues become messier. Impact analysis has nearly as hard a time escaping the gravitational pull of normative concerns as policy analysis. There may be wildly different beliefs about the causal mechanisms that connect means and ends, and these can (and often are) charged with political meaning. Judging policies as successes or failures on the basis of an empirical test first requires knowing what goals to measure and how to measure them; that choice alone may determine whether an impact analysis concludes that a particular policy is working or not. In education policy, for example, deciding whether to measure educational performance using standardized tests, graduation rates, or some other metric can provide contradictory notions on whether particular educational policies are achieving their desired objectives (Smith and Granberg-Rademacker 2003).

In this chapter we address the key issues and conceptual frameworks involved in trying to evaluate the actual impact of public policy and try to come to some understanding of how policy scholars go about answering the question "What have we done?"

Impact Analysis and Program Evaluation

Impact analysis is actually one part of a much broader field of policy studies called program (or policy) evaluation. Program evaluation, like many concepts in the field of policy studies, is defined in various ways. Such definitions include the "effort to understand the effects of human behavior, and in particular, to evaluate the effects of particular programs . . . on those aspects of behavior indicated as the objectives of this intervention" (Haveman 1987); the "assessment of the overall effectiveness of a national program in meeting its objectives, or an assessment of the relative effectiveness of two or more programs in meeting common objectives" (Wholey et al. 1970, 15); and the "systematic assessment of the operation and/or the outcomes of a program or policy, compared to a set of explicit or implicit standards, as a means of contributing to the improvement of the program or policy" (Weiss 1998, 4). What the various definitions of program evaluation tend to have in common, and what conceptually separates program evaluation from other types of policy studies, is its focus on the consequences of actually initiating a public policy or program and the judgment of these consequences based on some (normative) yardstick (Scriven 1967; Lester and Stewart 2000, 126).

As a field, program evaluation is perhaps the most Lasswellian of all areas of policy studies. At its core, program evaluation is an explicitly normative enterprise; the motivation is the desire to compare *what is* with *what should be*. Program evaluation is thus ultimately about determining the worth of a program or policy on the basis of some criteria; it is the systematic attempt to assess whether a program or policy is "good" or "worthy" (Scriven 1967; good discussions of purposes of evaluation and the normative and subjective issues that motivate it as a field of study can be found in Talmage 1982; Mark, Henry, and Julnes 1999; Patton 2000; and Fitzpatrick, Sanders, and Worthen 2004, 4–8). Yet in making such assessments, program evaluators employ the full range of (especially quantitative) methods of social science.

Unfortunately, as the most Lasswellian of policy studies it is also the most amorphous—even more so than policy analysis. The demand for evaluation is ubiquitous within the public and private sectors; meeting that demand means evaluations can range from academic studies, to reports by management consultants, to formal program reviews by the Government Accountability Office, to informal assessments by program managers. It is reasonable to portray the general field of program evaluation as more applied than academically oriented, a point that a number of well-known introductions to the field make explicit. Weiss (1998, 15), for example, argues that program evaluation differs from more academic approaches to studying policy because of its fundamentally pragmatic raison d'être. According to Weiss, evaluation is aimed more at informing and improving policy than at generating knowledge per se, and the knowledge generated by program evaluations is often seen as policy and program specific, rather than cumulatively building into a body of generalizable knowledge that applies across different policies and programs. This narrow theoretical focus may explain why program evaluations are often oriented less toward academic publication and more toward applied audiences.[1]

In one sense, program evaluation is probably as old as organized human activity. Figuring out what worked (or did not) and why was as important to the Romans as it is to modern-day public authorities. Formal evaluations, especially in the education field, have a history of at least 150 years, dating back to Horace Mann's annual report on education in Massachusetts in the 1840s (Fitzpatrick, Sanders, and Worthen 2004, 31). The modern discipline of evaluation, though, traces its roots to many of the same origins as policy analysis: It grew out of a recognition that social science could be useful in guiding public policy; got a significant boost in the 1960s because of demand to assess the impact of large new federal social welfare programs; and developed into a profession with dedicated graduate programs and publications in the 1970s, 1980s, and 1990s. Like the whole field of policy studies, even as graduate curriculums expanded and journals proliferated to disseminate evaluation theory and practice, program evaluation struggled to define itself as a field. Evaluation has been described as a "transdiscipline" that is employed across fields in a comparable sense to logic or statistics (Fitzpatrick, Sanders, and Worthen 2004, 42).

Although there is some conceptual core to the notion of program evaluation, it is also clearly something of an elastic concept that can mean different things to different people. Subsumed under the umbrella of "program evaluation" are a number of distinct ex post conceptual approaches that extend beyond impact analysis. Unfortunately, there is no universally agreed upon definition of the scope and particular subfields of policy evaluation, though a number of typologies seek to clarify these conceptual differences and provide some order to the field (e.g., Trisko and League 1978; Scriven 1991; Mohr 1995; Bingham and Felbinger 2002, 4–8; Smith and Licari 2007, 161–164; Dunn 1981/2011). The most common of these efforts is a pair of twinned categorizations: formative and summative evaluations, and process and outcome evaluations.

Formative and Summative Evaluations

Formative and summative evaluations are distinguished by timing and the intent of the individual conducting the study. Studies are undertaken in the early stages and are intended to inform the development of a program or policy. The evaluations are timed to be in medias res, as opposed to ex ante or ex post. A formative evaluation is undertaken when critical decisions have been made and a program or policy has at least some embryonic implementation but is not so developed that policymakers cannot make adjustments to the policy, taking advantage of empirical study to better match means to the desired ends.

Summative evaluations are done at a different part of a program or policy life cycle; their basic role is to decide whether to expand, contract, terminate, or continue a program. They are done when a program or policy is relatively mature and are intended to assess the overall worth in the context of whatever values the program or policy is being judged by. While timing clearly differentiates summative and formative evaluations, intent is the more important discriminator. Formative evaluations essentially ask: "Should we change anything that we are doing?" Summative evaluations ask: "Should we keep doing what we're doing, do something different, or stop doing it altogether?" Scriven (1991, 19) put the difference between formative and summative evaluations this way: "When the cook tastes the soup, that's formative evaluation; when the guest tastes it, that's summative evaluation."

Process and Outcome Evaluations

Another useful way to categorize evaluation studies is to split them into process and outcome evaluations. Process evaluations focus on what a policy is actually doing, whereas outcome evaluations focus on what a policy has actually achieved.

Process evaluations assess policy actions' program activities with an eye toward these sorts of questions: Are program staff adequately trained to do the job? Is the program/policy operating according to the rules/laws/obligations that govern it? Are contractual obligations being met? Is the policy serving the target population it is supposed to be serving? (Weiss 1998, 75; Bingham and Felbinger 2002, 4). The basic function of a process evaluation is to see whether the actions of those charged with putting a policy into practice (typically a public agency) match the plans and goals that justified the policy in the first place. Process evaluations, then, are oriented toward issues such as compliance (assessing whether a policy or program meets the laws and regulations that authorize and govern its operation) and auditing (assessing whether a target population is receiving the resources or services mandated by the policy or program). A good deal of what is being termed here as process evaluation overlaps with the study of policy implementation; implementation is discussed in depth in Chapter 7.

In contrast to a process evaluation, an outcome evaluation seeks to measure and assess what a policy has actually achieved. Impact analysis is a specific form of outcome evaluation, that is, a quantitative outcome evaluation. These are the sorts of questions that motivate an impact analysis: Is the policy having any impact on the problem it was designed to address? If it is having an impact, how much of an impact? If it is not having an impact, why not?

To understand the process/outcome distinction, consider the following example. An increase in drunk driving has become a high-profile issue for a municipality. An ex ante policy analysis concludes that the most efficient way to lower drunk driving rates is to implement a program of checkpoints on key roads and heavily advertise that the police are cracking down on drunk driving. Accordingly, the police department implements random checkpoints on these roads and begins a public relations campaign, warning drivers that law enforcement is making a point of catching drunk drivers and that the consequences of being caught driving while under the influence involve significant costs for those convicted. A process evaluation of this policy would focus on issues such as whether the checkpoints comply with the civil rights of the drivers, whether they are placed in the best spots to catch drunk drivers, and whether there are enough of them to significantly increase the probabilities of catching drunk drivers. An impact analysis, on the other hand, will focus on whether the number of drunk drivers has decreased as a result of the checkpoint policy, and if so, by how much (Smith and Licari 2007, 162).

Dividing the policy evaluation field into formative/summative and process/outcome categories helps impose some order on a sprawling area of policy studies. However, there is also clear overlap among these categories, and this can lead to confusion. Some scholars seem to view summative/formative studies more as process evaluations (e.g., Scriven 1991), whereas others view formative and sum-mative evaluations as particular types of outcome evaluations (e.g., Mohr 1995, 32). Weiss (1998, 32–33) has suggested that though it is possible to conceptually distinguish between the two pairs of terms based on timing, evaluator intent, and phase of the policy, the most useful way to think about policy evaluation is in process and outcome terms. The original purpose of policy evaluation, after all, was to assess outcomes, to figure out the consequences of public policy. Process studies fit naturally into this effort, because they can help explain why the conse-quences of policy are what they are.

There are three basic approaches to process and outcome program evalua-tions, which can be distinguished by distinct questions. The first is the descriptive evaluation approach, which seeks to describe goals, processes, and outcomes rather than form judgments about them. At the core of the descriptive approach are questions about whether something *is*: Is the goal (or are the goals) clearly articulated? Is the goal (or are the goals) clearly communicated? Is there a plan for assessing progress or success? Is there clear accountability? The second ap-proach is normative. At the core of normative program evaluations are questions about the worth of what is being done: Is the goal realistic? Does the policy ad-vance socially desirable goals? Finally, the impact approach focuses on the out-comes of a policy: To what extent did the policy achieve its goals? How can variation in this outcome be confidently assigned to the policy? Exactly how much of the variation is attributable to the outcome or policy?

Generally speaking, descriptive and normative approaches tend to use qual-itative methods and fall into the formative/process categories of program evalu-ation (though with plenty of exceptions). Impact approaches are concentrated in the outcome category and, at least according to Mohr (1995, 32), are consid-ered summative if they only assess whether a policy had a particular outcome and formative if they also explain why. Impact analysis is the rationalist project's core ex post approach to forming evaluative judgments of public policy and as such is the focus of most of what follows.

Impact Analysis

An impact analysis is always built around three core elements: the problem, the activity, and the outcome of interest. The problem is some predicted outcome or condition that is considered unsatisfactory and that is expected to remain un-satisfactory without the intervention of a public policy or program. The activity is the human-directed events that constitute the policy, that is, the state-directed actions undertaken to address the problem. The outcome of interest is the variable that is actually measured to evaluate the impact of the program on the problem (Deniston 1972; Mohr 1995, 3; Imbens and Wooldridge 2008).

Impact analysis, then, goes about systematically answering the question "What have we done?" by identifying and measuring some outcome of interest and empirically testing its relationship to the activity of the program or policy. This sounds simple enough in theory but can become complex very quickly in practice. For one thing, an impact analysis depends heavily on how an analyst chooses a dependent variable, that is, an outcome of interest. The outcome of interest has to serve two critical functions. First, it has to operationalize an aspect of the problem. Second, it has to be a variable that can be causally linked to the program or policy. This choice becomes complicated because the problems public policies are designed to address are often complex and multidimensional, and because programs and policies often have multiple, vague, or even contradictory outcomes. This is because public policies often have unclear goals, or multiple goals that are not prioritized or may even be contradictory (Hogwood and Gunn 1984, 234). This lack of clarity in goals injects an element of choice and subjectivity into the selection of an outcome of interest. The choices on the dependent variable can be echoed with the key independent variable(s). To take away any valid inferences, a researcher has to isolate the effects of the policy under study, not just from all the potential nonpolicy causes of the outcome of interest but from other policies or programs that may be aimed at the same problem.

As Mohr (1995, 25) has pointed out, a central problem here is that outcomes and problems are not necessarily the same thing. It is surprisingly easy to measure outcomes that do not really represent the targeted problem or to choose an outcome that captures a relatively tangential impact of the program or policy. Test scores, for example, are widely employed as a general yardstick of educational performance and as such are frequently employed as the outcome of interest in impact analyses of education policies. Yet it is not clear that these tests even measure what they were designed to measure, let alone capture some vague and general concept like "educational performance" (Lemann 1995; Rothstein 1997; Ravitch 2011).

Choosing an outcome of interest is further complicated by the fact that one policy may produce more than one outcome, and a single outcome may be influenced by more than one public policy. Mohr (1995, 39) even made a conceptual distinction between multiple outcomes and single outcomes with multiple elements. As an example of the latter he used the utilization rate of hospitals, an outcome of significant interest in health-care policy that consists of three separate parts: the number of patient admissions, length of stay, and resources used in the hospital. These are not separate outcomes, but rather interdependent elements of a single outcome.

The bottom line is that analysts typically have a range of options for how to operationalize an outcome of interest, and this choice can predetermine the conclusions of the study. Smith and Granberg-Rademacker (2003), for example, used six measures of educational performance to test a range of hypotheses about education policies and found that the link between these activities and educational outcomes was critically dependent on the choice of outcome of interest and on the mix of policy activities included. These differences were not just in statistical significance but in substantive direction: the sign of the coefficients in their regression models switched directions across different model specifications. In other words, they concluded that the answer to "What have we done?" across a range of educational policies was a cautious "it depends," mostly on how a researcher operationalizes the outcome of interest and specifies the causal model used to explain it.

These sorts of challenges open impact analysis to the same sorts of postpositivist criticisms leveled at policy analysis. The sophisticated quantitative techniques that characterize impact analysis present a scientific veneer, but lurking underneath are a set of normative biases that help predetermine conclusions (see Fischer 2003). This has led to some cynicism about the objective worth of not just impact analysis, but program evaluation generally. James Q. Wilson (1973b) long ago proposed two immutable laws of policy evaluation. Wilson's First Law is that all policy interventions produce the intended effect . . . if the research is done by those who support the policy. Wilson's Second Law is that no policy intervention works . . . if the research is carried out by third parties who are skeptical of the policy. Wilson argues that the First Law is driven by data supplied by the agency managing the policy or program, a time period selected to maximize the policy's intended effect, and a lack of attention to alternate causes of the outcome of interest. The Second Law is driven by independently gathered data, a time period (typically short) that minimizes the impact of the policy, and a strong focus on variables that could also be causally linked to the outcome of interest. Wilson (tongue only partly in cheek) suggested that any program evaluation not explained by one of these laws is explained by the other.

Wilson's Laws are cautionary tales for the "evidence-based program evaluation" movement, which has gained traction among government agencies world-wide over the past few decades. The basic aim of evidence-based program evaluation is to empirically assess "what works," that is, to provide reasonably objective yardsticks of policy or program performance so best practices can be emulated elsewhere and poorly performing programs can be identified and modified or shut down. This approach is largely rooted in the rationalist paradigm—that is, in quantitative impact analysis—and has been an important element of the new public management (NPM) movement in public administration (Davies, Nutley, and Smith 2000; Reid 2003; Head 2008). However, Wilson's Laws, along with findings such as those reported by Smith and Granberg-Rademacker, suggest that the quality of the evidence for "what works" is heavily dependent on who is doing the analysis, who is interpreting that analysis, and what choices an analyst makes about measurement and model specification.

The central problem, in other words, is not the method per se, but the subjective influences of political perspective and context that influence how that method is employed or interpreted. The primary job of an analyst operating from the rationalist framework (ex ante or ex post) is to provide policymakers with "honest numbers," defined as "policy data produced by competent researchers and analysts who use sound technical methods without the application of political spin to fit partisan needs" (Williams 1998, ix). Walter Williams, a primary advocate of this rationalist approach to analysis and evaluation, sees its main challenge not in the rationalist methods or training of analysts but in political spin and the incentives of partisan need. Policymakers do not always want honest numbers, because they are politically distasteful. As Brian Head (2008, 5) puts it, "Some policy positions are 'data-proof' or 'evidence-proof', in the sense that their evidence 'base' has been narrowed or buttressed by political commitments." In this sort of political context, the temptation for policy analysts is to substitute neutral competence (analysis based solely on expertise) with responsive competence (expertise deployed to serve partisan preferences). Williams claims that bad public policy is often supported by vast reams of supposedly rationalist research that in reality is tailored to sell an underlying political objective (Jones and Williams 2007). This, of course, undercuts the very notion of the rationalist project and makes "honest numbers" anything but.

Yet many scholars argue that the largely quantitative methods employed by policy analysts are perfectly capable of producing honest numbers, that is, data analysis that is not unduly spun or squeezed by partisan perspective (e.g., Williams 1998; Mohr 1995; Angrist and Pischke 2008). Producing those honest numbers, though, depends on the logic and theory underpinning impact analysis.

The Logic and Theory of Impact Analysis

The objective of an impact analysis is clear: to determine whether a policy had an impact on an outcome of interest, and if so, by how much. Impact analysis is thus explicitly causal analysis, the goal of which is to make an assessment of whether X (a program or policy) caused Y (an outcome of interest), and if so, by how much. Impact analysis thus depends critically on how it addresses the logic of causality. How do we know when X has caused Y?

The concept of causality used in impact analysis is articulated most clearly by such authors as Campbell and Stanley (1966) and Mohr (1995), and more broadly by King, Keohane, and Verba (1994), Angrist and Pischke (2008), and Freedman (2009). All of these works exhibit a common logic for establishing a causal claim that is broadly shared throughout the social sciences. Generally speaking, three elements are needed to support the claim that X causes Y: temporal precedence (if X causes Y, X must precede Y), covariation (if X causes Y, then Y will change when X changes), and co-occurrence (if there is no X, there is no Y). The first two of these elements are, at least in the abstract, comparatively easy to empirically establish in ex post evaluations of public policy. We expect X (the program or policy) to precede observed changes in Y, because the policy exists to bring about those changes and because no such changes are expected until X exists. Establishing covariation in X and Y is trivial in quantitative terms as long as adequate measures of the policy activity (X) and the outcome of interest (Y) are available. Correlation coefficients, difference of means tests, and the like are often enough to test a statistical relationship between policy and an outcome of interest, and the full range of quantitative tools available to social science can be brought in as needed.

The critical challenge in making a causal claim, then, comes down to generating an estimate of the counterfactual, that is, estimating what happens to Y in the absence of X. Assuming such an estimate can be generated, the impact of a policy boils down to the difference between the observed level of Y (the resultant), with an estimate of Y when there is no X (the counterfactual). To use Mohr's (1995) notation, $I = R - C$ (impact equals resultant minus counterfactual). An impact analysis systematically answers the question "What have we done?" by identifying the key causal claim between policy activity and the outcome of interest, estimating a counterfactual, and comparing the counterfactual with the resultant. These needs create the two central theoretical challenges of impact analysis. First is the need to identify the key causal link between policy activity and outcome of interest. A variety of conceptual frameworks can be employed to achieve this goal, though the generic approach is to employ program theory (discussed in detail below). Second is the need to generate a valid estimate of the counterfactual. This is typically handled through careful research design, and for impact analysis this relies heavily on reasoning borrowed directly from the scientific method (for primers on the logic of the counterfactual and its importance in impact analysis, see Mohr 1995; Morgan and Winship 2007; Angrist and Pischke 2008; Imbens and Wooldridge 2008).

Before examining program theory and research design, though, it is important to note that there are other approaches to policy evaluation that do not rely on the counterfactual to establish causality. These approaches tend to be qualitative (indeed, the absence of a counterfactual has been used to conceptually define qualitative approaches to program evaluation; see Mohr 1995, 1999). These alternate approaches can usefully be described as "diagnostic" because they approach causality in much the same way that a medical diagnosis is done. Causality, in this approach, is inferred from symptoms or from the physical traces of policy activity (these traces are sometimes referred to as "signatures" in policy literature; see Scriven 1967; George and McKeown 1985 for discussions of this approach to causality).

The diagnostic approach to causality is probably more intuitive than the counterfactual approach. Mohr (1999) uses the examples of a person dying after a heart attack and a lamppost falling over after being struck by a car. The cause of death in a heart attack is established by noting symptoms consistent with this problem prior to death or through an autopsy that shows damage to the heart. When a car hits a lamppost, we can readily establish a physical cause of the lamppost falling over: the car smashed into it. Compare these examples of establishing causality with the counterfactual approach. The counterfactual approach would require estimating whether the individual would have lived or died without having a heart attack and estimating whether the lamppost would have fallen over without a car smashing into it. Stated like this, the counterfactual approach seems not only fussily complicated but downright counterintuitive.

But consider a public policy, say, a drug treatment program designed to target long-term drug users and keep them clean. One way to figure out what this program has done is to take a diagnostic approach: interview the people administering the treatment to get their assessments of the program's effectiveness, do the same with drug users enrolled in the program, and find out how many people enrolled in the program return to using drugs compared to those who stay drug free for a certain period of time. From these data an analyst can fashion an empirically supported answer to the question of what the program has done.

Let's say, however, that the people who administer the policy (the program staffers) view it as very successful, the program's clients (drug users), view it as moderately successful, and 50 percent of the people who enroll fall back into heavy patterns of drug use. What does this mean? Can we claim that the program is responsible for helping half of its clients kick their drug habits? What if the only people who seek out the program's treatment are individuals who genuinely want to be drug free and are committed to doing whatever it takes to achieve this goal? Should the program be judged a success because it helps half of its clients, or a failure because it does not address the needs of the other half? It is difficult to extract from this sort of mixed picture a clear notion of program impact; subjective perspective clearly plays a role in making this determination. From a post-positivist perspective, this is perfectly acceptable. Actually, it is probably more accurate to say that from a post-positivist perspective, there is no real alternative. If truth or reality is constructed from individual viewpoints, there is no independent, objective reality that has a privileged claim to the truth. From a rationalist perspective, though, there is a big problem. To really assess impact we need to know not just how the program changed the behavior of the people who actually attended, but how it would have changed the behavior of those who did not. If we have reasonable estimates of that—in other words, reasonable estimates of the counterfactual—the program's impact can be assessed independently of participant or stakeholder perspective. The counterfactual approach, in other words, argues that careful estimates of R − C can be perspective free, or at least more perspective free than any other alternative (for a good introduction to the formal logic of this argument, see Angrist and Pischke 2008).

The counterfactual approach to determining the impact of our hypothetical drug program would identify the outcome of interest (say, the rate at which drug users seeking to kick the habit stay drug free for a certain period of time) and seek to compare the observed outcome of interest with the counterfactual. A valid approach to the counterfactual might be an estimate of the level of drug use for the same sort of population treated by the program in the absence of that program. In this approach, the judgment of what the program has or has not done boils down to R − C, an impact that can be quantified and readily attributed to the target policy. The big assumption here, of course, is that both the outcome of interest identified and the estimate of the counterfactual are meaningful (i.e., reflective of the underlying problem and the activity designed to address it) and valid. Such claims to validity are often debatable.

This makes the role of theory and research design absolutely critical in supporting the inferences drawn from impact analysis. Impact analysis requires a conceptual framework that identifies the correct outcome of interest and explains its causal relationship with the policy activity, and it needs a logical design for generating empirical estimates of this outcome of interest in the absence of that activity. The theoretical frameworks that supply causal explanations for impact analysis come from a number of places. Some are generalizable frameworks, or theories that make some claim to a universal explanation of human behavior. Public choice and institutional rational choice, for example, are predicated on a universal set of assumptions about human behavior (that humans are rational utility maximizers). This universal notion of why humans do what they do can be employed to help explain how and why institutional reforms would be expected to change certain behaviors. If these behaviors can be encapsulated in an outcome of interest variable, then a causal link between policy activity and outcome is established that can be empirically tested. For example, consider a regulatory policy that fines industries for emitting certain pollutants. The causal expectation here is that fines will create a rational incentive to reduce pollution. Isolating the unique impact of this regulatory policy on the variation in pollution levels provides empirical evidence of what the policy has (or has not) done.

Again, this sounds simple and straightforward in the abstract, but it can be highly complex in practice. For one thing, theory has to be able to identify the problem and the outcome of interest, which, as we've already seen, is not such an easy thing to do, especially within the boundaries of a single policy or program. Rather than generalizable frameworks such as rational choice, impact analysis is often guided by program theory.

Program Theory

Program theory constitutes "the set of beliefs that underlie action" (Weiss 1998, 55). Such beliefs do not have to be generalizable; they may be specific to the single program or policy under consideration. These causal beliefs do not even have to be correct. Program theory assumes that simply the existence of a policy represents a theory in the sense of a causal claim linking inputs to outputs. If policy is purposive, by definition it seeks to achieve some goal or objective. Logically, then, a policy represents some expectation that the activities it mandates will cause those objectives to be met. Impact analysis does not require a single program theory; there may be several theories that can be empirically tested.

A fairly standard approach to program theory is to construct an outcome line. In its simplest form, an outcome line is an exercise in backward induction. It begins with the ultimate desired outcome and from this starting point works backward, building a causal chain out of links consisting of activities and outcomes. The notion of an outcome line is readily grasped through an example. Consider a policy that seeks to increase teacher salaries as a means to increase student achievement. How will increasing teacher salaries increase student achievement? What justifies any public policy that seeks to achieve higher levels of student achievement? There are a number of potential answers to such questions, but from a society-wide perspective, higher levels of student achievement are associated with positive social outcomes, such as higher economic productivity and competitiveness, greater civic engagement, and a reduction in social ills ranging from criminal activity to teenage pregnancy. Let us assume that the ultimate desired outcome is greater economic productivity. How do higher teacher salaries result in this ultimate outcome? An outcome line links the policy to the desired outcomes in the following manner:

> Higher teacher salaries (activity) → more qualified individuals attracted to teaching as a career (outcome) → schools hire more qualified teachers (activity) → more qualified teachers in the classroom (outcome) → more qualified teachers provide superior learning experience (activity) → student achievement increases (outcome) → students use human capital to advance their economic prospects (activity) → economic productivity increases (outcome)

Though an extremely simplified example, this gets across the basic idea of program theory and an outcome line.[2] The outcome line makes explicit the causal beliefs that link the policy to its desired objectives. The immediate advantages of an outcome line are that it can help identify the outcome of interest and can alert a researcher to the activities and outcomes that may lie between the policy and this outcome of interest, that is, the dependent variable of an impact analysis. To use an outcome line to find the outcome of interest, simply start from the right and work leftward through the outcomes. The outcome of interest is the outcome where 1) all outcomes to its right are considered immaterial (we do not care what those outcomes are, or even if they occurred); and/or 2) we are willing to assume that all outcomes to the right will happen if this outcome is achieved. In Mohr's (1995) terminology, the outcome of interest is the leftmost "inherently valued" outcome. In our example, working from left to right, "student achievement increases" is a likely candidate to be this leftmost inherently valued outcome and is thus identified as our outcome of interest.

Our outcome line, though, makes clear that the causal link between the policy and the outcome of interest is not direct; a number of linked activities and outcomes have to fall into place. Mohr (1995, 32) calls outcomes that are prerequisites for the outcome of interest to be achieved policy "subobjectives." Subobjectives can be important, especially if the policy is found to have little or no impact on the outcome of interest. This is because they can provide crucial information about why this impact did not occur. If increasing teacher salaries did not attract more qualified people to the teaching profession, the causal beliefs linking policy to outcome of interest break down very early in the outcome line. This raises a question of how an analysis should treat subobjectives: Should they be measured and included in an empirical analysis? It depends. If the central objective is simply to empirically assess whether the policy had an impact on the outcome of interest, then subobjectives can be ignored. If the objective is to also explain why (or why not) the policy caused changes in the outcome of interest, subobjectives should probably be accounted for.

Program theory constructed in this fashion has much to recommend it. It specifies the causal reasoning that justifies a policy and helps identify the outcome of interest. However, program theory is also the target of some justified criticism. Program theory is often very narrow in the sense that it is a causal explanation limited to a single policy at a single time in a single place. This makes it an unlikely basis for building cumulative knowledge; a general theory of why policy does or does not work is unlikely to be fashioned out of outcome lines like the one given above. Program theory is also criticized for presenting an oversimplified model of reality. Student achievement is a complex phenomenon, and no outcome line is going to capture exactly how a single variable is going to shape that phenomenon simply because policymakers can manipulate that variable. Finally, program theory is vulnerable to a full range of post-positivist criticisms about what outcomes and activities are selected to be included in the causal chain. Program theory, remember, is often an unabashedly normative notion of how the world works; it is a framework that makes explicit causal beliefs. These beliefs, and thus the program theory, can arise from a number of different sources, including the biases of the analyst. Some critics raise doubts about any individual's ability to consistently identify the true causal mechanisms at work; the world is simply too complex and multivariate (see Shadish, Cook, and Leviton 1991; Cook and Shadish 1994).

Impact analysis, however, does not rely on program theory or an outcome line to make a formal assessment of causality. It uses these conceptual tools to identify the outcome of interest and the causal beliefs linking it to the policy activity. It seeks to assess causality, that is, whether X brought about changes in Y, by generating a valid estimate of the counterfactual. If X (higher teacher salaries) causes Y (greater student achievement), then Y should look different if there is no X. Once the outcome of interest and the causal beliefs are identified, the key issue in making a formal assessment of whether X has an impact on Y, and if so by how much, is the estimate of the counterfactual. That is more an area of research design than program theory.

Research Design in Impact Analysis

In impact analysis, research design can be defined as the system or means used to estimate a counterfactual. Any impact analysis research design faces the same crucial challenge: how to create equivalency; that is, how to create a counterfactual that is equivalent in all aspects to the resultant except for the presence of the public policy or program. There are three basic designs to achieve this end—experimental, quasi-experimental, and correlational—and seminal works linking these approaches to the counterfactual concept of causality employed in impact analysis include Campbell and Stanley (1966), Cook and Campbell (1979), Mohr (1995), and Shadish, Cook, and Campbell (2002). Though developed somewhat independently, there is a parallel literature in economics that applies the same logic of causality in policy analysis, though often applying it with considerably more methodological firepower and sophistication (see Imbens and Wooldridge 2008). All three frameworks seek to estimate an equivalent estimate of the counterfactual; the key difference among the research designs is how the equivalent comparison group is created.

The true experimental design is widely considered the flagship approach to impact analysis (Rossi and Freeman 1993, 307; Angrist and Pischke 2008). In experimental designs the target population is randomly assigned into treatment groups (those who actually receive program benefits) and control groups (those who receive no program benefits). Any observed difference in the outcome of interest is assumed to be a product of random chance (which can be assessed statistically) or caused by the policy. The experimental group's measure on the outcome of interest is thus used as R, and the control group's measure as C, and the impact of the policy as R – C. Though experimental designs come in numerous variants, all share the same basic logic; that is, the power of randomization creates real equivalency between control and experimental groups, allowing for valid comparisons of R and C (see Morton and Williams 2010; Mohr 1995 for thorough discussions of variants of the experimental design).

Of course the power of experimental designs is predicated on the assumption that an analyst (or some other central authority) actually has the ability to randomize subjects and thus manipulate the key independent variable (i.e., who does or does not get the policy benefits). When these assumptions hold, experimental designs can represent a social science analogy to the laboratory benchmarks of the hard sciences and justifiably can be considered "flagship" or "gold standard" means of estimating a counterfactual. In the policy realm, however, it is relatively rare for an analyst to have this sort of control. There are good practical, legal, and ethical reasons for this. Randomly withholding, say, educational benefits from a group of disadvantaged youths in order to assess the impact of a reading program will strike many of those assigned to a control group (and certainly their parents) as unfair and may be considered unethical by the governing policy authority or an institutional review board. Even when such control is granted, running such experiments can be resource intensive— a pilot jobs program that involves randomly selecting participants from a designated sample, for example, may take months to implement and may require considerable funding.

Though challenging to execute, experimental designs are not impossible, and true randomized field trials have yielded important insights into the impacts of a wide variety of public policies (for a review, see Burtless 1995; Angrist and Pischke 2008 also provide some instructive "real-world" examples). In the field, however, it is often difficult to sustain the assumptions of randomization that provide validity to the experimental design's claims to causal explanation. In education, for example, there have been a number of randomized field trials aimed at assessing the impact of school vouchers on outcomes of interest such as academic achievement. These were possible because the demand for vouchers in some programs exceeded supply and they were thus awarded by lottery—in effect, random assignment. At first blush, this seems like a perfect opportunity to leverage the power of experimental design to get a true estimate of the impact of vouchers. Given the significant controversy over what vouchers do (or do not) contribute to educational outcomes, such an impact analysis could make an important contribution to a high-profile policy debate. The experimental nature of these sorts of field trials, however, tends to break down quickly. To begin with, the experimental and control groups are not necessarily representative of the target population—all public school students—but just those actively seeking a voucher, and there are good reasons to suspect the latter group is systematically different from the former. Attrition also tends to be a problem; as much as 50 percent of those who received vouchers dropped out of the program within a semester or so (i.e., they returned to their assigned public school). If there are any systematic commonalities to those who drop out—again, there are reasons to believe this is the case—randomization is lost and with it the power of experimental designs (Ladd 2002; Metcalf, Beghetto, and Legan 2002).

One of the great advantages of quasi-experimental designs is that they avoid many of the practical limitations of putting experimental designs into practice. At their core, quasi-experimental designs follow the same structure as experimental designs, except for randomization.[3] Rather than randomization, equivalency is created by systematically selecting a comparison group (in quasi-experiments, the counterfactual group is called a comparison rather than a control). Obviously the key issue in quasi-experimental designs, then, is how the comparison group is selected. There are numerous options. Comparison groups can be selected on the basis of their similarity to the experimental group on a set of reference variables. For example, the impact of a community policing program might be assessed by comparing crime rates in cities of roughly similar size and demographics, some of which have a community policing program and some that do not. Similarly, a group of individuals may be systematically assigned to experimental (or treatment) and comparison groups so that both are balanced in terms of socioeconomics, age, gender, or whatever variables are believed important to creating equivalency.

Among the most common quasi-experimental approaches in impact analysis are versions of interrupted time series analysis, which at heart is a simple before-and-after comparison.[4] The basic idea is to take repeated measures across time on the outcome of interest for the unit of analysis, with the introduction of the program or policy occurring somewhere in the middle of those repeated measures. The counterfactual here is intuitively equivalent, because it does not just represent a similar group to that which actually received policy or program benefits—it *is* the same group. Consider, for example, the problem of assessing the impact of a crime policy on state crime rates. In an experimental design an analyst would randomly assign these policies to states and observe the crime rate differences between states with and without this particular policy. No central authority—let alone any single policy analyst—has the power to randomly assign policies to sovereign governments, so the experimental design is impractical. A quasi-experimental option is to use a time trend on crime rates that is bisected, or interrupted, by introduction of the policy. So there is a time series of crime rates over, say, forty years, and the policy is adopted at year twenty. The counterfactual is estimated using the measures before the policy, the resultant using the measures after its introduction.

This approach is attractive because impact analyses can take advantage of the fact that outcome of interest measures exist for many public policies and programs before and after they were adopted. The major problem, of course, is that the world is not static, and outcomes of interest like crime rates can vary considerably across time for a lot of reasons beyond the introduction of policy. An interrupted time series design as just described would likely take the form of a multiple regression analysis that included controls for other causes of crime rates. This shifts the design away from a quasi-experimental design, where equivalency is achieved through careful selection of the group or unit of analysis used to estimate the counterfactual, to a purely correlational design, in which there are no real controls or comparison groups. Technically a correlational design is one in which there is no centralized selection of who does or does not receive program benefits; individuals (or social aggregates) decide themselves whether to adopt or take advantage of the policy. There are no consciously selected control or comparison groups; all an analyst can do is observe and try to create equivalency by statistically controlling for alternate causes of the outcome of interest. Because there is no conscious selection underlying the estimate of the counterfactual and no real manipulation of the key independent variable—just observations of variance—the correlational design has the weakest claim to generating valid estimates of the counterfactual.

Assuming equivalence can be achieved statistically, correlational designs do provide valid estimates of a counterfactual (see Mohr 1995; Angrist and Pischke 2008). However, in most cases correlational designs practically translate into garden variety multiple regression analyses, which are always vulnerable to specification debates. In other words, there is usually some basis for claiming that equivalency has not been achieved, because some important cause of the outcome of interest has been excluded from the model, or because some irrelevant variable has been included. As the preceding discussion suggests, the line between quasi-experimental and correlational designs is not clear-cut. Impact analysis routinely makes use of statistical control techniques even in experimental designs (randomized field trials of school vouchers, for example, have used statistical controls to control for attrition in the experimental or control groups). This makes the counterfactual concept of causality vulnerable to post-positivist criticisms that values can readily creep into even a well-intentioned and executed impact analysis; because inferred impacts are critically dependent on these controls, the choice of controls can determine the conclusions of an impact analysis. Proponents of straightforward quantitative impact analysis acknowledge such possibilities but argue that "normative creep" can be reduced (if not eliminated) by subjecting ex post conclusions to the same sorts of sensitivity analysis that is common to ex ante prescriptive studies. In short, if choice of statistical controls can manipulate the estimate of the counterfactual, then the analysis should be run with different sets of controls to make their influence clear (see Smith and Granberg-Rademacker 2003).

Assuming that, regardless of research design approach, a valid estimate of the counterfactual is obtained, an impact analysis will provide a precise estimate of the effect of a program or policy: impact equals resultant minus counterfactual ($I = R - C$). If the goal(s) of the policy can be expressed as a point estimate of the outcome of interest, the effectiveness of the policy can also be quantitatively assessed through an effectiveness ratio: effectiveness = $R - C / P - C$ (where "P" is the planned or projected level of the outcome of interest). An effectiveness ratio is intuitive; it represents the proportion of the policy's goal that has been achieved on a given outcome of interest. A policy with an effectiveness ratio greater than 1 has exceeded its goals (it is more than 100 percent effective); a ratio that is less than 1 is short of the planned level of the outcome of interest (see Mohr 1995 for an in-depth discussion of these measures).

This, ultimately, is what impact analysis strives for: "honest numbers." More formally, it seeks a precise, quantitative answer to the question "What have we done?" The utility and validity of that answer is tied to a number of issues, but most critical are the counterfactual notion of causality and the strength of the research design. Without a valid estimate of the counterfactual, $R - C$, regardless of the sophistication of the methods and measures, is at best an educated guess.

Conclusion

A central focus of ex post facto policy studies is the impact of a public policy or program. Public policies are purposive social mechanisms; they are designed to change the existing state of the world. Exactly what policy is directed toward and what it is expected to change are all issues that can be considered ex ante, but adopting and implementing a program even on the basis of careful policy analysis is no guarantee that it will actually achieve its objectives. The fundamental question of ex post policy studies, then, boils down to this: "What have we done?"

Impact analysis offers a systematic framework to provide answers to this question. It is useful because it is not tied to any single causal theory; rather, it is based on a logical understanding of causality. Impact analysis does not require a universal theory, or even a universal normative yardstick like efficiency, as a basis for judging policy. What it needs is some notion of the causal beliefs linking a policy activity and an outcome of interest. These beliefs do not even have to be correct; they simply have to provide an explanation of why X is expected to change Y. This does not require a general theory such as rational choice; the causal beliefs linking X and Y can just as easily be drawn from ideology or broader political expectations. What impact analysis seeks to test is the empirical validity of these causal claims, regardless of their origin.

To do this, impact analysis relies on the counterfactual notion of causality. This is why research design is such a critical element of impact analysis; a research design constitutes the means to estimate the counterfactual, and a valid estimate requires less of a perfect theory but more of a robust research design. Impact analysis is subject to a broad set of objections from post-positivist critics. These criticisms have some merit. An impact analysis is wholly dependent on generating a valid estimate of the counterfactual, and this is only possible if the correct activity and outcome of interest have been identified and accurately measured, the causal link connecting them is accurately understood, and these elements are brought together in a robust and well-thought-out research design. This constitutes a lot of "ifs."

Still, impact analysis is unusual in the field of policy studies in that it offers a comparatively clear and clean systematic framework, one supported by well-thought-out internal logic and readily amenable to a wide variety of theories and quantitative methods (see Imbens and Wooldridge 2008). As such, impact analysis offers a compelling epistemological framework for generating and defending answers to the core question of ex post policy studies: "What have we done?"

Notes

1. That said, there are a number of field-specific policy evaluation journals, the most prominent of which is the *American Journal of Evaluation* (AJE), published under the auspices of the American Evaluation Association. The AJE publishes a broad variety of papers on the methods, theory, and applications of evaluation, many of them academic. The intended

audience of the AJE, though, is meant to be as broad as possible, certainly far beyond the realms of academia. Currently there are easily a dozen or more professional journals dedicated to evaluation studies, including *Evaluation and Program Planning, Evaluation Practice, Evaluation Review,* and *Evaluation Quarterly.* Some of these journals are devoted solely to evaluation in specific policy areas, such as *Studies in Educational Evaluation.*

2. Similar examples are found in well-known program evaluation texts such as Weiss (1998) and Mohr (1995).

3. Virtually every experimental design has a direct quasi-experimental analog (see Mohr 1995).

4. Although less common than interrupted time series designs, regression discontinuity designs are similar conceptually and methodologically. They arguably produce more valid estimates of the counterfactual but require an analyst (or some other central authority) to exercise assignment control, though in regression discontinuity this is on the basis of an assignment variable (e.g., the neediest get the program) rather than randomization. For a good overview of the pros and cons of experimental versus quasi-experimental designs, as well as the pros and cons of various quasi-experimental approaches, see Shadish, Cook, and Campbell (2002).

CHAPTER 7

How Does It Work? Policy Implementation

Chapters 5 and 6 focus on separate ends of a policy chain. On one end is the problem of deciding what should be done. On the other is the problem of figuring out what has been done. In between are a lot of decisions and actions that causally connect one end of this chain to the other. Implementation research seeks to make sense of this space between government intention and policy impact.

This is a complicated and muddled piece of political geography. From an implementation perspective, policy begins rather than ends with a formal declaration of what government is going to do. When Congress passes a law to, say, decrease pollutants in public waterways, the legislature does not adjourn to carry water filters down to the bank of the Potomac. The declaration of intent—the passage of a law—has to somehow be translated into reality.

That translation is typically assigned to an executive branch agency (or agencies; implementation is often plural bureaucracy-wise). Under ideal circumstances, that agency has a two-stage challenge in implementing the policy intentions of the elected branches of government. First, it has to figure out exactly what the elected branch wants to do. Second, it has to figure out a way to do it.

Even under ideal circumstances, implementation is not easy; a law that is fairly unambiguous about what should be done is invariably light on the specifics of how to do it. Agencies formally fill in these details through the process of formulating rules. Rules state the specific actions government will take, and formulating them involves a quasi-legislative process whose machinery mirrors the broader legislative process: hearings are held, lobbying is conducted, and there is give and take among interested parties with competing agendas (see Kerwin and Furlong 2010). Assuming the rules are realistic and have unambiguous guidelines practical enough for line-level bureaucrats to follow, and further assuming that these same bureaucrats are committed to putting the rules into action, there still remain some potentially difficult coordination issues. Different units within agencies may interpret the rules differently, and even the most detailed set of rules cannot cover all contingencies likely to arise in the running of public programs.

Ideal circumstances, needless to say, are fairly rare. More common are vague laws, overlapping jurisdictions, competing priorities for agency attention, and a thousand and one decisions that have to be made a long way from the formal rule-making process (not to mention the formal legislative process).

Surprisingly, policy scholars were relatively slow to recognize the importance of this bureaucracy-dominated gap between policy adoption and policy outcome. Conventional wisdom (not entirely correct, as we shall see) is that the systematic study of policy implementation did not begin until Jeffrey Pressman and Aaron Wildavsky's seminal study (1973)—in other words, a couple of decades after Lasswell called for a separate discipline of policy studies, and well after the laying of formal foundations for the rationalist project in policy evaluation and analysis. Once policy scholars turned to implementation, however, they immediately recognized its importance: the story of public policy success or failure is often the story of implementation. Thus the key focus for implementation studies is figuring out how a policy works, or more accurately given the often noted failure bias of implementation studies, how a policy does not work.

Three Generations of Implementation Studies

Although it is one of the most complex areas in policy studies, implementation is the rare policy field wherein definitional issues are relatively straightforward, at least as they pertain to the core concept. Widely cited definitions of implementation include those suggested by Mazmanian and Sabatier (1983, 5), Ferman (1990), and O'Toole (1995), all of which focus on the gap between policy intent and policy outcomes. O'Toole's (1995, 42) definition serves as a good representative example, stating that policy implementation "refers to the connection between the expression of governmental intention and results." Although numerous scholars proffer more detailed definitions, all are variations on this basic theme. Implementation is what happens after government declares a formal intent to do something and before a policy outcome has been produced.

As mentioned in the previous chapter, the field of policy evaluation overlaps considerably with implementation studies, especially in the sense of taking stock of agency actions to see if they should be adjusted to improve outcomes. Specifically, what we termed process evaluation in the last chapter is clearly oriented toward assessing programmatic activities that link policy intent and policy outcome. Key questions of process evaluation—Do program staff know what they are supposed to be doing? Are they qualified to do it? Do they have the necessary resources to carry out that task?—are intimately linked to implementation success or failure. As such, our discussion of implementation studies covers some of the same ground as process evaluation, and at least for our purposes the latter should be treated as a subset of the former.

Implementation studies begin with the realization that formal adoption of a policy goal does not necessarily provide any direction on what should be done to achieve that goal. As Mazmanian and Sabatier put it, "Knowing the [policy] objectives . . . [gives] only a general hint of what will actually be done by the agency responsible for carrying out the program and how successful it will be at winning the cooperation and compliance of the persons affected by it" (1983, 4–5). The key research questions for implementation scholars like Mazmanian and Sabatier are closely linked to process evaluation concerns: "Could the outcome have been different? Can we learn from experience and avoid similar problems in designing future public programs?" (1983, 2).

The importance of implementation to policy success or failure is intuitively obvious. It matters little if the government has a clear notion of what should be done if the agency charged with implementing the law lacks the ability to actually do it. Assessing precisely what has been done provides important information, but understanding why outcomes were (or were not) achieved is critical if policy success is to be replicated or policy failure to be avoided. Given the obvious importance of implementation to policy success or failure, it is surprising to find that implementation studies (at least in mainstream political science) were relatively rare until the late 1970s and early 1980s, although when they did appear they made a big splash. The potential value of such studies was immediately clear: a systematic understanding of what connected policy intent to a successful (or unsuccessful) policy outcome would go a long way to fulfilling Lasswellian notions of what the policy sciences were all about. A systematic understanding of the core elements of effective implementation could make democratic policy-making work better.

Unfortunately such a systematic understanding remains elusive. The field of implementation studies is traditionally divided into three generations (see Goggin et al. 1990), and in this chapter we suggest that a fourth-generation implementation research agenda is currently active and under way. The story of implementation research across these four generations ranges from excitement about the possibility of breaking new intellectual ground, to maturity and a more sober assessment of the intellectual challenges, to debate over whether implementation constitutes an intellectual dead end, to a new emergence that refocuses the study of implementation as the study of public management.

First-Generation Implementation Studies: Understanding Implementation Is Important

The first generation of implementation studies began with a seminal book by Jeffrey Pressman and Aaron Wildavsky (1973), *Implementation: How Great Expectations in Washington Are Dashed in Oakland*. The focus of the book was the federal government's attempt to create three thousand jobs in inner-city Oakland. What really motivated Pressman and Wildavsky was not this particular policy per se, but rather its surprising and spectacular failure to achieve its policy objectives. Pressman and Wildavksy (1973) argued that the focus of their case study was, in effect, a best-case scenario for policy implementation. To start with, there was general agreement on the objectives of the policy; no organized constituency sought to stymie its success. There was a reasonably unambiguous objective (create jobs in inner-city Oakland), and broad agreement that this objective was a worthwhile undertaking, especially in the particular political context of the time. Jobs had followed "white flight" out of the cities in the 1960s, and high unemployment and lack of economic opportunities had triggered civil unrest. Creating inner-city jobs was seen as a reasonable answer to "What should we do?"

The policy was also focused—it targeted a single city, Oakland, California—and it was (at least in theory) under the control of a single federal agency, the Economic Development Agency (EDA), which was committed to its success. Resources were not a problem; ample funds were available to support the program, and a lot of money was spent. Yet the policy failed miserably, producing few jobs and leaving much frustration in its wake. Pressman and Wildavsky wanted to know why policies like this, best-case scenarios with the stars seemingly aligned for success, failed. Their intensive case study brought the complex world between policy intention and policy outcome to the attention of a broad audience in political science. What they found was not pretty and laid the foundation for an explosive growth in implementation studies.

The central lesson to be taken from Pressman and Wildvasky was that complexity of joint action is the central obstacle for effective implementation. In the federal system of the United States, this means that virtually any domestic policy is dependent upon multiple layers of government and its agencies. Interactions among these various government entities are complex, and coordination is difficult. Potential roadblocks to implementation range from jurisdictional turf battles, to resource constraints, to clashing management styles.

For example, Pressman and Wildavsky (1973) found that broad agreement on ends does not necessarily translate into agreement on means. Just because all parties support the same policy outcome does not mean they agree on the best way to go about achieving that goal. Each government agency can have its own perspective, not just on how things should be done, but on who should do them. Different levels of government, and different agencies at the same level of government, may also have very different priorities. Whereas all may generally agree that a particular policy objective is worthwhile, they may prioritize that objective differently. Government agencies tend to be committed to multiple programs and policies, and the level of commitment to a specific program or policy is driven by agency perspective. Getting all of these agencies to adopt a general plan on means, synchronize their priorities, and generally share the same vision of a policy or program turned out to be the governmental equivalent of herding cats.

Perhaps the most cited lesson from Pressman and Wildavsky's (1973) study was their insight into decision points and the importance of control and coordination. Creating jobs through public works and other programs in Oakland required the involvement of state and local authorities; and other federal agencies also inevitably became involved. To get anything substantive done thus required getting a wide range of agencies at different governmental levels to approve key implementation decisions. Pressman and Wildavsky found that the more approvals have to be granted for an action to be taken, the higher the likelihood is that action will *not* be taken. To quantify this point, Pressman and Wildavsky provided an example in which thirty decision points had to be cleared, involving seventy separate required agreements before an action could be approved and undertaken. Assuming a .95 probability of approval at each agreement point, Pressman and Wildavsky calculated that the probability of a particular proposal running this bureaucratic gauntlet and actually being implemented was .000395 (1973, 106–107). In other words, when dealing with a dispersed decision-making system, one's chances of getting anything done are low—often astonishingly low—even when most people want to do it. Even if the odds are overcome, getting anything done is going to take a long time. Pressman and Wildavsky estimated that each of those seventy agreements would require one to six weeks to secure, which resulted in an estimate that the Oakland project would face four and one-half years' worth of delays. Their estimate proved to be fairly accurate (1973, 106–107).

A contemporary first-generation study that is still widely cited in the implementation literature is Martha Derthick's (1972) examination of a federal program to build model communities on federally owned land in urban areas. This was a project that grew out of President Lyndon Johnson's administration in the late 1960s and was designed to address the social and economic problems that developed in the wake of urban sprawl, which created low-density suburbs surrounding a socioeconomically depressed urban center. The program began with lofty ideals and goals, to address a growing metropolitan crisis by building self-contained, centrally planned "new towns" that would be socially and racially integrated. Like the EDA's attempt to generate jobs in Oakland, the program was a spectacular failure, and Derthick's examination of the implementation process echoes the lamentations of Pressman and Wildavsky.

Derthick was particularly attuned to the opposing perspectives at different governmental levels and to the difficulties of centralized coordination of implementation. What looked like a good idea from the federal level encountered stiff opposition at the local level. Conservationist groups wanted to protect the open lands, and neighborhood associations feared the new housing plans would bring racial imbalance. This led to intense opposition and conflict at the local level, which translated into strong local government resistance to the federal plans. This opposition had really not been accounted for in the federal government's vision of the policy, and it had trouble adjusting to the reality on the ground (Derthick 1972, 98). What began with noble and idealized hopes sputtered and sank because of the difficulties of implementation.

Though Derthick's and Pressman and Wildavsky's studies reflected some important differences in context, they shared some key takeaway points. First and foremost was that not enough thought and attention was devoted to implementation, given its importance to policy success. While planners and academics lavished attention on how to decide what to do and how to assess what had been done, there were too many assumptions and not enough knowledge about what would happen between these two points in the policy change. The overwhelming impression from reading Derthick and Pressman and Wildavsky is that the real surprise wasn't that public policies failed; it was that they ever worked at all. These studies threw a spotlight on implementation as a key reason for policy failure, and they also offered prescriptive advice on how to increase the odds of policy success: cut down on decision points and push control and authority downward to allow those closest to the project to make important decisions quickly and effectively.

More important for a book on the theories of public policy, Derthick, and especially Pressman and Wildvasky, hinted that a systematic understanding of cause and effect in implementation might be possible. This suggested that general frameworks of implementation could be constructed, and a more valuable contribution of the policy sciences to successful democratic policymaking would not be hard to imagine. A general theory of implementation could help avoid repeats of the Oakland and new towns policy failures by laying out detailed steps for executing a particular policy or program, making democratic policymaking more effective. This was just the sort of contribution the Lasswellian ideal envisioned for the field of policy studies. By the end of the 1970s the race was on to construct a general framework of implementation, a systematic understanding of how policies worked.

Second-Generation Studies: Understanding Implementation Is Complex

First-generation implementation studies made important contributions, but they suffered a number of critical drawbacks. Most important, they were largely case studies and as such were bound by time and space. They contributed a depth of understanding about what worked (or more often, did not work) for a particular program at a particular time, but not much could be systematically generalized to other programs in other contexts. The conclusions and prescriptions drawn from studies such as Pressman and Wildavsky's provided motivation for constructing a theory of implementation, rather than an actual framework of cause and effect.

Noting these drawbacks, and with the attention of policy studies fully engaged with the problems of implementation, a second generation of implementation studies shifted focus from the examination of specific policies to the construction of general theories of the implementation process. One of the first notable attempts to construct such a framework was Eugene Bardach's *The Implementation Game* (1977). This study took an extended critique of Derthick and Pressman and Wildavsky as a jumping-off point for building a general understanding of implementation.

Bardach (1977) sought to make sense of implementation by classifying it into a series of games. He used the metaphor of games because it focused analysts' attention on the actors involved in implementation: the stakes they played for; the rules they played by; and the tactics, strategies, and resources each brought to the table. Using these as raw materials, Bardach sought to create a basic typology of implementation games. Like Derthick and Pressman and Wildavsky, Bardach focused on what in implementation caused policy failure. He argued that four basic "adverse effects" can occur in the implementation process: 1) the diversion of resources, 2) the deflection of policy goals, 3) resistance to control, and 4) the dissipation of personal and political energy (1977, 66). He categorized his description of games according to each of these adverse effects.

For example, the "budget game" diverted resources. The budget game springs from the incentives government agencies have to "move money." Unlike tangible policy outcomes, which can take years to show up, expenditures can be used as short-term assessment measures. Spending money shows that something is being done, even if it is not exactly clear what, why, or how it will support the ultimate policy objectives. Bardach pointed out that in the Oakland jobs project studied by Pressman and Wildavsky (1973) the EDA put resources into specific job-creating projects not because they were systematically assessed to be the best for these purposes, but because they were the projects that were ready to go. There was political pressure to be seen as doing something, and funneling money in jobs projects created the impression of purposive action, even if not many jobs ended up being created. Bardach saw this as one example of a general game played by all government agencies that serve as conduits of public money: "moving money somehow, somewhere, and fast, even at the price of programmatic objectives, is the characteristic strategy of virtually every government agency that channels grants to other levels of government or to nonprofit institutions" (1977, 72). Other games Bardach identified included "piling on" (deflecting goals by using new programs as Trojan horses for an agency's preferred goals), "tokenism" (resisting control by making only token efforts to achieve programmatic goals), and "tenacity" (dissipating political energy by blocking progress of a program in an attempt to extract self-interested terms or concessions that may or may not be related to policy goals).

Bardach, in short, saw implementation as an extension of politics. He sought to impose theoretical order on this complex world of negotiation, scheming, and jockeying for favor by classifying behavioral patterns that had been repeatedly observed within and between the actors given primary responsibility for implementation, namely government bureaucracies. Other frameworks shared the basic perspective that implementation was an extension of politics but expanded the cast of actors. Giandomenico Majone and Aaron Wildavsky (1979), for example, argued that implementation should be viewed as an evolutionary process. It is shaped by general policy that is formally adopted but encompasses a wide range of goals, interactions, and dispositions, all of which are complexly connected. Rather than an agency treating formal policy adoption as a set of marching orders, they saw agencies, the target populations of policy, and even policymakers as having to adapt to the goals and expectations created by policy. For studies like Bardach's and Majone and Wildavsky's, the key explanatory target is the behavior of implementers. This makes sense as a dependent variable, because as Pressman and Wildavsky amply demonstrated, the behavior of the implementers is absolutely critical to success.

Other approaches to theory construction, however, targeted policy outputs and outcomes as the key dependent variable. A quite different approach was taken by Daniel Mazmanian and Paul Sabatier, who sought in *Implementation and Public Policy* (1983) to lay down a series of empirically testable causal hypotheses about implementation. Mazmanian and Sabatier argued that there are three basic perspectives on implementation. First is what they term the "center," or the perspective of the initial policymaker. Second is the perspective of the "periphery," or the lower-level bureaucrats whose behavior actually translates the policy into action. Finally there is the perspective of the "target group," or the people at whom the policy or program is aimed.

Implementation, Mazmanian and Sabatier argued, looked very different depending on perspective. From the center, implementation is a top-down phenomenon. The goal of implementation is to achieve official policy objectives, to translate the intent of a formally adopted policy into action. From the perspective of higher-level officials or institutions, then, the key issue is how to get lower-level officials and institutions to act in a manner consistent with that intent. From the periphery—the basic perspective taken by Bardach—implementation is all about how lower-level officials and institutions adapt to the shocks to their environment caused by higher levels introducing new policies and programs. From the target group perspective, implementation is about how the policy affects their lives (e.g., do the services provided by, say, a jobs training program actually increase the target population's employment prospects?). Mazmanian and Sabatier recognized considerable overlap in these perspectives; if the official goal is to get jobs for the unemployed, then the perspectives of the center and target population will obviously have much in common. However, they also recognized the difficulty in combining all three perspectives simultaneously into a single study or theory. Accordingly, Mazmanian and Sabatier's framework tended to reflect a center perspective (1983, 12–13).

Mazmanian and Sabatier's framework took a distinct center-perspective bias for the simple reason that they viewed the achievement of formal policy objectives as the key dependent variable of implementation studies, not the behavior of the implementers: "In our view, the crucial role of implementation analysis is the identification of the variables which affect the achievement of legal objectives" (1983, 21). Accordingly, the explanatory goal of their framework reflected the desired outcomes of the implementation process. These outcomes were subdivided into five distinct elements: the outputs of implementing agencies, the target population's compliance with these policy outputs, the actual impacts of policy outputs, the perceived impacts of policy outputs, and major revision in the statute (1983, 22). These constituted the dependent variables the framework sought to explain. Even a casual consideration of these five dependent variables should give some notion of the complex task undertaken by Mazmanian and Sabatier, and by extension the whole project of constructing a generalizable theory of the implementation process. Embedded within those dependent variables, for example, is arguably the whole field of policy evaluation (assessing actual policy impacts), as well as large areas of policy analysis (major statute revisions raise the question "What should we do?" or at least "What should we do differently?").

Mazmanian and Sabatier created a systematic sense of the independent variables driving the implementation process by categorizing them into three broad categories: the tractability of the problem, the ability of a statute to structure implementation, and nonstatutory variables that affected implementation (1983, 20–42). The tractability of the problem referred to the social problem the policy officially targeted. The bottom line is that some social problems are easier to deal with than others. The problems may be persistent social ills that any single program or policy is unlikely to cure (e.g., poverty), the technology to address the problem may be imperfect or nonexistent (e.g., replacing polluting fossil fuels with renewable alternatives), and the behavior required of the target population to achieve official policy objectives may be unrealistic (e.g., getting drivers to obey a uniform national speed limit of 55 mph).

The ability of statutes to structure implementation depended on another set of key variables independent of the tractability of the problem. First and foremost was the transmission of clear and consistent objectives; it is impossible to implement a formal policy objective if no one is sure what that objective is. Second, there had to be a real causal theory connecting the actions of policy to the desired policy objectives. It is unrealistic to expect to achieve policy objectives without a basic understanding of what will cause the desired outcomes. Other variables included in this category were allocation of adequate financial resources, recruitment of the right set of implementing agencies, and laying down clear lines of coordination and control among the implementing actors. Collectively, these elements constituted the "statutory coherence" hypothesis, which posited that the outcomes of the implementation process were partially determined by how (or if) the statute clarified objectives, understood what needed to be done to realize those objectives, identified the actors qualified to take these actions, allocated them adequate resources, and established a system of control and accountability.

Non-statutory variables included public support and the leadership and competence of implementing officials. A good program with a realistic objective can still fail if its managers are incompetent, uninterested, or distracted by other priorities. Even committed and competent managers have a hard time achieving policy objectives that are resisted by the public. Prohibition, for example, was a spectacular failure not because the federal government was incompetent, but because the public refused to stop consuming alcohol.

Mazmanian and Sabatier's (1983) theory is notable not just for being one of the first comprehensive theoretical frameworks of the implementation process, but because it highlights two critical issues that second-generation implementation studies never fully resolved: perspective and complexity. It was, and is, not clear what perspective—center, periphery, target population, or some combination—provides the best starting point for building implementation theory. Mazmanian and Sabatier and others seeking to propose systematic and testable causal relationships tended to favor the top-down approach that came with a center perspective (e.g., Berman 1980; Nakamura and Smallwood 1980).

Others, however, made a strong case for a "bottom-up" starting point, using the periphery or the target population as the best platform for understanding implementation. One of the best-known advocates of the bottom-up approach is Michael Lipsky (1971, 1980), whose notion of the street-level bureaucrat created a powerful case that Mazmanian and Sabatier's periphery was anything but peripheral when it came to determining what happened in implementation. For Lipsky, the key actors in implementation were not the people who made the policy, but the people who actually did the implementing.

Street-level bureaucrats represent the primary interface between citizens and government: "Most citizens encounter government (if they encounter it all) not through letters to congressmen [*sic*] or by attendance at school board meetings but through their teachers and their children's teachers and through the policeman on the corner or in the patrol car. Each encounter of this kind represents an instance of policy delivery" (1980, 3). These individuals, argued Lipsky, are primary shapers of policy delivery because of the simple fact that they make the decisions on the spot. Lipsky went even further, arguing that they are primary policy*makers*, not just implementers. A legislature may pass a speed limit of 55 mph, but that policy is utterly dependent on diligent enforcement by a traffic cop. If that individual police officer only stops cars traveling in excess of 60 mph, then that officer has effectively set a speed limit—a public policy—different from that set by the legislature.

Lipsky also noted that a natural tension exists between policy actors closer to the center and those closer to the periphery. The street-level bureaucrat is frequently dealing not just with ambiguous policy but also with the ambiguous nature of day-to-day reality. Policy and rules dictated from the center may seem unclear, unfair, or impractical to the street-level bureaucrat charged with implementing them. Those serving on the front lines of policy delivery are often short of resources, understaffed, and required to deal with an endless series of decisions (stop the car going 57 mph?) that in effect are policymaking decisions. This creates friction between the center, which seeks compliance with formal policy objectives, and the periphery, which seeks the autonomy to deal as it sees fit with the day-to-day dilemmas of the job.

For the "bottom-uppers," it is at the street level where implementation really happens, and to favor a center over a periphery perspective is to ignore the practical realities of delivering public services. A number of scholars pitched the argument that because implementation was ultimately dependent on street-level bureaucrats, they had to take center stage in any theory of the implementation process (e.g., Hjern 1982; Hjern and Hull 1983). Actually, the bottom-uppers' argument went even further. Given that street-level bureaucrats were clearly making policy, and given that compliance issues with the center were virtually inevitable, it made sense to start thinking of implementation as an important stage of the policy formulation process. In other words, they advocated transforming the periphery's implementation perspective (and the target population's) into a key issue in the process of resolving "What should we do?" The conclusions of, say, a traditional cost-benefit analysis could change radically depending on the periphery's perspective on how (or if) a policy option could/should be put into practice. As the street-level bureaucrats ultimately made these decisions in practice, it made sense to include them in policy formulation discussions, for the simple reason that any policy was doomed to failure if they could not adapt its objectives to local conditions.

This latter point was not entirely new. One of the key lessons drawn from studies like Derthick's and Pressman and Wildavsky's was that there should be a lot more attention paid to the practicalities of implementation in the policy formulation debate. The key question for policy scholars was how to provide a framework for doing that in a manner that was reasonably generalizable and systematic.

Although the top-downers generally acknowledged the points of the bottom-uppers, there remained resistance to swapping one perspective for the other. The top-downers were trying to figure out how to translate formal policy objectives into reality; their focus was on how to translate the intent of policy into action *after* the formal policy objective had been decided. Bottom-uppers did not want implementation so confined: they wanted the periphery and the target population perspective incorporated into all stages of the policy process, and they argued that implementation had to be considered holistically. Top-downers were more focused on outcomes, bottom-uppers on the behavior and choices of implementers. We also see something of the split between the rationalist and the post-positivist camps in policy studies. Top-downers, with their focus on empirically testable causal relationships, tended to fit comfortably within the rationalist project. Bottom-uppers, with their desire to bring traditionally unrepresented viewpoints into the entire policy process, tended to use more of a post-positivist lens to look at policy (deLeon 1999a).

The top-down versus bottom-up debate has never been fully resolved, though both sides acknowledge the validity of the opposing perspective, and over the years something of a truce was declared. A number of attempts have been made to synthesize the two approaches, notably by Sabatier (1988, 1997; see also El-more 1985; Matland 1995). Yet a full reconciliation of the two viewpoints has not been achieved. The "correct" or "best" dependent variable for implementation studies—policy outcome or implementer behavior—is still a matter of disagreement, as is the best epistemological approach (rationalist or post-positivist; see discussion below). Many ended up viewing the whole debate as an unfortunate distraction, claiming the underlying issue was more one of degree than kind. Few top-downers rejected the notion that street-level bureaucrats played a key role in implementation, just as few bottom-uppers rejected the notion that achieving formally adopted policy objectives was an important driver of implementation. O'Toole described the whole debate as more about how to look at implementation rather than a disagreement about what is or is not important, arguing (perhaps optimistically) that policy scholars had "moved past the rather sterile top-down, bottom-up dispute" (2000, 267).

Whereas the top-down/bottom-up controversy sputtered, if not to a reconciliation, at least to an amicable cohabitation, the second big issue raised by theory-building efforts like Mazmanian and Sabatier's remains stubbornly at the forefront of implementation studies. Basically, by organizing the wide range of variables critical to implementation into a causal framework, second-generation research made crystal clear the enormous complexity of implementation. In their framework, for example, Mazmanian and Sabatier (1983, 22) specified five dependent variables. Under the three broad categories of causal determinants of these dependent variables (problem tractability, ability of statute to structure implementation, and non-statutory variables affecting implementation) were a total of sixteen broadly described independent variables. None of the latter specified a clear, generalizable measure. Indeed, as their own empirical work demonstrated, operationalizing the concepts at the heart of their framework was a formidable measurement challenge, and bringing them together for parsimonious quantitative analysis created research design and methodological issues.

If building generalizable frameworks of implementation was the central challenge of second-generation studies, testing them would prove to be the central challenge of third-generation studies.

Third-Generation Studies: Understanding Implementation Is . . . Impossible?

Dividing the evolution of implementation studies into three distinct generations is usually attributed to Malcolm Goggin and his colleagues (1990), who saw the decades straddling the turn of the twenty-first century as ripe for a fruitful maturation of the field. Writing at the tail end of the 1980s, they foresaw a third generation of implementation studies that would develop causal hypotheses and rigorously test them. In this fashion, third-generation studies would clarify a generalizable understanding of successful implementation. In other words, they would ultimately produce a theory of how policy actually works (or does not). The central aim of third-generation studies, they argued, "is simply to be more scientific than the previous two [generations] in its approach to the study of implementation" (Goggin et al. 1990, 18).

Goggin and colleagues believed public policy studies during the 1990s would "very likely be defined by its focus on implementation. The nineties are likely to be the implementation era" (1990, 9). This did not exactly turn out to be the case. Within a decade, several leading figures in the field—including Goggin and his colleagues—were publishing laments about the demise of implementation studies and urging its reconsideration to scholars who had more or less declared the enterprise dead (see Lester and Goggin 1998; deLeon 1999a; deLeon and deLeon 2002). What happened?

The central problem had already been identified by Mazmanian and Sabatier (1983). Once the distraction of the top-down/bottom-up controversy was set aside, the complexity of the implementation process seemed to mock the very notion of a parsimonious and generalizable framework. It was not just the issues of research design and concept measurement (though these were hard enough); it was the sheer number of variables. Frameworks such as those proposed by Mazmanian and Sabatier (1983), and third-generation follow-ups such as those proposed by Goggin and colleagues (1990), struggled to make parsimonious sense of implementation. To encompass all the apparently essential elements of implementation, theoretical frameworks had to carry so much causal water that they sprang leaks at the seams.

Good examples of this come from a number of studies that in spirit, if not chronologically, fit with Goggin and his colleagues' notion of third-generation implementation studies. There were a number of attempts in the 1980s and 1990s to test Mazmanian and Sabatier's framework on various policy issues (e.g., Bullock 1981; Rosenbaum 1981). These generally found support for the framework, but all faced significant difficulties in operationalizing concepts and executing a comprehensive test.

A good example is Deborah McFarlane's (1989) work. Rather than test the entire framework, McFarlane focused on the statutory coherence hypothesis. In the Mazmanian and Sabatier framework, the ability of a statute to structure implementation specified seven elements of statutory coherence: 1) clear goals, 2) adequate causal theory, 3) adequate resources, 4) hierarchical integration of implementing agencies, 5) decision rules for agencies that supported implementation, 6) commitment of implementing agencies to the policy objectives, and 7) formal participation by constituencies supporting the policy objectives. What McFarlane sought to do was operationalize each of these concepts and empirically assess its ability to predict the policy outputs of implementing agencies.

In brief, the findings were supportive of the statutory coherence hypothesis, and thus of the Mazmanian and Sabatier framework. Of more interest for present purposes, however, were the caveats McFarlane carefully placed on her findings. Notably, the choice of dependent variables was driven in no small part by the practicalities of data availability and served as a proxy for just one of the five dependent variables in the framework (1989, 417). The operationalization of independent variables "was problematic . . . the measures utilized were crude . . . there is considerable distance between the measures employed and the broad concepts embodied in the statutory variables" (McFarlane 1989, 418–419). In other words, even a limited test of the framework posed significant conceptual, measurement, and methodological issues. McFarlane expressed hope that future refinements could improve the tractability of the framework for comprehensive empirical studies, but follow-ups ran into very similar issues (e.g., Meier and McFarlane 1996).

The third generation certainly did not fail because of lack of effort. Considerable energy was expended on rigorous theory development and empirical testing, not just testing implementation frameworks developed in second-generation studies, but using other frameworks—especially economic-based frameworks like game theory and principal agent theory. At least in a formal sense, none seemed to satisfactorily offer a general understanding of implementation. As O'Toole (1995, 54) put it, "implementation networks contain complications that modeling can neither ignore nor fully address." That serves as an apt epitaph for the high hopes of third-generation implementation research.

In the end, then, third-generation studies did not die because their core research agenda was falsified; they simply stuttered to a crawl because implementation resisted parsimonious explanation. In a much-cited review of more than one hundred studies, O'Toole (1986) discovered more than three hundred variables being forwarded as key determinants of implementation process and outcomes. Creating coherent structure out of those materials is, to put it mildly, a daunting task. Or as Peter deLeon put it, "What the contemporary policy implementation community is seemingly confronted with is an acknowledgement . . . of what the early implementation scholars apparently knew best, as reflected in their case study approach: that the complexity of the implementation process is more than daunting, it is apparently impenetrable" (1999a, 319).

Third-generation studies ultimately ended up with a less-than-satisfying answer to the core question "How does it work?" The consensus response seemed to be, "we're not really sure." Sometimes it was even worse than that. Lin (1996) suggested not only that the difference between implementation working and not working was more about luck than design, but also that careful design might do more harm than good: "successful implementation is often accidental, while failed implementation is the result of design" (4).

Implementation studies, needless to say, did not develop into the central focus of policy studies as Goggin and colleagues (1990) had hopefully forecast. Indeed, in the years following this prediction, numerous policy scholars expressed skepticism about the ability of implementation studies to move significantly beyond the achievements of the second generation. Implementation studies were seen as failing to achieve conceptual clarity (Goggin et al. 1990, 462); unlikely to reach a comprehensive, rational explanation of implementation in the foreseeable future (Garrett 1993, 1249); and, more bluntly, "an intellectual dead end" (deLeon 1999a, 313).

A Fourth Generation?

Despite the struggles it encountered at the end of the twentieth century, the field of implementation studies did not entirely founder on the difficulties faced in the third-generation project. New theoretical ground continued to be broken. For example, Richard Matland sought to sidestep the entire frustrating problem of complexity and a seeming lack of generalizability by rethinking the whole notion of what a comprehensive conceptual framework of implementation should look like. Rather than specifying causal relationships between large numbers of variables, he proposed a typology in much the same way Theodore Lowi (1964) had sought to do for policy as a whole (see discussion in Chapter 2). The basic idea was to classify policies in a two-by-two matrix of implementation approaches based on levels of policy conflict and ambiguity. This simple and creative classification sought a middle ground between some of the earlier arguments that divided bottom-uppers and top-downers. For example, policies with low ambiguity and low conflict were ripe for top-down implementation, because this was a context in which implementing agencies knew clearly what had to be done and how to do it. Policies with high ambiguity and high conflict, on the other hand, were more suited to a bottom-up approach. Matland argued that in this sort of policy context it is the "coalitional strength" at the local level—think Lipsky's street-level bureaucrats—that determined policy perspectives. This typology, in other words, pointed to where the arguments of the bottom-uppers and top-downers might be most usefully applied in implementation studies.

Matland was far from the only scholar to try to drag implementation studies out of the dead ends and mazes where third-generation research seemed to have left it. James Lester and Malcolm Goggin (1998) experimented with a matrix approach similar to Matland's, arguing that successful implementation was driven by government commitment and institutional capacity. Laurence O'Toole (1995) used a rational choice lens to examine implementation, with some success. Denise Scheberle (1997) sought to create a systematic framework based on the levels of trust among and involvement by implementing officials. Many, though, were skeptical of these efforts to break the big third-generation problem and actually fuse everything into a parsimonious and general conceptual framework of implementation. At the turn of the twentieth century, a number of the leading names in implementation studies openly began to question what they saw as an increasingly flagging research agenda. These included Peter and Linda deLeon (deLeon and deLeon 2002), who posed the question, "What ever happened to policy implementation?" and Lester and Goggin (1998), who wrote a provocative essay dividing implementation scholars into four distinct camps based on whether they had a positive or negative view of the continuation of implementation research and whether they believed significant modifications in implementation theory were needed.

Those with negative views were divided into "skeptics," who believed that to go forward, implementation research needed major theoretical and conceptual changes, and "terminators," who wanted to discontinue implementation research as currently conceived and re-envision this entire sector of the policy process. Those with positive views were divided into "testers," who wanted to continue rigorous empirical testing of existing frameworks like Mazmanian and Sabatier's, and "reformers," who were still committed to the earlier high promise of implementation research, but also saw the need for theoretical formulation and more empirical work.

Lester and Goggin (1998) put themselves in the reformers camp and sought to rally the third-generation troops for another sustained intellectual assault on generating theories of implementation. Specifically, they called for organizing research around the dependent variable of implementer behavior, which meant dropping implementation's traditional focus on policy outcome as the key explanatory target, essentially following Lipsky's lead and making implementation the study of individuals. "The essential characteristic of the implementation process," Lester and Goggin argued, "is the timely and satisfactory performance of certain necessary tasks related to carrying out the intents of the law. This means rejecting a dichotomous conceptualization of implementation as simply success or failure" (1998, 5). Having clarified the dependent variable, they called for the development of a "parsimonious, yet complete, theory of policy implementation and a set of testable hypotheses that explain variations in the way implementers behave" (1998, 6).

Response to Lester and Goggin's essay provides a fascinating insight into the state of implementation research at that time. Some responded to the call. Winter (1999), for example, seconded the call to make behavior the central dependent variable of implementation research, especially variations in implementer behavior. Some had a more mixed reaction. Peter deLeon (1999c) argued that he was not a skeptic in the sense that he viewed implementation studies as of central importance to the policy process, both in practical and theoretical terms. However, he admitted this positive view was more about the potential of implementation research rather than its current practice: "One need not go much beyond [the Lester and Goggin article] to see the vast and amoebic array of policy implementation essays and books that, to most observers, would comprise a largely aimless wandering in search of some consensus" (deLeon 1999c, 7).

Others were largely negative, including Kenneth Meier (1999), who rejected the tester label Lester and Goggin pinned on him and confessed to being a "stealth terminator." He argued that the key dependent variable in implementation studies should remain policy outcomes, not implementer behavior, and expressed a strong skepticism about implementation theory as it currently stood, describing it as "forty-seven variables that completely explain five case studies," suggesting the need for a fresh start. Meier argued that third-generation implementation studies had ended up taking the wrong path. In trying to provide a comprehensive and generalizable explanation, it was not suffering from a lack of insights, but rather from a surfeit of them. In short, the frameworks and empirical models were reflecting the complexity of implementation rather than actually explaining it. The only real hope for implementation studies, he argued, was to keep the dependent variable focused on policy outcomes but expand its scope to include anything that happens in the policy process after formal adoption. This meant, in part, embracing the lessons and theories of more applied disciplines. Perhaps insights from areas like public management and public administration research, along with a lot more empirical studies, could help prune the lengthy list of variables clogging up insight-heavy implementation frameworks. Meier stated the case, then, that the top-downers remained the best hope for generating cumulative knowledge about implementation.

In the past decade or so a number of such scholars have been forging something of a new path that essentially takes the road urged by Meier: keeping the dependent variable focused on policy outcomes; incorporating insights from public administration and other literatures; and using empirical analysis to bring a few key variables into focus, as opposed to adding yet another group of contenders to an already growing list. This effort is best exemplified by an extensive research agenda undertaken by Meier and Laurence O'Toole that focuses on public management as the "missing link" in implementation research (O'Toole and Meier 2011; see also Hicklin and Godwin 2009). The essential theoretical assumption of this research is fairly easy to convey: a key element of implementation—perhaps *the* key element of implementation—is the quality of the public managers responsible for running programs. Or as Meier (2009, 7) puts it in discussing educational policies and programs: "Good managers can work in poor environments with few resources and get significant value added; good managers can take the deck they are dealt by the state legislature and generate three of a kind or possibly a full house."

The importance of public management to successful implementation is hardly news from a public administration standpoint, but until relatively recently its importance to implementation had been given much lip service and comparatively little empirical attention in the policy literatures. Over the past decade O'-Toole and Meier, along with an expanding list of other scholars, have done much to remedy this. The empirical investigations of management led scholars to focus on things like the credentials, salary, and turnover of administrators charged with implementing public policies and programs, as well the degree to which these managers were networked with each other. All of these things, along with various other dimensions of public management, have consistently been linked with policy outcomes—in other words, they seem to play a consistent role in influencing the success or failure of public policies. Much of the original work was focused on managers in public education, but the basic framework has long since been expanded to agencies and policies at all levels of government and even internationally (Nicholson-Crotty and O'Toole 2004; Petrovsky 2006; Avellaneda 2009; Walker, O'Toole and Meier 2007; O'Toole and Meier 2011). It is worth underlining the clear implication of this research agenda: There actually exists a truly generalizable element of implementation, one that can be readily and parsimoniously captured in conceptual empirical models. This does not completely solve the problem that stymied third-generation studies; there is more to implementation than public management, and though it is maturing rapidly, this is still (at least in the field of public policy) a relatively new literature. Nonetheless, it represents a significant advance that demonstrates an emergent fourth generation is reinvigorating implementation studies.

Conclusion

Reports of the impending death of implementation studies—not uncommon a decade or so ago—have clearly been exaggerated. Perhaps they always were. Indeed, some scholars argue that implementation studies have always been in a constant state of ferment, experiment, and advance. The problem has not been lack of empirical and theoretical advance, per se, but the lack of it being done in the field of policy studies. Outside of policy studies, implementation research has never lacked for adherents, mostly because of its obvious practical and applied importance (see Saetren 2005). Though not always viewed as "implementation" research by policy scholars, serious thinkers in public administration and other more applied fields have always given high priority to the systematic study of how government decisions are translated into policy outcomes (e.g., Waldo 1946; Redford 1969).

It is little surprise, then, to find policy scholars increasingly incorporating, adapting, and extending models and concepts from those fields. The major problem of third-generation studies, that implementation simply seemed to be too complex to explain in relatively parsimonious conceptual frameworks, seems to be yielding, at least a little. The new work in public management clearly shows that there is at least a possibility of a generalizable dimension of implementation, one that may be at least somewhat amenable to manipulation by policymakers and thus systematically tweaked to improve policy outcomes. This suggests implementation studies are perfectly capable of creating cumulative knowledge and more than deserving of continued attention by policy scholars.

CHAPTER 8

Whose Values? Policy Design

The tension between the rationalist project and its post-positivist critics is, as previous chapters have highlighted, a consistent theme in policy studies. Yet although there is considerable debate over the appropriate role of values in the method and epistemology of policy studies, there is general agreement that public policy itself is value-based. If politics is defined as the authoritative allocation of values, then public policy represents the means of allocating and distributing those values (Easton 1953; Schneider and Ingram 1997, 2). But exactly whose values are sanctioned by the coercive powers of the state? This is a central question of policy studies that cuts to the heart of power relationships within society.

Policy design is an umbrella term for the field of policy studies devoted to the systematic examination of the substantive content of policy. From a rationalist perspective, policy is purposive—it is a means to achieve a desired end, a solution to a problem. Policy design scholars readily accept the notion that policy is purposive, but they argue that the substance of policy is much more complex and nuanced than the instrumental assumption of rationalists. Rather than identifying the goal (or problem) and trying to assess what should be done, policy design scholars look for the "blueprint" or "architecture" of policy. Policy from this perspective is more than an instrumental means to a desired end; it symbolizes what, and whom, society values. Policy design scholars recognize the instrumental dimension of policy, but are more focused on identifying and interpreting the symbolic elements. Policy design, and the design process, can shed information on why particular outcomes of interest were or were not achieved, but it is more revealing for what it says about who does, and who does not, have political power, that is, the ability to have a preferred set of values backed by the coercive powers of the state.

A wholly rationalist view of the policy process suggests that decisions about policy design are made by comparing potential solutions to defined problems, and that policy actors and citizens react to such decisions using similar criteria. The policy design perspective sees such assumptions as naive and incomplete. In the political arena, even the most scientific ("objective") evidence tends to be used subjectively and selectively, championed and accepted when it supports preexisting assumptions about the world and how it works, and rejected when it counters these assumptions (Schneider and Ingram 1997). Objective, or at least falsifiable, claims about policy often tend to be secondary considerations even when they do enter the political arena; often the symbolic cues stemming from policy are more appealing than policy facts (Edelman 1990; Weston 2007). The decision about policy such as, say, the Patriot Act, tends to be structured not by objective analysis of its expected impact on a particular set of problems, but rather by the symbolic and emotional freight of what it means to be a patriot in a time of grave threat to national security.

These symbolic and emotional dimensions are, according to the policy design perspective, highly revealing about the real purposes of public policy, which may be some distance from the putative goals expressed by the policy. Indeed, policy design scholars argue that the values embedded in policy design reflect what political struggle is all about. For example, rational actor models of political participation indicate that citizens engage in politics to express their policy preferences and, accordingly, will vote out those officials with policy preferences that are different from their own. The field of policy design flips this argument on its head. Values are embedded in policy design, and elected officials and policymakers strategically use these values to secure or maintain political power. Citizens, in turn, tend to be more responsive to value-based arguments than to arguments highlighting the costs and benefits of a particular policy program (see Weston 2007).

The ability of elected officials to use values and symbols to their advantage when crafting public policy has attracted numerous scholars to the study of policy design. Some are interested in explaining political, social, and economic disparities and see the underlying structure of policymaking as contributing to these inequities. Others are interested in trying to bring certain values (egalitarianism, diversity, participation) to the policymaking process. Still others are interested in exploring the conflict between the values they see in mainstream social science methods and theories and the democratic values they believe should be central to public policy. What ties all of this together is a core research question: Whose values does public policy promote? This chapter explores scholarly contributions regarding what values are inherent in policy design and how those values are constructed and believed to affect the targets of public policy.

Objective Policy Design?

Policy design refers to the content of public policy. Empirically, this content includes the following observable characteristics: target population (the citizens who receive the benefits or bear the costs of the policy), the values being distributed by the policy, the rules governing or constraining action, rationales (the justification for the policy), and the assumptions that logically tie all these elements together (Schneider and Ingram 1997, 2). Though observable, the content of public policy is not viewed objectively by citizens and policymakers, nor is it based on rational considerations. Instead, the process of assembling policy content is based on highly subjective interpretations of who justifiably deserves the costs or benefits of a policy, what values should be backed by the coercive powers of the state, and who (or what) should have their freedom of action promoted or constrained to uphold those values.

Central to this framework is the notion that language is used as a means for justifying and rationalizing actions or outcomes through the use of powerful imagery and narratives. Leading the way in this approach is the work by Murray Edelman (1964, 1990). His *The Symbolic Use of Politics* (1964) first addressed the theme of the intersubjective nature of policy and politics. Subsequent work focused on the "political spectacle," or the notion that nothing in the political world is objective; all facts are subjective. Instead of policy design reflecting the needs of society, Edelman presented a political world in which governmental action is not based on a rational response to societal problems. Symbols and language are used to perpetuate political status and ideology. Language is a means of evoking "favorable interpretations" (Edelman 1990, 103). What does this mean for the study of policy design? According to Edelman, actions taken by the government are based on alternatives and explanations that promote favorable measures but maintain unresolved problems (1990, 18). The construction of the political spectacle is intended to protect immediate interests in an unpredictable world.

Following Edelman, other scholars noted the ability of policymakers to manipulate the policy process. Most notable is the work of Frank Fischer. In *Politics, Values, and Public Policy* (1980), Fischer argued that values are embedded in the policy process, and policymakers appeal to certain values when designing public policy. Decisions about problem definition, alternative selection, and policy evaluation are based on the deliberate use of values and the subjective interpretation of those values. For Fischer, the process of policy evaluation is best described as "political evaluation" (1980, 71). Policymakers construct realities that minimize political costs and maximize political gain.

Edelman and Fischer paint a very nuanced and chaotic picture of how the content of public policy is assembled, one in which debates between policymakers over who should receive policy benefits are based on subjective, rather than "rational," arguments. This fits well with Frank Fischer and John Forester's (1993) work on the "argumentative" turn in policy analysis. Similar to Edelman's work on the intersubjectivity of public policymaking, Fischer and Forester argue that language shapes reality. Politics is based on arguments over who gets what, when, and how. Fischer and Forester wrote that these arguments spill over to the policy process and affect the way policymakers define a problem and select solutions to problems. Like Fischer and Forester, Charles Anderson (1979) argued that policy evaluation is highly subjective and highly normative, and that language is the key to understanding the policy process. Writing at roughly the same time as Fischer, Anderson argued that "policy analysis has less to do with problem solving than with the process of argument" (1979, 712). Policymakers and analysts use language to craft a reality that fits with their policy design rather than crafting policy design that fits with reality. Problem definition is subject to framing and the deliberate use of narratives, symbols, and stories to shape reality (see also Hajer and Laws 2006).

Put simply, policymakers approach the content of public policy from the value-laden perspective, from a notion of what the world should look like, not from a hard-nosed, objective notion of a societal problem and a systematic analysis of its potential policy solutions. Policy design is an instrumental, cost-benefit exercise, but it is based on the deliberate use of values and symbols to achieve a particular outcome. In other words, policy outcomes are judged in a relative context; there is no one objective way to view policy design. This has serious practical implications in terms of judging whether a policy is effective. If policymakers make political or normative decisions instead of rational judgments about public policy, how do we effectively evaluate public policy? Or more simply, how do we know if a policy is "good" or "bad"?

The underlying similarity among all the aforementioned scholars is their resolve to move away from strict, empirical analyses of public policy. Policy analysts should instead embrace theoretical approaches, ranging from post-positivism, to critical theory, to deconstructionism, to hermeneutics. Edelman (1990) offered a prescription for the future that calls for an "awareness" and understanding of conflicting perspectives in the decision-making process (130). Such awareness calls for a focus on what serves an individual's and a community's long-term self-interest, as well as a need to recognize that reality is constructed through "art, science, and culture" (Edelman 1990, 130). Policy scholars must employ a "multimethodological" approach (Fischer 1980, 11). Cost-benefit analyses assume policy design can be viewed through a single, objective lens. To accurately study policy design, a methodology that accounts for multiple perspectives is required. For Fischer, the multimethodological approach, one that accounts for intersubjectivity and the deliberate use of symbols and language, is the most comprehensive and realistic means for analyzing public policy. As Anderson (1979, 22) puts it, "Policy making is understood as a process of reasoned deliberation, argument and criticism rather than pragmatic calculus." Because the policy process is inundated with values, the methodology required to study the policy process must account for such intersubjectivity.

In the title of this chapter we posed the question: "Whose values?" For Edelman, Fischer, and others, this is the critical question, both whose values are being supported or distributed by the policy and whose values are being used to judge the relative success or worth of the public policy. Values permeate the policy process, and what values are important will vary according to the observer. Reality is constructed by each observer (Edelman 1990, 101). Distributing benefits to low-income families may be perceived by some as perpetuating shoddy lifestyle habits; others see such benefits as a corrective measure for poorly designed institutions. Whereas an economist might describe a particular policy as successful or efficient, an analyst trained in sociology might view it as inequitable or damaging to the fabric of a community (Anderson 1979, 714). As Edelman (1990) stated, "Reason and rationalization are intertwined" (105). Put another way, "Political language is political reality" (Edelman 1990, 104). These early policy design scholars were simply pointing out what is most likely obvious to any policymaker: policy design is a messy, political, value-laden process.

The "Paradox" of Policy Design

Scholars such as Deborah Stone (2002) contend that the rational evaluation of policy design and the policy process is simply not possible. For Stone, the "policy paradox" represents the ambiguous nature of public policy. Nothing in the process is clear-cut; all policies present a "double-edged sword" (Stone 2002, 169). Rational, market-based approaches to policymaking are insufficient and inaccurate because they treat the policymaking process like an "assembly line" (Stone 2002, 10). Her approach is based on two premises: 1) that economic frameworks rooted in rational choice theory (the foundation for analysis and evaluation methods such as cost-benefit analysis) are inadequate for evaluating public policy; and 2) that society should be viewed through the lens of a "polis" and not the market. For Stone, policymaking is best defined as "the struggle over ideas" (2002, 11). The policy process is characterized by a combination of rational decision making based on scientific calculations and political goals derived from social interaction and "community life" (Stone 2002, 10). The polis, or political community, allows for both perspectives when evaluating public policy. In this regard, Stone's argument is similar to the work of Edelman and Fischer. Policy design must be viewed through multiple perspectives; there is no one rational or objective way to evaluate public policy.

For Stone, the policy process is irrational at both the agenda-setting and decision-making stages. As other scholars have noted, how a problem is defined affects whether the policy receives a favorable reaction from elected officials and citizens (Baumgartner and Jones 1993/2009; Kingdon 1995). For Stone and Fischer, the use of symbols, images, and narratives most strongly affects the problem-definition stage of the policy process. Indeed, Stone (2002, 133) writes that problem definition is "the strategic representation of situations." When a policymaker uses the image of a "welfare queen" to talk about equity in distributing welfare benefits, she is clearly pushing for more stringent welfare benefits. However, when a policymaker uses images of families with young children in homeless shelters, she is trying to shift the basis of the debate from inequitable distribution of benefits to compassion and fairness. At the decision-making stage, the policy process is not rational because alternatives are not considered equally. Policymakers tend to use political language and ambiguous goals that do not allow for rational cost-benefit comparisons. Policy problems tend to be written as narratives, with numbers being used selectively to support the story line. Metaphors, such as the "war on poverty" or the "war on drugs," are political tools deliberately designed to elicit support for certain policies (Stone 2002, 154). Similarly, Stone noted how policymakers often use a synecdoche such as the "welfare queen" to push for tougher restrictions on the distribution of welfare benefits (2002, 146).[1]

Stone's argument extends to policymakers as well as to the targets of public policy. To determine whether a policy will be effective, policy analysts must understand the target's viewpoint. Contrary to predictions of the rational actor model, behavior does not always change based on monetary costs and benefits (Kahneman 2011). Rewards and sanctions tend to have different meanings for different populations, and such populations tend to act strategically. As an example, Stone notes how the Clinton administration incorrectly assumed welfare recipients would work more if the penalty for working while receiving benefits was reduced. Instead, Stone argues, it is more likely that such recipients worked as a means of having enough money to put food on the table. Thus, decreasing the penalty for working while receiving benefits would be an ineffective policy, because most welfare recipients work in response to their daily needs rather than existing welfare provisions (Stone 2002, 279).

The paradox of Stone's *Policy Paradox* is that whereas public policy is often justified as adhering to one of five democratic values (equity, efficiency, security, liberty, community), in reality there is widespread disagreement over what is equitable, what is efficient, what is secure, what liberates, and what constitutes community. A rational evaluation of public policy implies a common understanding of these democratic goals. Such a view is shortsighted and naive, however. Disagreements arise between citizens, between policymakers, and between citizens and policymakers over the definition of these values.

As an example of the problem of achieving the goal of efficiency, Stone asks the reader to consider the efficiency of a public library (2002, 62–65). How should policymakers (librarians) spend savings resulting from the restaffing of the library? To achieve efficiency there must be an agreement on the goals of the organization. Should it increase the number of books? If so, what type of books? Should the library seek to reduce the amount of time necessary to locate materials? Should it focus on goals as perceived by library staff or as perceived by citizens? As with the values of equity, liberty, and security, efficiency requires agreement about the goal of the organization. Efficiency is usually defined as inputs over outputs. But for most public organizations, there is disagreement over desired output, and this is exactly Stone's argument. What output should be the focus of the public library? How easily a citizen can find a particular book, video, magazine, or newspaper? Quality of the book collection? Because there is unlikely to be consensus on which output to use, making calculations about efficiency become impossible. It requires complete information, a state that is rarely achieved in the polis. Thus, the paradox of using these goals as justification for policy design is that citizens and policymakers are most likely to disagree on how best to achieve these goals. People want democratic values to guide the policy process; they are simply unable to agree on how they should be reflected in policy design. There will always be disagreement about what constitutes a good outcome.[2]

Stone has raised awareness of the competing perspectives on seemingly agreed goals. The market model, according to Stone, indicates a zero-sum relationship between equity and efficiency. To efficiently distribute welfare benefits means that not all of those who qualify for such benefits will receive them. Stone rejected this model in favor of the polis model, which states that policymakers use symbols when designing policy to perpetuate existing stereotypes. According to Stone, the democratic values of equity, efficiency, security, liberty, and community not only guide policy design but also serve as goals and benchmarks. Policymakers and citizens want the content of public policy to reflect democratic values, but agreement on whether such values are reflected in policy content is rare.

Other scholars have picked up on Stone's paradox. H. George Frederickson (2007) comments that "results-driven management" approaches are naive because they ignore the very problem identified by Stone. Frederickson points out that "public administrators catch criminals, put out fires and even try to prevent them, teach children, supply pure water, fight battles, distribute social security checks, and carry out a thousand other activities—all outputs" (2007, 11). Applying the value of efficiency, how do we analyze such outputs? For a local fire department, should efficiency be defined by response time to fires, the number of fires put out per month, or the number of complaints by local citizens? These choices are important because they can determine whether a policy is judged as efficient or not, and more generally whether the policy is judged as good or bad. Frederickson also applied this notion to breast cancer research by medical research organizations. Should such organizations be held accountable according to "the percentage of women of a certain age receiving mammograms or the percentage of women of a certain age with breast cancer" (2007, 11)? In this case the organization must choose between "agency outputs" and "social outcomes" (Frederickson 2007, 11). Although Frederickson focused on the problem of achieving consensus on accountability, the problem could just as easily be applied to the concept of efficiency. The point is that attaching too much weight to specific measures of policy output overlooks the diversity of outputs produced by public organizations and the different values citizens and policymakers attach to such outputs.

At the heart of Stone's argument is the notion that public policy should be accountable to a diverse set of interests. However, as Frederickson's argument suggests, the value of accountability suffers from the same problems as those of equity, efficiency, security, and liberty. In January 2002 President George W. Bush signed into law the No Child Left Behind Act as a means of increasing the accountability of K–12 education. Since that time, administrators and parents have clashed over how accountability should be defined. For some, any measurable improvement is a sign of success; for others, test scores are the only appropriate measure. Making the problem even more difficult is the fact that schools tend to face what economists label "economies of scope." A school that focuses its resources on increasing graduation rates may see a subsequent decrease in test scores as marginal students are kept in school. Similarly, schools interested in increasing test scores may see a rise in truancy rates as marginal students are not encouraged to stay in school, particularly on test days (see Wenger 2000; Smith and Larimer 2004). Although policymakers, school administrators, and parents agree on the need to increase school efficiency and effectiveness, all three groups tend to define such values differently.

Scholars from other subfields have also recognized the dilemma in attempting to implement objective means for evaluating public policy. Going back to the work of Woodrow Wilson, public administration scholars have long argued that the dichotomy between politics and administration is a false one. Instead, administration is infused with political battles, creating problems when attempting to evaluate the efficiency of public policies. Policymakers need to recognize that citizens value processes and outcomes differently. Citizens and policymakers are likely to disagree about the importance of policy outcomes, and such disagreement is "probably the rule rather than the exception" (Bohte 2007, 812).

Because there is no one agreed-upon definition of efficiency or equity, policymakers are free to use symbols and to craft language in such a way as to create certain policy images. These policy images then serve as representations of the policy generally. Whether a policy is judged as good or bad or is considered a success or failure is ultimately a value choice. Normative or value judgments, in addition to rational judgments, influence public policy decisions. Although efficiency arguments tend to guide policy analysis, Stone makes a strong case that what constitutes efficiency, as well as other democratic values, is also a value choice.

Social Constructions and Target Populations

To understand and analyze the policy process requires an understanding of the way in which policymakers create and use measures for policy evaluation. How we characterize groups of individuals is based on multiple perspectives of the problem, as well as symbolism and the strategic framing of interests. Peter May (1991) writes of such a strategy when distinguishing between "policies with publics" and "policies without publics." Policies with publics, that is, policies with established constituencies, face a different set of design constraints than policies without publics. Although policies without publics do not have to adhere to the expectations of interested advocacy groups, they must also avoid inciting conflict that gets the attention of previously uninterested groups. The point is that policy design does not operate independently of politics. The process of policy design requires an acute awareness of how the public and the political world will respond to policy proposals and the narratives surrounding them.

What to include or exclude from the policy process is based on individual interpretation and contrasting worldviews. Although Stone did not completely discount rational decision making, she argued that the political community has a profound impact on the policy process. Key to Stone's argument is the notion that policy design is based on the politics of categorization: "what needs are legitimate" (2002, 98) and "how we do and should categorize in a world where categories are not given" (380). Anne L. Schneider and Helen Ingram (1997) made use of Stone's (1988) original notion of the politics of categorization. However, unlike scholars discussed in the previous two sections, who primarily focused on the values of policymakers, Schneider and Ingram focused both on the deliberate use of values by policymakers as well as how such values are translated and interpreted by citizens, the targets of public policy.

Schneider and Ingram argued that only by evaluating policy content and substance is it possible to discern how and why policies are constructed. Using "policy design" as the dependent variable and "social construction" as the independent variable, the authors characterized the policymaking process as "degenerative"

(1997, 11). Policies are designed by public officials to reinforce social constructions of various groups in society, described as "target populations." In addition, science is often used to further stigmatize these groups as "deserving" or "undeserving." As the authors note, science is exploited as a means for justifying policy, not for verifying specifics of the most appropriate means available, as would be expected in the rational actor model. Science is used only when it is "convergent with the policy options that create political capital for policy makers" (Schneider and Ingram 1997, 12).

Policy designs are constructed and interpreted according to favorable meanings based on societal perspectives of target populations. Schneider and Ingram create a 2 x 2 matrix consisting of political power and deservedness (deserving and undeserving) to identify four main types of target groups: advantaged, contenders, dependents, and deviants (1997, 109). Advantaged groups include scientists, business owners, senior citizens, middle-class taxpayers, and the military. Contenders, like advantaged groups, have a lot of political power, but are perceived as less deserving than advantaged groups. Examples include labor unions, gun owners, and the insurance industry. Dependents are those groups that lack political power but are positively socially constructed (e.g., mothers, children, including at-risk children, students, and the mentally disabled). Although individuals with disabilities seeking public education would fall under the heading "dependents," distributive policies to this group have lacked sufficient resources, because special education advocates are "weakly represented," thus yielding few political opportunities (Schneider and Ingram 1997, 126). Finally, deviants lack both political power and a positive social construction; thus they are perceived as politically weak and undeserving. Welfare mothers, criminals, terrorists, gangs, and illegal immigrants tend to fall within this classification (examples are from Schneider and Ingram 1997, 109; Ingram, Schneider, and deLeon 2007, 102; Schneider and Sidney 2009, 107).

These four categories are fluid and subject to change. Ingram, Schneider, and deLeon (2007) later distinguished between big business and small business, with the former being classified as contenders and the latter as advantaged. Advocacy groups tend to be the most fluid. For example, environmentalists in Schneider and Ingram's early classification are classified as having moderate political power and are perceived as deserving, resulting in a classification somewhere between contenders and deviants. Later revisions by Ingram, Schneider, and deLeon (2007) placed environmentalists clearly in the contender grouping. Even within categories, groups can affect how other groups are socially constructed. Tracing the history of the social construction of welfare recipients, Sanford Schram (2005) argues that because welfare was constructed as being synonymous with African Americans, the social construction of African Americans suffered. This had significant repercussions, because they suffered in terms of political power. Because welfare recipients were categorized as dependents, African Americans were initially socially constructed as a dependent population. In a subsequent revision, "black" and "middle class" were added; they occupy the space between advantaged and dependent social constructions, both groups perceived as deserving with moderate political power (Schneider and Sidney 2009, 107). The 2 x 2 social construction matrix, as originally conceived, continues to struggle with questions about where to place groups that include multiple target populations, for example, black, middle-class taxpayers.

The social construction of target populations implies that public officials purposefully construct policy designs based on a "burden/benefit" analysis of political opportunities and risks of the four categories of target populations (Schneider and Ingram 1997, 114). Advantaged groups tend to be targets for distributive policies that allocate benefits with little or no costs. Because advantaged groups are high in political power, policymakers benefit by minimizing policy costs and maximizing policy benefits to such groups. Contender groups also tend to receive policy benefits, but these benefits are not as explicit as for advantaged groups. Contenders tend to be perceived as "selfish, untrustworthy, and morally suspect" (Ingram, Schneider, and deLeon 2007, 102) and thus less deserving than advantaged groups. As a result, policy burdens tend to be more publicized than policy benefits. Indeed, as Ingram, Schneider, and deLeon point out, "benefits to contenders are hidden because no legislators want to openly do good things for shady people" (102).

Both advantaged groups and contenders tend to have a high degree of political power; the only difference is that the former are perceived as deserving, whereas the latter are perceived as undeserving. Unlike these two groups, the other two groups in Schneider and Ingram's framework lack political power. Dependent groups such as the poor, homeless, and unmarried lack political power but are socially constructed as deserving. Although benefits distributed to dependent groups tend to be more explicit than those distributed to contenders, dependents' lack of political power prevents such groups from receiving maximum policy benefits. The problems of dependent groups are perceived as the result of individual failings rather than social problems. Doling out benefits to the poor or people on welfare is politically risky, because such benefits are perceived as addressing individual problems at the expense of the public good. Dependent groups are also the first to see their benefits cut in times of fiscal crisis (Schneider and Ingram 1993, 345; Ingram, Schneider, and deLeon 2007, 103). Finally, deviants, as would be expected, receive few if any policy benefits. Instead, policymakers tend to be more interested in ensuring that "burdens" are distributed to such groups. Deviants "deserve to punished," and any policies that deviate from such expectations are likely to lead to negative political consequences for the policymaker (Schneider and Ingram 1997, 130).

Consider the recurring discussion over the voting rights of ex-felons. Although few would dispute that such individuals fit neatly within the deviant category, there is considerable variation across states regarding the restoration of voting rights for this target group. In some states, voting rights are restored automatically following completion of a sentence and parole, whereas other states require a more onerous application process, the end result of which is many ex-felons being disenfranchised for life. For some, voting rights represent a path back to citizenship; for others disenfranchisement is a suitable penalty for past behavior. Politicians, usually governors, thus face a choice: restore voting rights (a benefit) to an undeserving and deviant population (ex-felons), or require a stringent application process (a burden). In 2012, in two states where ex-felons' right to vote had previously been automatically restored, governors reversed such policies (Ghuman 2012), in effect securing political gain by doling out a burden to an undeserving group.

Schneider and Ingram's research is unique for the two-stage research process it employs. In the first stage, the researchers treat policy design as the dependent variable and social constructions as the key independent variable. How groups are socially constructed (deserving or undeserving) ultimately affects policy design (the distribution of policy benefits and burdens). The second stage of Schneider and Ingram's work is to treat policy design as the independent variable and test for any effects on perceptions of citizenship and democratic efficacy. The authors posited that individuals placed in politically powerless groups (dependents and deviants) have a negative view of the political system, resulting in political apathy and low levels of political participation. Target populations learn their position in society as deserving or undeserving (Schneider and Ingram 1997, 103), and this has real implications for attitudes toward government.

Joe Soss (2005) conducted a direct test of the second stage of Schneider and Ingram's framework. Soss drew on interviews with recipients of Aid to Families with Dependent Children (AFDC). Because AFDC recipients depend on caseworkers for benefits, Soss argued that these individuals lack a sense of self-worth, resulting in negative or apathetic views about the political system. Indeed, recipients appear to sense that they have been categorized as members of a negative or "stigmatized" group (Soss 2005, 316). As a result, they are less likely to participate in government or to view such participation as meaningful. Earlier work by Soss (1999) also found that perceptions of policy designs directly influence perceptions of political efficacy. As Soss wrote, "policy designs teach lessons about citizenship status and government" (1999, 376). If applied to the voting rights of ex-felons, the example noted above, Soss's work suggests that, all else being equal, felons in states with automatic restoration will hold more positive views toward government than felons in states in which the process is more complicated.

By distributing costs and benefits to target populations according to whether they are perceived as deserving or undeserving, elites reinforce power relationships. In turn, this shapes political participation as the targets of specific policies develop positive or negative attitudes toward government and their ability to effectively influence governmental activity. The work by Soss, as well as early work by Schneider and Ingram, clearly implicates the connection between the study of policy design and the study of democratic citizenship and whether the actions of government fulfill democratic values. Ingram and Schneider (2005b, 6) later argued that the "degenerative" nature of public policy is worsened by the path-dependent nature of social constructions. Social constructions become embedded in society, rarely questioned and rarely subject to change. Implicit in this reasoning is the notion that any policy proposals that match existing social constructions will be passed unanimously by a legislative body. And in fact some scholars have found a direct relationship between policy style and the likelihood of degenerative politics, particularly for groups constructed as undeserving (Mondou and Montpetit 2010). But can social constructions change? Can the targets of public policies expand or contract?

According to Peter May, the answer is yes. Social constructions are not static; instead, policymakers adjust beliefs about policy problems in response to incoming stimuli, evidence of what May (1992, 332) described as "social learning." Social learning is different from instrumental learning. Although both entail forms of what May has described as "policy learning," instrumental learning is more reflective of the rationalist approach to policy analysis, emphasizing the means for solving policy problems and learning through policy evaluation. Social learning is more goal-oriented, focusing on the cause of the problem and beliefs about target populations. May has cited as evidence of social policy learning cases in which the targets of policy proposals change or beliefs about the goals of the policy change (1992, 351). Policy learning is considerably more likely for "policies with publics" (May 1991), because such policies allow for a give and take and an updating of beliefs about established groups.

Learning, however, is not limited to policy content. Unlike policy learning, "political learning" concerns the ability of policy elites to craft politically feasible policy proposals. Political learning and policy learning are distinct but interrelated concepts; with a change in beliefs about the goals of a policy, policy elites may adopt new strategies for pushing a particular policy. Although May has admitted that evidence of policy and political learning is difficult to systematically and empirically assess, his model provides a theoretical basis for how target populations are socially constructed and that such social constructions are subject to change.

Nicholson-Crotty and Meier (2005) addressed this issue, agreeing that policymakers deliberately use social constructions to craft public policy, but contending that the process is more complex than suggested by Ingram and Schneider. At issue is the notion that policy proposals designed to burden deviant groups will face little or no resistance in becoming public policy. Nicholson-Crotty and Meier instead have argued that three conditions must be met before this transition takes place. First, the group must be perceived as "marginal" by those who hold political power. Second, there must be a "moral entrepreneur" who actively seeks to link the actions of the group to larger societal problems. This individual must possess political power or be a well-respected expert. Nicholson-Crotty and Meier discussed the role of James Q. Wilson as a moral entrepreneur in assisting the passage of crime legislation in 1984 as an example. Wilson, because of his role as a well-respected academic, was able to shape the discussion to link criminal behavior with the decline of community values (Nicholson-Crotty and Meier 2005, 237). Finally, there must be a "political entrepreneur." This individual is similar to Kingdon's (1995) policy entrepreneur, in that he or she attempts to convince other policymakers that the proposal represents sound public policy. In short, policymakers use social constructions to design public policy, but the link is more nuanced than originally argued by Schneider and Ingram.

A more recent example is illegal immigration policy in the United States. "Illegal" immigrants tend to be socially constructed as deviants (Schneider and Sidney 2009, 107). Empirical and anecdotal evidence, however, suggests that this social construction can be changed through the use of symbols and emotion, as well as by powerful political actors. Examining policies on in-state tuition status for undocumented students in the American states, Reich and Barth (2010, 428) show that, in the case of Kansas, powerful advocacy groups were able to construct these students as "proto-citizens." The result was a more favorable policy outcome; undocumented students were now seen as deserving of a policy benefit (a break on tuition). Perhaps bowing to the political pressure of a presidential campaign, President Barack Obama declared on June 15, 2012, that undocumented workers who came to the United States as children would no longer be deported. The president's comments on the new policy are noteworthy for their attempt to shift the social construction of a group previously seen as undeserving: "They pledge allegiance to our flag. They are Americans in their hearts, in their minds, in every single way but one: on paper" (Foley 2012).

The point is that the construction of target groups is not static or clear-cut; there is no hard and fast empirical boundary between groups. The "rich," for example, hover between the advantaged and contenders groups (Schneider and Sidney 2009, 107) and could easily be socially constructed as either deserving or undeserving. "Pregnant teens" occupy space between dependents and deviants, their deservedness dependent on whether they are constructed as being in a tough position and worthy of society's help or simply irresponsible, their plight the result of immoral or unethical behavior. Some groups are targeted for policy benefits, whereas others are targeted for policy burdens. These decisions are not based on rational cost-benefit analyses, but rather on socially constructed realities. Although "policy learning" does occur (May 1992), so too does political learning; thus there is no guarantee that policymakers will make decisions on the basis of what is good public policy. And even though it may be more practical and logical to design policy that redistributes benefits to groups that are rationally justified as suffering from societal problems, political risks often dissuade rational officials from pursuing such action (Schneider and Ingram 1997, 115). The lack of democratic values and the subsequent lack of interest in politics also have real practical implications for democracy.

"Democratic" Values and Policy Design

In liberal democracies, the normative underpinning of public policy should be democratic values. As a normative claim, this is a supportable argument. But how do we test it? Do public policies indeed reflect democratic ideals? Stone's work questioned whether there can ever be agreement on what constitutes such democratic values as equity or liberty. Schneider and Ingram have also stressed that the values inherent in policy symbols are undemocratic. Unique to all of these scholars is an explicit call for a more democratic policymaking process; from problem definition to policy design, democratic values should be inherent in the policy process. So, if democratic values should guide the policy process, but clearly do not, how do we correct this?

As discussed previously in this chapter, many scholars agree that quantitative approaches to the study of public policy, such as cost-benefit analyses, ignore the intersubjectivity guiding the policy process (see Fischer 1980; Edelman 1990). Up to this point, we have emphasized the theoretical solutions to this dilemma, most notably post-positivist methodology such as constructionism and hermeneutics. For Peter deLeon, however, this intersubjectivity and deliberate use of values and symbols have resulted in a growing separation between government and its citizens, requiring a more practical response.

Drawing on Harold Lasswell's notion of the "policy sciences of democracy," deLeon (1995, 1997) argued that the policymaking process has shifted away from core democratic values. For deLeon, the move toward a more positivist approach to the study of public policy has resulted in a non-Lasswellian shift. DeLeon saw the policy sciences as captured by two dominant approaches, utilitarianism and liberal-rationalism, both of which have increased the distance between citizens and their government. Utilitarianism, because it advocates a strong role for the market and relies heavily on data, ignores "human factors" (deLeon 1997, 53). The utilitarian approach ignores the wishes of ordinary citizens and how citizens interpret policy messages sent by governing elites. This leads to policy research that is "methodologically rich and results poor" (deLeon 1997, 55). The solution? According to deLeon, a more involved citizenry.

On a theoretical level, deLeon called for post-positivist methodology, particularly the use of deconstructionism and hermeneutics, to more appropriately link the policy sciences with democratic values. DeLeon, however, also offered a practical solution for more democratic policy design. The lack of democratic values creates an apathetic public, and to correct this, the study of public policy must be characterized by open discourse between citizens and policymakers, an approach that would be labeled participatory policy analysis (PPA), the notion of directly engaging citizens in public policymaking. DeLeon cites numerous examples in which citizen panels have been constructed to assist in policy design and the result has been a more satisfied citizenry. The underlying assumptions of PPA are that citizens want more involvement in the policymaking process, and that such involvement will ameliorate growing disenchantment with government institutions and the government elite.

For policy design scholars such as Schneider and Ingram (1997) and Soss (1999, 2006), apathy breeds lack of interest and the desire to withdraw from political life, further perpetuating a cycle of undemocratic policymaking. PPA moves the citizen from a passive, reactionary role in the policy process to an active, decision-making role. Paraphrasing John Dewey, DeLeon asserted: "The cure for the ailments of democracy is more civic participation" (1997, 43). More citizen participation in the policy process increases citizen satisfaction with the political process *and* creates better public policy.[3] Only through citizen engagement will the policy sciences truly reflect democratic values. deLeon's (1997) call for PPA has fueled research examining the effects of citizen participation on improving policy responsiveness and overall citizen satisfaction with the policymaking process (see also Fung and Wright 2003a; Macedo 2005). Even public administration scholars have advocated a more citizen-oriented approach to policy design. For example, Schachter (2007) argues that the only way for an organization to agree on efficiency is through input from stakeholders. For policy design to reflect the preferences of citizens, they must be involved in the policy process.

Refining their earlier work, Ingram and Schneider (2006) later called for a more explicit and active role for citizens. Like Peter deLeon, Ingram and Schneider view the study of public policy as a normative exercise: "The public must become more directly involved in holding government structures accountable" (Ingram and Schneider 2006, 182). They have explicitly argued that policy design should serve democracy and policy analysts should "design policy that will better serve democracy" (2006, 172). Furthermore, "citizens ought to view their role as citizens as important" (Ingram and Schneider 2006, 172). Later revisions by Schneider and Sidney (2009) do not shy away from a more normative basis for policy design theory. More attention should be given to positive social constructions as a way to serve democratic ends, notably increasing participation and openness (Schneider and Sidney 2009, 111). Policy design shapes the connection between citizens and government. Thus, the primary means for improving policy design and increasing citizen satisfaction with government is through citizen engagement in the policy process. Similar to deLeon's PPA approach, Ingram and Schneider contend that when citizens are given a voice in the policy process, they will "be encouraged through this policy change to engage in discourse" (2006, 176).

Rather than a positivist approach, PPA and revisions to policy design theory were purposeful attempts to introduce normative arguments, particularly those linked to democratic participation. The policy process rarely fits with the market model of economics, in which goals are clearly defined and alternatives considered comprehensively in an objective costs-and-benefits manner. Instead, it is a battle over what values should guide the policy process. Schneider and Ingram have made a strong case that democratic values should be involved in policy design. However, in their view, policy design tends to be based on constructed realities that benefit advantaged groups. The result is undemocratic policy design and a self-perpetuating system of "degenerative politics." Not only are values and symbols present in the policy process, they are used deliberately by policymakers. For Schneider and Ingram, the current state of policy design is both undemocratic and non-pluralist. Policy designs impart messages to target populations about their status and how others think of them, and current policy designs teach powerless groups (dependents and deviants) that mobilization and participation are useless. As Ingram, Schneider, and deLeon stated, "Messages convey who belongs, whose interests are important, what kind of 'game' politics is, and whether one has a place at the table" (2007, 100). For deLeon, the only way to change such messages is through a more policy active citizenry. When citizens participate in the policymaking process, their sense of efficacy and trust in government increases, making the policy process more democratic as well as improving the overall quality of policy design. Schneider and Sidney conclude by stating that "a key element to policy design theory is the integration of normative and empirical analysis" (2009, 112). Whether such a normative framework that allows for objective quantitative testing is possible, however, remains to be seen.

Narrative Policy Framework

To this point, the focus of policy design theory has been how to analyze policy content, and what effect, if any, such content has on the participation of targeted groups. But are there patterns in policy design as an instrument of policy change? To answer this question requires an understanding of how the stories and narratives surrounding policies are processed by actors in the political system.

Michael Jones and Mark McBeth (2010) made the first attempt to create a systematic framework for examining the role of narratives in policy design. The narrative policy framework, or NPF, posits that stories, symbols, images—the basic components of a narrative—can be studied in an empirical and quantifiable fashion to offer insight into how and why policy change occurs. Acknowledging potential criticism from the positivist crowd, Jones and McBeth lay out a framework that is, in their terms, "both empirical and falsifiable" (331). The basic structure of the NPF is that policy narratives, when structured correctly, can affect individual public opinion as well as opinions within existing policy subsystems. Advocacy coalitions use policy narratives to expand or contract the size of the coalition to achieve a desired policy change. Jones and McBeth lay out eight hypotheses about how narratives affect individual opinion and are used by coalitions or groups. Key to all hypotheses is the effectiveness of the narrative. In short: How good or convincing is the story?

The NPF has been applied to various issues in multiple contexts (see McBeth, Lybecker, and Garner 2010; McBeth et al. 2007; McBeth, Shanahan, and Jones 2005). But what constitutes a good story? What are the key elements? Jones and McBeth note that to achieve individual policy change, the narratives must be persuasive, be compelling, fit with existing beliefs, and be from a trusted source (343–344). Shanahan, Jones, and McBeth (2011; see also McBeth et al. 2007) apply the NPF to the advocacy coalition framework, asking: How do coalitions use narratives to change core beliefs, allowing for policy or political learning, and ultimately result in policy change? One particularly intriguing hypothesis concerns the "power of characters." Narratives with powerful characters will be more effective in influencing and changing public opinion (Shanahan, Jones, and McBeth 2011, 553).

The NPF confirms an idea that political psychologists and neuroscientists have been batting around for some time. To change public opinion requires less emphasis on policy details and more on telling a good story. All good stories have intriguing heroes and villains, and research indicates that such stories have profound effects on our evaluations of political candidates (Weston 2007). As Jones and McBeth note, all narratives share four basic elements: a setting or context, a plot, characters, and a moral (2010, 340–341). The NPF hypothesizes that when combined in a compelling manner, those four elements can change public opinion. Nowlin (2011, 53) sees the NPF as an "emerging trend" for improving theories of the policy process. But the NPF, and policy design theory generally, tell us little about why such change is possible. Turning to evolutionary theory, scholars have remarked extensively on the groupish nature of our ancestors, resulting in a strong predisposition to consider and discuss life in group terms (Boehm 2012; Wilson 2012). Humans are predisposed toward "tribalism," or the tendency to distrust out-groups and take satisfaction in benefiting at the expense of out-group members (Wilson 2012, 61). There is also a strong predisposition to avoid feelings of shame within one's in-group, leading to acts of kindness and even altruism (Boehm 2012). For policy design theory, such arguments suggest policymakers able to construct narratives that exploit such tendencies will be more likely to achieve desired policy changes.

Testing Policy Design Theories?

In one sense, there is universal agreement about the claims that emerge from the field of policy design. Most policy scholars agree with Edelman, Fischer, and Stone that policymakers make deliberate and selective use of facts, stories, and images to support particular policies. Most policy scholars agree with Schneider and Ingram that policymakers distribute policy burdens and benefits in such a way as to maximize political gain. Political scientists have long noted that elected officials are driven primarily by the desire for reelection (see Mayhew 1974). So it is no surprise that elites will attempt to embed certain values within policy designs that reinforce existing perceptions and avoid negative repercussions. Yet positivist social scientists view the frameworks discussed throughout this chapter with skepticism—the concepts are too amorphous to systematically guide research, and the methods lack the empirical rigor associated with the rationalist project. The frameworks do nothing to resolve concerns that a post-positivist approach to policy design theory would be non-falsifiable and too normative.

Testing the policy design theories discussed in this chapter, like constructing the theories themselves, is a messy process. To be considered a legitimate subfield, policy design has to offer some predictability to the policy process. As has been discussed, early policy design scholars argued that policymakers craft stories to fit with existing policies. So, can we predict what values, stories, narratives, and images will resonate with citizens? The narrative policy framework is an attempt to do just that by equating narratives with individual belief systems. The NPF allows for hypothesis testing at both the individual and subsystem levels, and scholars are developing a clear empirical track record regarding the use and effectiveness of certain narratives. But questions about the type of narratives most likely to change public opinion are left unanswered. A more complete answer requires a more interdisciplinary approach, one that will most likely need to incorporate key elements of psychology and neuroscience. As discussed previously, people are predisposed to think in groupish patterns (Wilson 2012), and narratives that exploit this tendency are more likely to find receptive audiences. Policymakers able to cast target groups as out-groups will find it easier to direct policy burdens to such groups. The warfare narrative discussed by Wilson (2012) has deep psychological roots stemming from our evolutionary past, and indeed has already been used by policymakers ("war on drugs," "war on poverty," "war on terror," etc.). Future work should continue to examine how cognitive structure affects the processing of policy narratives.

Other questions remain, however. Are post-positivist methods such as constructionism or hermeneutics more appropriate for certain stages of the policy process? Schneider and Ingram have argued that social constructions and policy design reduce democratic participation. Perhaps, but by how much? What type of participation? Soss (2005) has provided a solid first cut at these questions using survey research, but questions still remain. How much variation in participation levels is there between deviants and dependents, between contenders and advantaged groups? What constitutes evidence of "social learning" or "political learning"?

DeLeon's PPA faces perhaps the greatest difficulty, as it seems to raise more questions than it answers. For example, who should participate? How much participation? At what stage of the policy process? About what decisions? The assumption underlying this solution is that citizens, if given the chance, want to be involved in policymaking. However, research on public attitudes toward government suggests otherwise. Drawing from extensive survey and focus group research, Hibbing and Theiss-Morse (1995, 2002) find that in fact most citizens do *not* want to be involved in the policy process. What they want is the comfort of knowing that policymakers are looking out for their best interests. Most citizens are not comforted by what they see in the policy process. As a result, they feel forced to pay attention to politics, not out of a desire to participate but to keep policymakers in check. Joining groups is not the answer to increased satisfaction with government, because homogenous groups tend to reinforce the perception of a commonality of interest where one does not exist (Hibbing and Theiss-Morse 2005). Thus, whereas deLeon has argued that increased levels of citizen participation will improve satisfaction with government, Hibbing and Theiss-Morse argue that rarely do citizens want to participate, and only do when they feel it is necessary to prevent self-interested behavior on the part of elites. Even Deborah Stone (2002) would most likely take issue with deLeon's recommendation for more citizen involvement. As her discussion of ensuring equity in school board elections demonstrates, even when most parties are in agreement on the need to be inclusive, conflict arises over what constitutes equitable public participation.[4]

A central problem for the policy design project is that its conceptual frameworks frequently do not generate clean, empirically testable hypotheses; ultimately its empirical claims are not particularly empirical. This is not wholly surprising given its emphasis on the subjective nature of reality, but it provides no clear basis for sorting out which claims or perspectives are the best basis for judging policy. The rationalist project, for all of its shortcomings, offers a steady platform for generating comparative judgments of public policy and has a central notion of a value to guide such judgments: efficiency. Policy design theory so far has no equivalent internal conceptual gyroscope.

Conclusion

Although descriptions of the policy process and policy design are not neat and clean, they do move us closer to understanding the content of public policy and what it means for understanding power relationships in society. One of the clear lessons of policy design research is that those who wield political power are able to construct a reality that fits with their proposed policies. Policy design theory is perhaps best understood as the politics of defining goals or the politics of categorization. Stone sums up this argument quite nicely: "Policy is precisely this deliberate ordering of the world according to the principle of different treatment for different categories" (2005, ix).

Policy design theory also contributes significantly to the study of how citizens form perceptions about their government. Policy designs are utilized to reinforce existing power relationships and perceptions of the appropriate role of government. As Schneider and Ingram (1997) and Soss (2005) noted, values are often embedded in policy designs, and these values have important implications for democratic participation. In fact, most policy design scholars agree that the study of policy design provides evidence of nondemocratic values in the policymaking process and non-pluralistic competition, and that policy is often used to reinforce nondemocratic values (see Schneider and Sidney 2009; Schneider and Ingram 2005). Policy evaluations are based on political evaluations. Schneider and Ingram provide a framework for testing whether these political evaluations have damaging effects on political participation and attitudes toward government.

If the policy process is based on constructed realities and intersubjective interpretations, the obvious question is: How does one determine whether a policy is effective? Edelman, Fischer, and Stone have laid the groundwork for a theory of policy design and policy analysis based on post-positivist methodology. Their primary interest is accounting for "constructed" realities when conducting policy evaluations. Even though Stone and Fischer paint a picture of the policy process that is based on a constructed reality, this does not necessarily mean the policy process is unpredictable. Rather, predictability increases once one recognizes the intersubjective nature of policymaking. Schneider and Ingram take this a step further by asking, given that policy design is infused with values, symbols, and stories, what effect this has on the targets of such policy. Under this framework, "policy design" is treated as both the dependent variable and an important independent variable.

As this chapter has made clear, a number of policy scholars see the content of public policies as undemocratic. Scholars describe the process of policy design as deliberate and manipulative, not a rational response to public problems. Policymakers use symbols and language to craft policy to perpetuate existing stereotypes. For most of these scholars, policymakers, analysts, and even other scholars should be more involved in accounting for the diversity of views shared by citizens affected by particular policies. One practical solution to this dilemma is the notion of more citizen involvement. There are, however, serious empirical roadblocks to this solution, notably the lack of evidence showing a strong desire on the part of citizens to participate in policymaking. By focusing on how images and stories interact with existing belief systems, the narrative policy framework is another step in the right direction in terms of improving the testability and falsifiability of the policy design framework. Though empirical in nature, the approach is still cumbersome and to date limited to case studies. The NPF is in part a call to create a subfield of public policy akin to political psychology, aptly named "policy psychology." Policy design theory is about how citizens and policymakers interpret and use narratives. To move beyond the case study approach requires a generalizable and more foundational knowledge base of human psychology. Advances in evolutionary science have only recently been adopted by policy scholars (see John 2003; Jones 2001; Smith 2006b). The evolutionary psychology framework provides solid theoretical footing for scholars interested in why people reason and think the way they do. If policy design theory is about how policymakers manipulate policy content, as well as the way in which citizens respond to such content, then policy scholars would be wise to look to evolutionary science for answers.

Notes

1. See also Gilens (2000) for a discussion of the way symbolic language such as "welfare queen" has been used to perpetuate existing stereotypes of welfare recipients and to decrease public support for increasing welfare benefits.

2. Bohte (2007, 812) also used Stone's library example to illustrate the difficulty of achieving efficiency in a public organization.

3. Other scholars (deLeon and Denhardt 2000) also criticize approaches that appear to strengthen the role of policymakers, such as bureaucrats, at the expense of citizens.

4. On a more practical level, Bohte (2007, 813) cautioned against too much citizen involvement, because citizens tend to lack knowledge of how policies will be implemented.

CHAPTER 9

New Directions in Policy Research

In this chapter we present alternative approaches to the study of public policy that are being developed in fields such as experimental and behavioral economics, evolutionary psychology, anthropology, and neuroscience. The driving force behind these developments is the claim that rational choice in both its classical and bounded variants has problems explaining a large portion of human behavior. Because these two general models of human behavior underpin a good deal of the most important conceptual frameworks in public policy (e.g., incrementalism, new institutionalism, the Tiebout model, punctuated equilibrium, and virtually all of the applied analysis frameworks originating in economics, such as cost-benefit analysis and welfare economics), their development obviously has the potential to significantly shape the field of policy studies. The central research question at the heart of these new theoretical approaches is this: Why do people do what they do? This question strikes to the heart of all the social sciences and is critical to the study of public policy.

The field of policy studies, like other social sciences, has long held the view that people tend to deviate from models of complete rationality. Where other fields such as behavioral economics and evolutionary psychology have surpassed policy studies, however, is in building a theoretical framework for explaining such deviations. That people do not conform to traditional models of rationality is taken as a given in what are considered to be some of the most prominent policy models, such as incrementalism, new institutionalism, and punctuated equilibrium. What is missing is a theory for systematically explaining such "irrational" behavior.

.   A quickly emerging and powerful tool for explaining deviations from the rational-comprehensive model comes from outside mainstream policy studies. For this group of scholars, people are still capable of making rational decisions, it is just that the type of rationality is more in line with what evolutionary psychologists refer to as "adaptive rationality" (Barkow, Cosmides, and Tooby 1992; Frank 2005) The basic premise of adaptive rationality models is that the human mind evolved in an environment of scarce resources, in which group cooperation was critical to survival. Because of this, humans developed a strong sense of fairness and concern for what others think (see also Boehm 2012; Wilson 2012). Importantly, and unlike the classical rationality often used in policy studies, adaptive rationality makes room for emotional considerations and cognitive shortcuts.

Some scholars question whether these shortcuts are in fact "adaptive," noting that cognitive shortcuts often result in suboptimal decisions. Bryan Jones addresses the limitations of decision-making heuristics. While accepting the premise that people are incapable of making completely rational decisions, he contends that cognitive limitations prevent people from adapting appropriately to current situations. Instead, people tend to "adapt in disjointed ways" (Jones 2001, ix).[1] The inability of human beings to process information in a rational manner leads to a heavy reliance on decision-making shortcuts or heuristics. For Jones, these heuristics are not only deviations from the rational actor model but also are potentially bad policy decisions. So from this perspective, heuristics are not the best basis for decision making, which is to say that they are not the best basis for policymaking. The corrective for maladaptive decision making is well-structured institutions that help overcome the cognitive limitations and shortcuts inherent in how humans make choices.

An alternative view, however, is that heuristics are adaptive, at least on the individual level. The fact that they seem to be more or less universally employed indicates that there must have been selection pressures that identified some benefit to these cognitive shortcuts. Indeed, evolutionary psychologists can see these heuristics in a positive light, essentially as a means for making bounded rationality a functional and workable basis for decision making. Scholars in the ABC Research Group at the Max Planck Institute for Human Development, for example, have devoted two volumes to the research and development of the concepts of "Simple Heuristics That Make Us Smart" and linked them to the basic framework of bounded rationality (Gigerenzer and Selton 2002; Gigerenzer and Todd 1999b).

While the question of whether these heuristics "make us smarter" or lead us into making irrational decisions that need institutional correctives is the subject of some debate, there is no question that people often make bad or inaccurate judgments, particularly in conditions of incomplete information. Going back to Tversky and Kahneman's (1974) seminal work in this area, scholars outside of policy and political science have empirically documented the conditions under which predictions of the rational choice model are unlikely to be met. Yet with the exception of a few pioneering scholars like Jones, the field of policy studies has been slow to recognize, let alone adopt, conceptual frameworks developed in fields such as evolutionary psychology and behavioral economics. Dan Ariely's book *Predictably Irrational* (2009) is notable for the plethora of empirical evidence from lab and field experiments showing people's tendency to make "irrational" decisions (see also Brafman and Brafman 2008 for similar evidence). Evolutionary psychologists suggest such irrationality is the result of evolutionary pressures on the human mind (Barkow, Cosmides, and Tooby 1992; Kurzban 2010). Scholars in these fields are steadily accumulating systematic evidence that people act irrationally and are finding systematic patterns in this irrationality. At some point policy scholars need to incorporate such patterns into their conceptual frameworks in the field. In the sections that follow we draw on behavioral economics and evolutionary psychology to sketch out potential directions for a more interdisciplinary approach to policy studies that incorporates such approaches. In this regard we are similar to Somit and Peterson (2003a), advocating for a more prominent role for evolutionary theory. Where we differ, however, is in our emphasis on using the tenets of evolutionary psychology to inform existing theories of policy change.

The bottom line is that the rational choice model, for all its service to supporting policy theory, is not only descriptively unrealistic but incomplete. In the remainder of this chapter we discuss several well-established patterns in human decision making that we believe have the most relevance for explaining change in the policy process and policy decision making. The list is by no means complete, nor is it exhaustive. Rather, we believe it provides good starting points for retesting existing theories as well as building new conceptual frameworks. Following this section, we discuss the role of evolutionary psychology as a potentially fruitful avenue for theory building, with specific application to crime policy. Theoretical and empirical developments being made outside mainstream political and policy science offer important insights for understanding the policy process; we believe it behooves policy scholars to pay attention to such developments.

Policy Change, Irrationality, and Social Utility

Very simply, to become an issue, an idea must reach the governmental agenda. In Chapter 2 we discussed theories put forth by policy scholars about how an idea becomes an issue. For Baumgartner and Jones (1993/2009), agenda setting is a relatively stable process, with occasional punctuations usually sparked by a change in policy image. As noted in Chapter 4, for Kingdon (1995), policy change is the result of the merging of the three "streams" and the opening of a "policy window," the latter of which depend on the ability of a policy entrepreneur to successfully build support for a particular policy narrative. At the heart of each of these explanations is a focus on policy definition. As issues are redefined, they increase or decrease the likelihood of policymakers addressing them (see Stone 2002). Despite the explanatory power of these frameworks, questions remain: What causes people to pay attention to particular issues? Why do people tend to react strongly to some policy images rather than others? Why do issues that are defined as social dilemmas do better than issues defined purely in instrumental terms?

Baumgartner and Jones's punctuated equilibrium and Kingdon's streams approach do not address these questions. Instead, their interest is in describing macro-level policy change (Wood and Vedlitz 2007). What policy scholars need is a micro-level model of policy change that focuses on how individuals process policy information, particularly relating to policy image. B. Dan Wood and his colleagues have attempted to create such a model. Of particular interest is the finding that people tend to conform to the majority opinion. When presented with information about the predominant view of others on a particular issue, people tend to adjust their views to match those of their peers (Wood and Vedlitz 2007; see also Wood and Doan 2003). As such, we would expect people to moderate their individual policy attitudes to match those of their surroundings. From a rationalist perspective, this seems illogical. Why should the views of others matter when evaluating public policy? From the standpoint of social psychology and neuroscience, however, it makes perfect sense.

People tend to be hypersensitive to what others think of them, particularly within their own group (Cialdini and Goldstein 2004). In fact, such sensitivity goes beyond emotional reactions to include physiological change. Using brain imaging software, Eisenberger, Lieberman, and Williams (2003) show that social exclusion results in neural activity similar to that experienced during physical pain. That is, the brain processes sensations experienced by social exclusion as being analogous to those experienced during physical trauma. As others have commented on this evidence, repercussions stemming from the loss of an existing social bond are likely to be perceived as damaging to individual fitness, as are decisions to forego immediate tangible incentives (Panksepp 2003). Renowned sociobiologist Edward O. Wilson (2012) argues that such sensitivity is in fact perfectly rational from an evolutionary perspective. He argues that behavioral traits are in part the result of individual- *and* group-level selection; our long history as hunter-gatherers operating in small groups with scarce resources led to the selection of traits designed to promote the well-being of the group. Leading anthropologist Christopher Boehm makes a similar argument. Drawing on cross-cultural evidence, Boehm (2012) suggests our tendency to cooperate (e.g., act irrationality) is motivated by our strong desire to preserve our reputation within the group; we want to avoid shame and ostracism from other group members. What does this tell us about policy change? For one thing, it suggests that policy entrepreneurs able to cast an issue as a violation of norms of fairness toward in-group members or as unjustly benefiting members of a perceived out-group are likely to gain significant public attention. For models of policy change, this suggests that policy proposals often gain traction not because of their policy appeal but rather because others find them appealing. Policymakers who are able to craft proposals perceived as enjoying mass support are therefore at a distinct advantage.

The "policy sciences" were intended to improve upon the quality of public policy as a way of improving upon the human condition. To understand the human condition, however, requires an understanding of what makes people happy. Reviewing the extant literature in neuroscience, Rose McDermott (2004) writes that it is not material well-being or "economic indicators" such as income that produce happiness. Instead, happiness is related to what McDermott describes as "social support" (2004, 701). What does this mean for public policy? According to McDermott, "if happiness derives from social support, government should place less emphasis on incomes and more on employment and job programs, encouraging leisure activities . . . by supporting after-school programs and public parks—and supporting marriage and other family relationships" (701).

Humans are social creatures, deriving satisfaction from interactions with others. People tend to shy away from expressing preferences that are at odds with the rest of the group. And as Boehm (2012) documents, this tendency is a human universal and predates modern society. In fact, people will often incur material costs to maximize social benefits (see Smith 2006b). A simple way to maximize social benefits is fitting in with the group. The result is often that revealed preferences are at odds with private preferences. Kuran (1995) describes this tendency as "preference falsification." Particularly in public settings, people tend to withhold their true preferences to maintain a favorable reputation and avoid social ostracism. Rob Kurzban, an evolutionary psychologist, takes this a step further, suggesting that such irrationality is the result of the evolved "modularity" of the human mind (2010). As Kurzban proposes, we have multiple selves operating semi-independently. Our expressed preferences are dependent upon the context of the situation. In social situations, Kurzban suggests, it makes sense to go along with a group even if it means lying or deceiving others, as long as such behavior results in a social benefit. According to Kurzban, the mind may not even be aware of the lie. The evolutionary pressures of small group living put preserving a favorable reputation above all else. This means following the group even when it means making a poor or inaccurate decision. For Kurzban, it makes sense that the mind would not even be aware of such inconsistency; accurate information is "encapsulated" in another module not required for responding to the situation at hand (2010, 43).

Kuran's notion of preference falsification is significant when considered in the context of Baumgartner and Jones's punctuated equilibrium. Kuran's basic argument is that people tend to have an intrinsic utility (their true preference), a reputational utility (the result of how others will react to one's true preference), and an expressive utility (the utility of expressing one's true preference publicly). In a public setting, the choice between maximizing reputational utility or expressive utility tends toward the former. However, Kuran notes that this tendency leads to "hidden opposition to positions that enjoy vast public support" (1995, 335). As more people express an opinion, the pressure to maximize one's reputational utility, at the expense of intrinsic utility, increases.[2] However, if it is revealed that what most people prefer in private is shared by others, there is a potential for a "social explosion" (335). The premise behind punctuated equilibrium is that a change in policy image can cause a sudden change in policy. The theoretical basis for this sudden change most likely rests with people's willingness to maximize their expressive utility. Baumgartner and Jones give the example of nuclear scientists who were privately skeptical about the safety standards of nuclear power. Only after the Three Mile Island accident were they willing to express these reservations publicly. In other words, once the majority opinion shifted to be more in line with their private preferences, they were willing to maximize their intrinsic utility.

Kuran's work also speaks to Kingdon's (1995) model of policy change. To achieve significant change, specialists working in the policy stream must be able to recognize the opening of a policy window in the problem or political stream. The latter stream is determined in large part by public opinion, or what Kingdon has called the "national mood." Preference falsification is potentially problematic for policy specialists in two ways: 1) the national mood may not reflect the public's true preference for policy change, leading to unwanted policy (reputational utility is more beneficial than expressive utility); and 2) the national mood is highly volatile and can change without any action on the part of the policy specialist (a focusing event increases the costs of reputational utility, allowing for maximization of expressive utility).

For evolutionary psychologists such as Kurzban, the tendency to engage in preference falsification is hardwired into our brains. People tend to value being part of a group as much as or more than tangible benefits they may receive from a particular policy. Existing models of policy change, however, tend to rely solely on such benefits or environmental causes. Recognizing that preference falsification is endogenous to policy change will improve our understanding of why sudden and rapid policy change occurs.

Policy (All) Decision Making Is Emotional

The previous section suggests that human decision making in many situations is not rational and perhaps not even adaptive, particularly if decision making is made in a group context. If decision making is not rational, what is it? The most likely answer is that it is intuitive and emotional as well as (not instead of) rational.

Psychologist and Nobel laureate Daniel Kahneman's work (with Amos Tversky) on decision-making heuristics and biases is well known and probably most often cited by policy scholars when discussing the role of framing effects (see Kahneman and Tversky 1984; Tversky and Kahneman 1981). In *Thinking, Fast and Slow*, Kahneman (2011) draws on evidence accumulated since his early work with Tversky to explain these systematic deviations from rationality. Essentially, the argument is that human decision making is ruled by two distinct mental systems: "System 1" and "System 2." What Kahneman labels "System 2" is akin to the rational model; it is slow and deliberative, carefully weighing all alternatives. System 1, by contrast, is automatic and intuitive. As Kahneman explains, System 1 "operates automatically and quickly, with little or no effort and no sense of voluntary control" (20); System 1 is often the culprit behind the biases so well documented by Kahneman and his colleagues and is likely the source of maladaptive decision making identified by scholars like Bryan Jones. Avoidance of such biases or maladaptive thinking requires the activation of System 2, or rational thought. However, System 2 requires effort, and "one of its main characteristics is laziness, a reluctance to invest more effort than is strictly necessary" (31). Even when activated, System 2 does not impose complete rationality, but is often influenced by the intuitive leaps made by System 1. As Kahneman puts it, "the thoughts and actions that System 2 believes it has chosen are often guided by the figure at the center of the story, System 1" (2011, 31).

Kahneman's work essentially puts to bed any notions of a rational consideration of all alternatives or a rational evaluation of policy narratives. In fact, it would be difficult to compose a more damning critique of the role of rationality, as traditionally defined, in everyday decision making. Instead, System 1 is clearly suggestive of a direct and powerful role for intuitions and emotions in decision making. Perhaps the most compelling evidence for an emotional basis for decision making comes from leading neuroscientist Joseph LeDoux. Focusing on the amygdala as the emotional center for affects associated with fear, LeDoux (1996, 2002) finds that neural connections flowing from the cortical areas to the amygdala are weaker than connections flowing from the amygdala to the cortical regions of the brain. In other words, whereas the cortex and neocortex are assumed to represent the cognitive, reasoning portion of the brain—serving as a filter to guide rational decision making—the amygdala, representing a focal point for affective motivations, is capable of overriding conscious, rational processes. Stated differently, emotional processes exert a stronger influence over the process of discerning the context of external stimuli than do rational processes. Indeed, as LeDoux and others (see Damasio 1994; Fessler 2002) have observed, this process often occurs unconsciously (e.g., Kahneman's System 1), furthering the argument that emotions serve as powerful behavioral motivations in human decision-making processes.

As further evidence on this point, we turn to the work of clinical and political psychologist Drew Weston. Drawing on survey analysis, lab experiments, and fMRI brain scans of potential voters, Weston shows that people simply do not process political information rationally. Or, as Weston puts it, the "dispassionate mind bears no relation to how the mind and brain actually work" (2007, ix). To take one example from Weston's work, strong partisans, whether Democrat or Republican, ignore negative information, or information that would make their candidate appear inconsistent even if it is factually accurate. Moreover, such information is processed in areas of the brain primarily associated with regulating emotional states. More generally, Weston shows that emotional narratives are particularly compelling when trying to convince voters, because, as Weston writes, voters process information through "networks of association" (3), and facts simply do not make for good or easy to remember narratives. The facts surrounding any particular issue tend to be static. What is malleable is the image of an issue. Weston documents survey after survey showing that feelings toward particular candidates are much better predictors of voter choice than perceptions of more rational qualities such as candidate competence or stances on particular issues.[3] Feelings and perceptions are exactly the very items political strategists attempt to manipulate and control on a day-to-day basis during a campaign. Similarly, policy actors (e.g., the president, legislators, or the media) attempt to shape attitudes toward particular policies by constructing different narratives to describe who benefits and who will pay the costs (see Schneider and Ingram 1997). An "emotional brain," as suggested by Weston (and LeDoux), indicates such efforts will have a profound impact on how people view the acceptability of a policy, regardless of the facts.

So what do Kahneman, LeDoux, and Weston have to do with public policy? Take as an example the two dominant frameworks of policy analysis, cost-benefit analysis and welfare economics, which are designed with the explicit intention of removing emotion from the decision-making processes. Policy decisions should be made according to the estimated costs and benefits of available alternatives, with the most efficient decision (the one that minimizes costs and maximizes benefits) being implemented. From a rationalist perspective, cost-benefit analysis makes perfect sense. From a neurological perspective, it is at odds with how the brain actually works. Rather than focusing on costs and benefits, or economic rationality, the brain processes information in such a way that is more in line with "emotional rationality" (McDermott 2004).[4] Not only do emotions affect decision making, they tend to guide it, often with improvements in the overall outcome. The basic assumption of conceptual frameworks like welfare economics, institutional rational choice, the Tiebout model, and their prescriptive policy derivatives such as school choice, is that people are rational actors and will behave in ways that maximize their own economic self-interest.

The theory of emotional rationality suggests this is the exception rather than the norm.

In short, emotional triggers drown out rational considerations. McDermott writes, "Emotion remains endogenous to rationality itself" (2004, 693). A purely rationalist approach to policy analysis is essentially asking the human brain to override itself, or at the very least to put forth considerable effort. If emotions result in bad policy decisions, such an approach might be warranted. But as it turns out, this is not the case. Humans are capable of making intelligent decisions. As Damasio's (1994) research on patients with acute brain damage has demonstrated, people lacking areas of the brain associated with emotional responses are unable to engage in favorable social interactions—often exhibiting higher levels of unemployment and divorce. Work by Boehm and Kurzban also allude to the benefits of being guided by emotions in social situations.

In short, the fast-emerging consensus that emotions and intuition guide decision making casts considerable doubt on the assumptions of "classic" policy models. For example, the assumption of the Tiebout model is that people make mobility decisions based on the quality of service being provided—that people make rational decisions based on policy outputs. The same argument holds for proponents of school choice—parental decisions about which school to send their children to are based on school outputs such as test scores. As we discussed at length in Chapter 3, the assumptions of the Tiebout model and school choice models break down when subjected to empirical scrutiny. But what is the theoretical and empirical basis for this disconnect? The neurological role of emotions gives policy scholars an endogenous variable that will boost the explanatory power of policy decision models. Policy specialists hold that position alternatives in the context of emotional appeals are more likely to find receptive venues than if such alternatives are discussed in purely instrumental or rational terms. As Weston (2007) has shown, politicians who cater to emotions have more electoral success than those who focus on policy details, or what would be considered the "rational" part of public policy. We do not deny that emotional rationality opens the door for demagoguery on the part of politicians and policy specialists. But understanding that the potential for such demagoguery exists is likely the first step in understanding ways to correct for it. To do so requires a neurological understanding of how the brain processes incoming information, whether that information is policy related or not.

People do not make decisions based on policy outputs; they make decisions on the basis of emotions and the preferences of their group, however they define "group." For some, this might mean conforming to the preferences of their neighbors; for others the group might be the local PTA, a bowling club, or a reading group. That emotions guide the decision-making process has important implications for at least two major areas of policy scholarship: 1) agenda setting and 2) policy analysis. Models of policy change continue to be criticized on the grounds that they are not predictive. Yes, significant policy change can occur because of a focusing event or the merging of the three streams, but when is this likely to happen? The problem is that these models tend to be couched in a rationalist framework. If the frame of reference were shifted from economic rationality to emotional rationality, we argue, the predictive power of such models would increase. People make decisions not devoid of emotions or in a vacuum but rather with a very strong awareness of what those around them will think about their decisions and with a very powerful emotional base.

An Evolutionary Approach to Policy Science

Why is the brain wired to give social pressure and a concern for reputation within a group such prominence in decision making? Why are people so sensitive to the perceptions of others? The basic assumption of evolutionary psychology is that the human mind is a product of evolutionary pressures. The brain evolved to solve adaptive problems faced by our hunter-gatherer ancestors in the environment of evolutionary adaptation, or EEA (Cosmides and Tooby 1992; see also Barkow, Cosmides, and Tooby 1992). Individual preferences are a function of *both* the environment and what Cosmides and Tooby have called evolved "psychological mechanisms" (1992, 165). A main problem of the EEA was a reliable source of food. The scarcity of food resources required group cooperation and sharing to survive. A cognitive by-product of this environment was a strong tendency toward cooperation with one's in-group and a desire to maintain a favorable reputation among other group members. Scarcity of resources also created a hypersensitivity to fairness norms, a tendency that Boehm (2012) shows applies across cultures and attributes to the emergence of shaming tactics for violations of such norms. A group member who hoarded food in the EEA was essentially trading a public good for his or her own selfish ends. Because such behavior likely meant death for another group member, people developed a strong disposition for detecting cheaters in social situations, or what Cosmides and Tooby (1992) label a cheater-detection module.

Within political science, the framework of evolutionary psychology, particularly the notion of cheater-detection, is gaining traction as a useful tool for explaining political behavior. Alford and Hibbing (2004) propose that people are actually "wary cooperators." People will cooperate when others cooperate but will cease cooperation when others defect and will incur a cost to punish others for noncooperation. Alford and Hibbing further suggest that the model of the wary cooperator has important policy implications. Take, for example, compliance with tax policy. The wary cooperator model posits that we pay our taxes only because we assume others are doing the same (Alford and Hibbing 2004, 711). If it is revealed that others are cheating on their taxes by not paying, and getting away with it, the result is likely to be widespread disgust with government (this also fits with Kuran's model of preference falsification). The same holds for perceptions of welfare policy. Why does an image of a welfare recipient not actively seeking employment provoke such strong public reactions? Because such an image sets off our cheater-detection module—this is someone who is accepting benefits without incurring a cost. The "welfare to work" motto of the 1996 Welfare Reform Act passed by the federal government was most likely an attempt to allay fears that the policy was simply benefiting free riders (Rubin 2002, 196); the motto served to ease the reaction of our cheater-detection module. Humans seem to possess a strong disposition toward cooperation but also a high level of skepticism about others. From an evolutionary perspective, this is a highly adaptive strategy (Orbell et al. 2004). On the one hand, it leads to optimal outcomes, while at the same time preventing suboptimal outcomes as a result of being played for a sucker. In fact, the cheater-detection module allows humans to remember cheaters at a higher rate than they remember altruists (Chiappe et al. 2004), suggesting that strong reactions to the image of the lazy welfare recipient or the non-taxpayer are likely to be long-lasting.

If adaptive pressures on the mind produced behavioral outcomes and expressed preferences similar to those predicted by the rational actor model, this research could be ignored. Similarly, if adaptive rationality led to suboptimal outcomes, the evolutionary psychology framework could be dismissed. But as Cosmides and Tooby (1994, 329) have discussed, evolved modules, such as the cheater-detection module, actually lead to decisions that are "better than rational." For example, Gerd Gigerenzer and his colleagues have repeatedly demonstrated that people using "fast and frugal" decision-making heuristics are quite capable of making optimal decisions (Gigerenzer and Todd 1999a; see also Gigerenzer and Selton 2002). The reason is that adaptive pressures have selected for optimal cognitive mechanisms, which deviate sharply from the assumption of complete information in the rational-comprehensive model. These mechanisms are designed to efficiently and effectively solve social dilemmas, and they have important relevance for solving policy problems.

A prime example of adaptive rationality in action comes from the work of Elinor Ostrom and her colleagues on common-pool resource dilemmas. In the case of a common-pool resource, the rational actor model predicts an overuse of the resource. From a welfare economics perspective, to correct for such inefficiency requires external intervention. As we noted in Chapter 3, these dilemmas can actually be solved through mechanisms other than those predicted by welfare economics or cost-benefit analyses; simple solutions such as face-to-face communication and the threat of punishment are enough to prevent overuse and ensure cooperation (Ostrom, Walker, and Gardner 1992, 1994; see also Ostrom 2005). The question that is left unanswered, however, is: Why are such mechanisms so effective? Evolutionary psychology and the theory of the "wary cooperator" provide an answer to this question. Face-to-face communication creates a sense of group identity, which if violated is likely to lead to social ostracism. Adaptive psychological mechanisms have created behavioral predispositions that guard against ostracism-type behavior.

As an example ingrained in the minds of policy scholars, take March's (1994) "logic of appropriateness." According to March's theory, people tend to do what is perceived as appropriate for the situation. That is, they base their behavior on existing institutional culture and norms. Essential to this argument is an ability to read others' expectations and gauge what is acceptable and not acceptable within an organization. At a very basic level this is about the ability to fit within a group and identify with other group members. Evolutionary psychology and the theory of the "wary cooperator" indicate that humans possess a strong capacity for doing just that. In fact, the ability to mind-read has been found to be evolutionarily adaptive and fits within the broader framework of "Machiavellian intelligence" (Orbell et al. 2004, 14; see also Whiten and Byrne 1997). The EEA mandated an ability to join groups and sustain group membership. A failure to conform to group norms meant social ostracism and most likely death. Doing what is appropriate is about figuring out how to be part of the in-group and successfully navigating in-group relationships.

Biological and cognitive factors also provide enormous explanatory power to everyday policy decisions. To take one (overused) example, consider the decision to contribute to a public good such as National Public Radio (NPR). From a purely rational perspective, at the individual level, no one should contribute; they should free ride off others' contributions. But if everyone free rides, no one will contribute. The reality is that people do contribute and often can be cajoled into contributing through emotional appeals or social pressure. Why? The pressure to conform to the majority opinion, the fear of being labeled a "free rider" or not conforming to social norms in a public setting increase the likelihood of a negative reaction from one's peers.[5] Consider other donation drives that attempt to prime the emotion of shame by asking for donations over the phone or in person at the local grocery store. The idea is to put people in a situation that favors an emotional response, most likely a generous response. Behavioral predispositions against violating group norms are the result of evolutionary pressures and exert a strong influence on public preferences.

Knowing that people are adept at solving social dilemmas could also help to explain why people react to certain policy images in the way that they do. For example, Nelson (1984) argues that child abuse was able to reach the policy agenda only after it was redefined as a social dilemma. Similarly, the issue of providing education to children with disabilities only reached the national agenda after it was defined as a social issue (Cremins 1983). From a rationalist perspective, the framing of the issue is irrelevant. When issues are redefined as social issues with powerful emotional narratives, however, people are better able to understand them and are more open to addressing them (as Weston would predict). Although we acknowledge that policymakers can use this information to manipulate policy images in such a way as to trick citizens, we believe such an approach is still useful. In fact, as Paul Rubin (2002, 164–165) writes, this social element is built into policy decision making. Rather than relying on policy details, elected officials regularly bring in individuals affected by a policy or issue to give their personal testimony. As Rubin notes, from a rationalist perspective this does not make sense, nor should it affect the final decision. The details of the policy have not changed. Personal testimony, however, particularly on highly salient issues, shows people "identifiable" individuals who are affected by the policy (2002, 164). For those watching, the policy image has changed from an abstract problem to one with social and emotional implications. The result is that people will give more weight to one side of the argument, even though the details have not changed. Consider the effect of Ryan White on the image of AIDS as a national problem, or of celebrities testifying on Capitol Hill, such as Michael J. Fox testifying on the need for stem-cell research to help cure Parkinson's and other diseases, or actress Jada Pinkett Smith (married to actor Will Smith, who was seated right behind his wife) on human trafficking. These "identifiable" individuals focus attention and create the opportunity for a change in policy image, which according to Baumgartner and Jones (1993/2009) increases the likelihood of a change in policy venue and the potential for a policy punctuation. When viewed through the lens of evolutionary psychology and the neuroscience of emotion, this potential makes perfect sense.

That policy images can be manipulated to serve selfish ends also has theoretical roots in behavioral economics, specifically prospect theory, the underpinnings of which are rooted in evolutionary psychology (McDermott, Fowler, and Smirnov 2008). Kahneman and Tversky's (1978) widely cited article on this topic essentially gives policy advocates a blueprint for manipulating policy images to promote or hinder policy success (see also Kahneman and Tversky 1984; Tversky and Kahneman 1981). Prospect theory states that people will be risk-averse when faced with gains and risk-seeking when faced with losses. What Kahneman and Tversky demonstrated is that preference for a particular policy solution depends on whether that solution is framed in terms of gains or losses. When presented with a health crisis, subjects favored a solution that minimized risk when the solution was framed in terms of "saving" lives, but favored a riskier approach when the solution was framed in terms of the number of people who would die. Although mathematically the outcome of each solution set was the same, subjects reversed their preferences due to the framing of the solutions.[6]

When the risks and benefits of a particular policy are defined in social and emotional terms, they tend to be given more weight than in statistical models. The result is potentially inefficient policy. A story depicting the ability of a single individual to cheat the system is most likely to lead to calls for more oversight mechanisms, despite the fact that the costs of such mechanisms are likely to outweigh the benefits. Such biases in decision making have important policy implications. Rubin (2002, 175) documents the fact that during the 2000 U.S. presidential election, Vice President Al Gore attempted to counter then governor George Bush's argument to privatize Social Security by appealing to people's general tendency toward the status quo and loss aversion. As president, George W. Bush once again made a similar push for privatizing Social Security, and again, the tendency to overvalue loss and a preference for the status quo seems to have prevented such an overhaul, regardless of the potential benefits. In short, the adaptive rationality framework provides important insights for both policy scholars and policy elites seeking to better understand how people react to policy proposals and solutions.

Putting It All Together

Public policy is an aggregation of human decisions. But what do we know about the human decision-making process? From a public policy perspective, not much. We assume policymakers have preferences and will act on those preferences. The dominant theoretical paradigms within public policy (e.g., public choice, bounded rationality, welfare economics) tend to take preferences as a given; policymakers are assumed to be self-interested decision makers. Deviations from such predictions are assumed to be the result of environmental constraints such as institutional rules and norms. The last few decades have seen widespread rejection of the rational choice model on multiple grounds: 1) it generates untestable assumptions (Green and Shapiro 1994); 2) observed behavior in social dilemmas deviates widely from economic rationality (see Ariely 2009; Camerer, Lowenstein, and Rabin 2004; Kahneman 2011); and 3) what is viewed as "overcooperation" in social dilemmas makes sense from an evolutionary psychology perspective (Boehm 2012; Field 2004; Kurzban 2010). And though attempts have been made to discard the rational actor model in public policy, such attempts do not stray too far from rationalist assumptions.

Bryan Jones (2001, 2003) has pushed for a renewed emphasis on bounded rationality as a model for human decision making. Although Jones agrees with evolutionary psychologists that bounded rationality is a product of human evolution, he seems less interested in explaining why people deviate from the rational actor model than in redesigning institutions to account for such deviations. For Jones, preferences are taken as given, whether they conform to bounded rationality or complete rationality, and the means for achieving more efficient policy is through the manipulation of the "task environment." The task environment is akin to institutional rules and norms. Scant attention is given to the manner in which people are "bounded." Instead, the focus is on how institutional design can correct for cognitive limitations. As Jones (2001) puts it, "People can make better decisions, individually and collectively, because of institutions" (190).

Political scientist John Orbell and his colleagues (2004) have distinguished between "rationality in action" and "rationality in design." Rationality in action is grounded in the assumptions of the rational-comprehensive model, whereas rationality in design is based on the assumption that natural selection favored the development of certain cognitive mechanisms that improve the prospect of group living. Although Jones departs from rationality in action, he is unwilling to accept the premise of rationality in design, or adaptive rationality. The "task" environment is essentially an argument that decision making is the result of exogenous factors. Endogenous factors are taken as a given. Evolutionary psychology starts from a different premise. People are not bounded; rather, the human mind evolved certain mechanisms for solving adaptive problems. These mechanisms allow people to make good or appropriate decisions when faced with a social dilemma, decisions not normally predicted by rationalist models. Unfortunately, little effort has been made to incorporate endogenous variables relating to cognitive and biological mechanisms into models of policy change (for an exception, see John 2003).

Even though policy scholars have long been critical of the rational actor model (see Stone 2002), these critiques often fail to provide theoretical justification for why the rational framework should be rejected or what should replace it. Bryan Jones deserves considerable credit for taking a more interdisciplinary approach to understanding organizational behavior and policy decision making, utilizing empirical and theoretical models based in biology and cognitive psychology. Other policy approaches, however, have been less successful. For example, postpositivist approaches seem less interested in developing a unifying framework than in preserving the notion that reality, or at least political reality, is socially constructed. Such an approach does little to advance our understanding of how people process policy information. In fact, constructivism, hermeneutics, and intersubjectivity deny that any unifying framework is possible. Under these models, humans lack any universal preferences or tendencies. As the discussion in this chapter has demonstrated, people do not come to a policy problem with an empty set of preferences. Rather, human cognitive capacities are a product of human evolution. Theoretical insights from evolutionary psychology and empirical evidence from behavioral economics and neuroscience give policy scholars a foundation for how the public will react to certain variations in issue definition.

To be sure, cognitive approaches to policy change are creeping into the field of policy studies. Work by Leach and Sabatier (2005) holds promise for moving beyond strictly rational or environmental explanations of policy change. Utilizing both rational choice and social psychology, Leach and Sabatier identify factors that are critical to fostering and maintaining trust among policy elites. In particular, perceptions of fairness and legitimacy are better able to explain interpersonal trust than past policy outcomes. As a whole, however, policy studies appears stuck in what Cosmides and Tooby have described as the "Standard Social Science Model" (SSSM). Exogenous factors dominate models of the policy process; no attention is given to endogenous factors such as biological or psychological mechanisms. As such, the current state of policy decision-making research is largely descriptive, with little predictive power. Leach and Sabatier's work is important because it attempts to provide a testable theory regarding the formation and disintegration of policy subsystems—one that is balanced between exogenous and endogenous variables. Perhaps the greatest advance has been made by Albert Somit and Steven Peterson. As far we can tell, Somit and Peterson (2003a) offer the only book-length manuscript attempting to directly apply evolutionary theory to the study of public policy, specifically how evolutionary theory can be used to improve existing policies. Somit and Peterson (2003b) are much more explicit and direct about the need to jettison the SSSM. To better design public policy, and therefore better address individual and social problems, policy scholars should adopt what Somit and Peterson (2003b) describe as the "evolutionary model" (4). The authors draw heavily from the work of Cosmides and Tooby, arguing that good public policy starts with a solid understanding of how our evolutionary past constrains our modern preferences and behavior. Although such work is certainly a step in the right direction, we argue that more needs to be done to merge the assumptions of evolutionary psychology with existing theories of policy change; Somit and Peterson are less interested in theory building than in applying the evolutionary psychology framework to the design of public policy.

One of the main drawbacks of policy research is that it lacks coherent theory-building (Sabatier 2007a). When theory such as policy stages or policy typologies is criticized, rarely is a replacement theory put forth. The preceding discussion suggests that the raw materials for constructing replacement theories are readily available; they are just located outside of the fields of policy studies and political science. The main criticism of punctuated equilibrium and policy streams is that they fail to predict policy change. Emotional or adaptive rationality reverses models of decision making founded on rationalist assumptions. Emotions do matter, and they tend to operate a priori to rational thought. Public policies require the support of the electorate to be changed, maintained, or even adopted. Taking preferences as a given, as is done in rationalist approaches, leads to incorrect inferences about public policy preferences. Moreover, it is limited to a single set of covariates. Environmental variables such as institutional rules do explain a lot of what is known about policy change, but they provide only one side of the explanation. If we open the "black box," it is likely that we will increase the explanatory power of existing models of policy change as well as other policy-related models. For example, compliance with public policy tends to be grounded in perceptions of trust (Tyler 1990, 2001; Scholz 1998). Perceptions of trust are in large part based on perceptions of fairness, which according to evolutionary psychology are a function of evolutionary pressures in the EEA. Only by including nonrational, endogenous considerations such as emotions are we able to build a complete model of policy compliance. Simply showing that rationalist approaches are wrong is not enough. What is needed is a theory that can explain and predict how people will respond to policy images and outcomes. Such a theory is likely to be interdisciplinary in nature, with a strong emphasis on evolutionary psychology, neuroscience, and behavioral economics.

An Application to Criminal Justice Policy

What the preceding discussion suggests is that the power of conceptual models in public policy can be significantly improved by accounting for emotions and behavioral predispositions stemming from our evolutionary past. In this section we put such notions to the test. Specifically, we discuss three important insights from behavioral economics and evolutionary psychology in the context of criminal justice policy: 1) a tendency to seek retribution for unfair behavior, 2) the occurrence of criminal behavior, and 3) the inefficiency of jury trials.

First, regarding the tendency to punish others for unfair or uncooperative behavior, from social psychology we know that social norms have a strong effect on individual behavior (Cialdini and Trost 1998). People conform to the expectations of others, particularly when their behavior will be made public (Cialdini and Goldstein 2004; Whatley et al. 1999). The strength of a particular norm can be assessed by the level of compliance, particularly in the absence of others, as well as the degree to which others are willing to punish the noncompliant. We previously noted evidence supporting the notion that evolutionary pressures support the development of a mental module for detecting cheaters, particularly violators of fairness norms. Experimental and neurological evidence also indicates a strong desire to punish such cheaters.

In laboratory settings, people exhibit a strong desire to punish others for unfair behavior, even at substantial cost to themselves.[7] In fact, this tendency is so strong that it is evident in third parties, or individuals unaffected by the outcome (Fehr and Fischbacher 2004); persists even when allowing for a substantial increase in monetary stakes (Cameron 1999; Fehr, Fischbacher, and Tougareva 2002); and extends across cultures (Henrich et al. 2001). The desire to punish also has strong biological roots. Brain activity associated with unfair offers in two-person bargaining scenarios tends to be located in the anterior insula, an area of the brain considered to be the source of negative emotional states (Sanfey et al. 2003, 1756). The decision to punish, however, is reflected in areas of the brain commonly associated with anticipated satisfaction (de Quervain et al. 2004). Notably, this brain activity occurs only when subjects are allowed to "effectively punish," where punishment reduces the payoff of the noncooperator (de Quervain et al. 2004, 1254). In short, people tend to have a very negative emotional reaction to unfair behavior but a very positive reaction to punishment. Such anticipated satisfaction explains why individuals are willing to incur the short-term costs of punishing free riders with full knowledge that there will be no future payoffs for the punishing individual.[8]

This extreme sensitivity, both behaviorally and neurologically, to injustice begins to explain why people are quite willing to file grievances for even the smallest deviation from what they perceive as fair, perhaps also explaining why people are willing to go to court over what may seem like trivial matters. Others have also noted that despite its ineffectiveness as a deterrent mechanism, the public remains quite supportive of the death penalty, a position that defies rational explanation based on outcomes or efficiency but fits with evolutionary theory favoring a strong preference for swift and immediate justice (Alford and Hibbing 2004, 711). The desire to punish for violation of fairness norms can also be an efficient policy mechanism, because it can solve common-pool-resource dilemmas in the absence of an external authority (Ostrom, Gardner, and Walker 1994). The nature of punishment also seems to matter. Xiao and Houser (2011) demonstrate that "public punishment" (punishment is known to all group members) is significantly more effective at boosting contribution rates in a public goods game than private punishment (in which only the individual being punished is aware of the punishment).

Second, regarding criminal behavior, that evolutionary pressures favor a cheater-detection module is suggestive of a long lineage of cheating or criminal-type behavior. Criminologists are now beginning to accept evolutionary explanations for the occurrence of criminal behavior. In the EEA, high status was a means to reproductive success, and one way to gain status was to dominate other group members. That status-seeking is particularly prominent among males (Boehm 1999) suggests that males are more prone to dominating tendencies such as physical aggression (Ellis 2003). Criminologist Anthony Walsh writes: "Non-evolutionary theories cannot account for why men everywhere and always com-mit far more criminal and antisocial acts than females" (2006, 255). Lee Ellis (2003) provides further evidence of the hormonal and neurological basis for criminal behavior, particularly among males, and that criminal-like behavior can actually have reproductive benefits. On a less extreme scale, that people tend to cooperate in social dilemmas also presents an opportunity for deception (Walsh 2006). In fact, in laboratory settings people tend to be more concerned with appearing fair than with actually behaving fairly (Smith 2006b), which some have labeled "Machiavellian intelligence" (see Whiten and Byrne 1997; Orbell et al. 2004). Humans possess a strong tendency to cooperate, but also a strong tendency to exploit others' cooperation if such exploitation can go undetected, a strategy that would have been advantageous in an environment of small groups and scarce resources.

Finally, consider the method in which justice is delivered. We noted previously in the chapter that biases in information processing result in more weight being given to social or emotional cues, particularly when policies are associated with identifiable individuals (Rubin 2002). As Paul Rubin (2002) points out, jury trials are the essence of incorporating "identifiable" individuals and present jurors with the extraordinary task of attempting to make fully rational decisions despite strong behavioral predispositions to the contrary. In a jury setting the identifiable individual is sitting in the same room as the jury and in relatively close proximity. Such a setting, Rubin suggests, essentially ensures that less weight will be given to statistical models, with an overreliance placed on personal testimony. In a sense, jurors are put to the ultimate test; they are placed in an environment that stimulates neurological activity shaped by evolutionary pressures to be the best response to social dilemmas, and they are asked to ignore such influences. And in fact Rubin (2002, 176–180) argues that such jury bias can actually lead to overcompensation for damage payments. Rubin argues that because jury settings ignore social and biological pressures, they create an environment ripe for bad policy decisions.

Conclusion: Answering the Call for New Theory

Our argument, like so many others in economics and psychology, is that the empirical record of the rational-comprehensive model of decision making falls woefully short in both explanatory and predictive powers. A quick glance through the literature in economics (the disciplinary foundation for rational choice) makes it abundantly clear that the rational choice model of behavior is no longer viable. Over the last twenty years, numerous scholars have written about the need for better policy theory (Sabatier 1991b, 1999b, 2007a, 2007b; Hill 1997); some even calling for the incorporation of evolutionary theory (see John 2003; Somit and Peterson 2003a, 2003b). Though progress has been made in terms of criticizing initial attempts at theory, such as policy stages and policy typologies (see Chapter 2), a unifying approach to policy change is still lacking. In this chapter we suggest several new directions for policy theory, especially for human decision-making models that make use of insights from neuroscience, behavioral economics, and evolutionary psychology.[9] Several consistent themes emerging from these fields seem to have clear implications for policy theory. First, perceptions of others matter. The human brain evolved in an environment of scarce resources that necessitated group living for survival. As such, people tend to be highly sensitive to fairness norms and highly cognizant of their reputations with others. This translates into a strong desire to conform to the majority opinion as well as a strong skepticism about policies perceived to favor cheaters. Second, people do not process information in a manner consistent with the rational actor model that serves as the basis for many existing theories of public policy. Instead, people rely on heuristics and particularly emotions. Despite rationalists' fear that emotions result in suboptimal decision making, physiological and experimental evidence indicates that people do reason using emotional and other heuristics, and that such reasoning tends to result in outcomes that are "better than rational." Third, an overreliance on exogenous or environmental variables ignores the powerful influence of endogenous variables on information processing. Advances made in the fields of neuroscience, cognitive psychology, behavioral economics, and evolutionary psychology contribute to our understanding of how the public reacts to policy processes and outcomes. They also give policymakers insight into how to increase public awareness of an issue. For example, images that activate the cheater-detection module can potentially be utilized by policymakers seeking to increase opposition to a particular policy.

An interdisciplinary approach to public policy theory is not new. A generation ago Herbert Simon (1985) advocated a more psychological understanding of policymaking theory, and more than sixty years ago Harold Lasswell (1951b) argued that the "policy sciences" should be grounded in interdisciplinary theory. More recently, in his 2008 presidential address to the American Political Science Association, Robert Axelrod advocated the need for more interdisciplinary research. As Somit and Peterson (2003b) make clear, policy scientists have relied too heavily on environmental explanations of policy change. Bryan Jones's (2001) intended rationality model, despite borrowing from cognitive psychology and biology, gives disproportionate weight to institutional rules. We are not calling for discarding such variables; rather, we suggest that psychological and biological variables be given equal weight. Without straying too far into the nature versus nurture debate, we argue that the field of policy studies is ready for more nature to balance the nurture. Despite physiological evidence, social scientists have been reluctant to include emotions as primary influences on human behavior. Indeed, the debate between rational, cognitive processes and emotional, or affective, influences has assumed multiple forms: "passions vs. reason" (Frank 1988), "emotion vs. reason" (Damasio 1994), and "emotional vs. rational" (Marcus, Neuman, and MacKuen 2000), to name a few. However, as scholars have recognized the value of interdisciplinary findings, particularly those from evolutionary biology and neuroscience, models of human behavior are increasingly being advanced that theoretically and empirically account for the role of emotions in decision-making processes.

The field of public policy makes a lot of assumptions about human decision making. Policy scholars, however, are not experts on the way humans process information. To compensate, assumptions are built into policymaking models about how policymakers *should* make policy decisions. Not only are those assumptions about human decision making wrong, they are at complete odds with how the brain actually works. To make accurate policy prescriptions requires broad knowledge of human behavior. We applaud the work of Somit and Peterson (2003a) and argue that more effort should be devoted to incorporating such work into existing theories of policy change. Great strides have been made over the past couple of decades in understanding the human decision-making process, and Somit and Peterson (2003b) are to be commended for taking a truly interdisciplinary and evolutionary approach to policy design. Neuroscience, behavioral economics, and evolutionary psychology are at the forefront of answering the question: Why do people do what they do? These disciplines have already made great advances in developing theories for replacing the rational actor model as an answer to this question. We agree with Somit and Peterson that policy scholars ignore these advances at their own peril. Future work in policy theory would be wise to heed Lasswell's advice for a truly interdisciplinary approach to the field of policy studies.

Notes

1. Jones is not alone in this regard. Following Herbert Simon's (1947) initial emphasis on the limitations of human rationality, Newell and Simon (1972) documented the inability of people to adapt their decision-making heuristics to new situations.

2. That people respond to social pressure has been known in the field of political behavior for some time (see Huckfeldt and Sprague 1987; Kenny 1992; Schram and Sonnemans 1996). Yet there have been few attempts to incorporate this theoretical framework into models of policy change.

3. Gad Saad (2003) provides a summary of the physical characteristics, such as height, that also affect voter preferences.

4. Daniel Goleman (1995) has referred to the primacy of emotions and their role in optimal decision making as "emotional intelligence."

5. For example, publicly revealing violators of the norm of voting has been found to significantly increase voter turnout (Gerber, Green, and Larimer 2008).

6. Research in behavioral economics also points to problems with attempting to make policy evaluation decisions on the basis of consistent preferences. As it turns out, people assign different utilities to decisions on the basis of whether they have experience with the decision. This is known as "experienced utility." People who have experience with a decision or policy are more likely to avoid errors in assigning utility than people who have no such experience (Kahneman and Sugden 2005; Kahneman and Thaler 2006). Because of such cognitive biases, Kahneman and Sugden (2005, 175) have advocated a "day reconstruction method" for assessing utility, in which preferences are deliberately recalled on an "episodic" basis. This is done to avoid the tendency to focus on a particularly salient experience with the policy in question, a tendency known as "focusing illusion." Like the theory of preference falsification, experienced utility demonstrates the weakness of assuming consistent preferences, as is done in the rational-comprehensive model.

7. See Nowak, Page, and Sigmund (2000) and Guth and Tietz (1990) for evidence in two-person bargaining scenarios. See Fehr and Gächter (2000) for evidence in a public goods game.

8. See Smirnov (2007) for a discussion of this literature as it relates to political science.

9. See Crawford and Salmon (2004) for another attempt at bridging public policy and evolutionary psychology.

CHAPTER 10

Do the Policy Sciences Exist?

This book's central goal has been to explore the core research questions of public policy scholarship with an eye toward gaining the tools necessary to decide whether there really is, or ever can be, such a thing as an academic field of policy studies. The preceding chapters, we believe, marshal considerable evidence supporting an integrationist conception of public policy studies.

In Chapter 1 we identified the basic characteristics that identify an academic discipline: a core research question or a central problem, a unifying theoretical framework, a common methodological framework, and a general agreement on epistemology. Some of these characteristics clearly apply to policy studies. True, the field does not have a central research question, nor is it oriented to a single, overarching problem. Still, given what has been presented in the preceding chapters, we believe there is a strong argument that public policy does have a set of clearly identified research questions, and that these questions roughly define distinct scholarly domains. We do not always see a dominant theoretical framework within these domains, but there is considerable evidence of theory construction. In areas such as policy process and implementation, there are general notions of what a conceptual framework needs to do, even if no one has—yet—figured out how to perfect that framework. In all the dimensions of policy studies examined, we find lively debate over theory-building and extensive hypothesis generating and testing. At an absolute minimum, it is fair to say the process of constructing explanatory frameworks is an active and profitable enterprise of the policy sciences.

But what connects the disparate domains of policy studies? What stitches them together into something that can be defined and defended as a distinct field? The best answer to this question is to return to Lasswell's notion of the policy sciences as problem oriented. That orientation makes the field multidimensional by definition, in the sense that policy studies is not oriented toward *a* particular problem, but social problems (plural) more generally. What can be drawn from all areas of policy studies is a deeper applied understanding of how democracies deal with, have dealt with, or might deal with whatever problems society or a group within society believes is worth addressing. This is the common thread that connects all areas of policy studies, even the policy process literature, which to the novice can seem an overwhelmingly academic exercise wherein knowledge is pursued for its own sake. At a minimum, work such as Kingdon's (1995) and Baumgartner and Jones's (1993/2009) can be mined for a wealth of practical advice on how to get a democratic system to pursue a particular solution to a particular problem: have a solution, be ready to attach it to another problem, change indicators, be alert to focusing events, breach the subsystem monopoly, and seek a shift in venue. Though these are academic studies rather than how-to manuals for policy advocates, such works can be mined for exactly that kind of systematic advice.

Although the problem orientation is arguably a pretty thin way to connect the disparate research questions that orient different policy domains, it is no weaker (and perhaps a good deal stronger) than the bonds that hold together varied subfields in disciplines like political science, public administration, and sociology. The same defense can be made for public policy's lack of distinct methodology or the running epistemological battle between the rationalist project and its post-positivist critics. Whatever balkanizing influences such issues have on the field of public policy, they are not so different from those in related social science disciplines.

This same line of argument, however, also advances the perspective that policy studies does not add up to a coherent academic field. If its primary claim to be a distinct discipline boils down to "we're no worse than political science or public administration," then the field is in trouble. To stand on its own it must make a positive claim to unique conceptual, theoretical, methodological, epistemological, and empirical contributions; the negative defense that public policy is not any better or worse than related fields is ultimately not only unsatisfying but condemning. If policy studies conceives of itself as a decentralized patchwork of a discipline, content to borrow bits and pieces of whatever is useful or fashionable in other social sciences, it deserves its already-commented-on inferiority complex. The core case against treating public policy as a unique discipline boils down to this basic critique: What has the field of policy studies added to the cumulative store of knowledge that has not been borrowed from some other academic home? We believe the contents of this book suggest that a reasonable answer to this question is "quite a lot."

The Theoretical Contributions of Policy Studies

As detailed in Chapter 1, policy studies is viewed as a taker and user of theory rather than a producer. It is bad enough that this view is broadly shared among those outside the field, but it is accepted and affirmed by many within policy studies as well. The call for better theories comes from those identified with the rationalist project (Sabatier 1999a) and its post-positivist critics (Stone 1988, 3). The inability to construct general conceptual frameworks is blamed for lack of progress in areas like implementation, and the reliance on theories adapted and taken from other fields is a key reason why policy studies is perceived as parasitic to disciplinary hosts like economics and political science. Even in areas where policy studies indisputably generates unique theoretical frameworks, these are seen as too limited and tied to specific times and events to count as a real contribution (program theory being the obvious example).

It is true that policy studies has not produced a single generalizable framework that ties together all the causal relationships that fall within its area of interest. Even if we divide the field by central research questions, as we have done in this book, we find little in the way of a guiding conceptual framework within any of them.[1] Although we cede this argument, we believe criticisms from this quarter miss the point. No social science, with the potential exception of economics, has managed to establish a central theoretical orthodoxy. And even in economics there is considerable controversy about this orthodoxy's ability to adequately describe, explain, and predict the phenomena it is supposed to. Indeed, based on some of the research anchored in psychology and behavioral economics discussed in Chapter 9, the rational utility maximization-based orthodoxy of classical economics looks to be pretty shaky these days. Theory-wise, rather than the social sciences moving toward economics, economics seems to be moving toward the more theoretical free-for-all of the rest of the social sciences. Given its sprawling subject matter, the more vigorous than usual free-for-all scrum typifying theoretical development in the policy sciences seems not only unexpected, but healthy. What is remarkable about policy studies, and has been a constant theme throughout the preceding chapters, is the astonishing array of theoretical efforts and accomplishments the field has generated.

Consider policy typologies, generally reckoned (as detailed in Chapter 2) to have reached an explanatory dead end because of the inability to overcome the classification problem. What is important to keep in mind about the policy typology project is that it was not simply a theory of public policy; it was (and is) a general theory of politics. It did not borrow from political theory—it was not constructed by adapting preexisting theories from other disciplines—it was an original conception of the political realm that stood on its head the conventional wisdom about causal relationships in politics. The failure to live up to its tantalizing promise was not due to a failing in logic or an empirical falsification of its key axioms. It stumbled primarily because of a universal difficulty found in the study of politics: the inability to separate facts from values or perceptions from objective reality. Although this inability doomed the framework as a predictive theory, for two reasons it is unfair to label typologies as a theoretical failure.

First, typologies continue to provide a useful heuristic for making sense of the political and policy world. Categorizing policy as regulatory, distributive, or redistributive is a quick and intuitive means to make sense not just of policy outputs or outcomes but of politics in general. It is conventional wisdom to accept that redistributive policies produce different power relationships than regulatory policies, even if objectively classifying policy into these categories is all but impossible. Second, policy typologies continue to develop as a theoretical construct and have proven to be a remarkably resilient and useful way for researchers to conceptualize process, behavior, outputs, and outcomes in a broad swath of the political arena. For a "failed" policy theory, typologies have done a remarkable job of imposing systematic as well as intuitive order on politics and the policy process.

To take one example, a significant literature in morality policies has developed over the past two decades (e.g., Tatalovich and Daynes 1998; Mooney 2000; Mucciaroni 2011). Morality policy attracted the attention of scholars because of its increasing centrality to politics at this time; issues such as abortion, gay marriage, and the death penalty have become ideological and electoral rallying points.

These types of issues seemed to produce a particularly virulent form of political conflict, one that mobilized large numbers of people and resisted the sort of compromise typical of the democratic process. Morality policy scholars were interested in whether there was a particular form of policy issue that bred this sort of politics and if so, if it could be systematically described, put into a coherent conceptual framework, and used to explain (or even predict) political behavior and policy outputs. At its heart, the morality politics literature is oriented by a classic typology strategy: the attempt to systematically classify policy issues into morality and nonmorality types and to assess whether these classifications have predictive power. Though this literature ultimately stumbled over the same issue as Lowi's (1964) original framework—the problem of objectively classifying policy types—it provided some unique insights into why public policies fail, why they orient themselves to some problems rather than others, and why certain policies have such powerful mobilization characteristics and are resistant to compromise—and it even provided some evidence that policies could be classified systematically and empirically, if not wholly objectively (e.g., Meier 1994, 1999; Mooney and Lee 1999; Smith 2002; Mucciaroni 2011). These are significant achievements that drew their conceptual power from a framework developed and refined within the policy field.

Perhaps the classic "failure" of policy theory is the stages heuristic. The harshest critics of the stages approach are almost all policy scholars themselves, who argue that the stages theory is not a theory at all (e.g., Sabatier 1991b). As detailed in Chapter 2, these criticisms are not without justification. The stages approach is not predictive and does not generate falsifiable hypotheses; it is descriptive rather than explanatory in any real sense. Yet even if it is only a heuristic guideline to the policy process, it is a remarkably succinct means to impose meaning and order on an incredibly complex undertaking. Understanding public policy in all its dimensions is a daunting task when undertaken as a primary academic career; yet the basic gist can be conveyed to an undergraduate class in ten minutes using the stages framework. Whatever its drawbacks as a grand conceptual theory, this is not an insignificant achievement.

Moreover, the stages heuristic still serves as a useful means to conceptualize what the entire field of policy studies is all about. Figure 10.1 shows how most of the dimensions of policy studies discussed in this book might map onto the stages heuristic. All these dimensions are connected through the larger stages framework, each subfield focused on a particular element or set of elements that together constitute the stages approach. To be sure, there is overlap and redundancy,

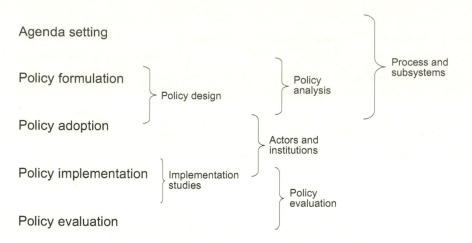

FIGURE 10.1 The Stages and Fields of Public Policy

and no single dimension encompasses every single stage of the policy process, but the stages framework serves as a useful umbrella to demonstrate what policy studies is all about.

Typologies and the stages framework, in short, have made and continue to make useful contributions toward helping scholars understand the complex world of public policy. More to the point, these conceptual frameworks were produced and developed primarily within the policy field; this is hardly the record of an academic discipline as theoretically devoid as policy studies is routinely described to be.

We have taken some pains in this book to point out that the theoretical contributions of policy studies are not limited to these two frameworks. Some policy theories build off conceptual foundations from other disciplines. Notable in this category is Kingdon's (1995) concept of policy windows, which builds from Cohen, March, and Olsen's (1972) garbage can model of organizational behavior. They also include Baumgartner and Jones's punctuated equilibrium framework (1993/2009), which builds from the bounded rationality concepts pioneered by Herbert Simon (1947) in public administration as well as work by Stephen Jay Gould in evolutionary biology.[2] Kingdon and Baumgartner and Jones, however, do considerably more than simply borrow an existing conceptual framework and apply it to a different dependent variable. In both cases, there is considerable theoretical refinement going on. Starting from the fairly raw materials of a new perspective on organizational process (Kingdon) or a well-established notion of how humans make choices (Baumgartner and Jones), these scholars considerably refined the starting concepts and emerged with original contributions to our understanding of where policy comes from, why government pays more attention to some problems than others, and why policy changes.

Even in an area like implementation, where hope of developing generalizable explanation was all but abandoned a decade ago, we see policy scholars reinvigorating an entire research agenda by not just applying, but refining and extending, conceptual models originating in other fields. The extension of public management theory into implementation studies is helping to address some of the tougher questions that have haunted implementation research for decades. Yes, it is true that we still do not (yet) have a comprehensive and generalizable theory of implementation, but the movement in the past decade has definitely been in that general direction. We certainly know a lot more about what is or is not important in putting a policy into action; the distance between Pressman and Wildavsky (1973) and O'Toole and Meier (2011) is enormous, with the latter filling in gaps not even conceived of forty years earlier.

Where policy scholars have made the fewest theoretical contributions is, ironically, in the realms of policy studies that have the most settled conceptual frameworks. Policy analysis, at least compared to other areas of the policy studies field, historically has something approaching a general theoretical gyroscope in the form of welfare economics. Though policy scholars have certainly refined the conceptual materials and made a number of contributions in terms of the methodology, it is reasonable to describe rationalist policy analysis as largely consisting of applied economic analysis (see Munger 2000). The stable platform of welfare economics, however, is being rattled by developments rooted in psychology and evolutionary theory. As we learned in Chapter 5, the work of behavioral economics is starting to reshape the long-standing conceptual stability of paradigms like cost-benefit analysis. This is opening up opportunities for noneconomists to make major contributions to developing conceptual frameworks of central interest to policy scholars. Bent Flyvbjerg, who has a PhD in urban geography and is a professor of management, not economics, developed reference class forecasting not from classical economic ideas, but from the work of psychologists Daniel Kahneman and Amos Tversky (whose work featured prominently in the discussions in Chapter 9). If geographers teaching management can use the work of psychologists to develop new conceptual tools of importance to policy studies, we see no reason why policy scholars should not be pursuing similar innovations. We are by nature interdisciplinary, and anyone who is a policy analyst or an impact analyst by trade is painfully aware of the drawbacks of conceptual frameworks in those fields (e.g., lack of forecasting accuracy, the often heroic assumptions required to make cost analysis tractable). There is no reason we need to accept those limitations or wait for someone else to fix those problems. In other words, even where policy scholars have not made important contributions, the future has plenty of opportunity to reverse that record.

Some of the harshest critics of policy theory (or the lack thereof) are post-positivist policy scholars, who are either skeptical that theories in the scientific sense are capable of explaining the world of politics and policy, critical that such theories and their associated methods undercut democratic values in the policy-making process, or some combination of both (e.g., deLeon 1997; Stone 1988; Fischer 2003). Yet the post-positivists are not antitheory; they just tend to argue that normative theory (as opposed to the positive theories of the rationalists) should provide the guiding framework for policy studies. Creating normative democratic frameworks for systematically understanding the complex world of public policy is not an undertaking for the fainthearted. Stone's polis model and the epistemological cases made by Fischer and deLeon have nonetheless had a significant impact on policy studies as a field that perceives what it is doing and why. If nothing else, the post-positivists have served to remind the theory-building rationalists that public policy in democracies must ultimately be judged not just by scientific values but also by democratic ones.

In summary, we believe there are plenty of examples to counter the argument that policy studies has done little to contribute to the systematic understanding of the political world. From our perspective, the real problem is not the field's inability to generate conceptual frameworks that result in genuine insights, so much as its sprawling subject matter. Policy scholars have made significant advances since Lasswell first envisioned the policy sciences. We know considerably more about agenda setting, decision making, implementation, impact, and evaluation than we did a half-century ago. Much of this book has been devoted to making exactly that point. Yet in the policy field, progress seems to be measured by what we have not done rather than by what we have. We have not produced a robust and generalizable theory of implementation or reconciled the paradox of science and democratic values. The field has no overarching framework for the policy process. This list of failures is all true enough. We have, however, provided a decent understanding of the reasons why implementation succeeds or fails and have been engaged in a serious and long-running debate over how science and democratic values can and should be balanced in policymaking. The field has produced a wide array of empirically testable conceptual frameworks (punctuated equilibrium, advocacy coalition frameworks, policy windows) that cover multiple stages of the policy process, even if they do not cover all of them. These are important contributions, and any discussion of the policy field's failures should rightly be balanced with an account of its successes.

Key Problems

Although we believe a spirited defense of the policy field's intellectual contributions is more than justified, this should not distract attention from the field's ongoing intellectual challenges. The purpose of this book is to demonstrate that policy studies does have a set of core research questions, has constructed useful conceptual frameworks to answer those questions, and has used these to accumulate a useful store of knowledge. Yet our examination has also clearly shown that the policy field consistently stumbles over a set of key conceptual and epistemological challenges.

Conceptual Challenges

The field of policy studies suffers considerably because of continuing vagueness about what it actually studies. As discussed in some detail in Chapter 1, no precise universal definition of "public policy" exists. A central problem here is making "policy" conceptually distinct from "politics." In languages other than English, "policy" and "politics" are often synonyms. In German, for example, "die Politik" covers policy and politics. In French "politique" does the same.

In English we have fairly precise definitions for politics. In political science the most commonly used are Easton's (1953)—"the authoritative allocation of values"—and Lasswell's (1936): "who gets what, when and how." Both of these essentially capture the same underlying concept: the process of making society-wide decisions that are binding on everybody. There is little controversy over these definitions or the underlying concept, and they are widely accepted by political scientists as defining the essence of what they study. But if this is politics, what conceptual ground, if any, is left for policy? This is a fundamental question for policy studies—indeed, it is probably *the* fundamental question—and it has never been satisfactorily answered. Astonishingly, the field as a whole seems to have lost all interest in seriously grappling with this question—as a subject it

seems to have quietly exited as a high-profile, or even low-profile, topic of scholarly exchange.[3]

If we distill the various definitional approaches summarized in Chapter 1, we
end up with a concept that can roughly be thought of as "a purposive action
backed by the coercive powers of the state." This definition (and those similar to
it) conveys the two basic concepts at the heart of policy studies: 1) public policy
is goal-oriented; it is a government response to a perceived problem; and 2) public policy, as Lowi (1964, 1972) argued, fundamentally rests upon government's
coercive powers. What makes a policy public is the fact that, even if we oppose
the purposes of policy, the government can force us to comply with it.

We fully recognize that the validity of this definition is debatable (e.g., what
about purposive inaction? Should that not count as policy too?). Our purpose
here is not to end the definitional debate, but rather to point out its importance
in distinguishing policy studies as a distinct academic field. If this definition, at
least for the purposes of argument, is accepted as a reasonable expression of the
concept at the heart of policy studies, how is it really different from the concept
of politics? Does it not simply restate, perhaps in a more narrow and focused
way, "the authoritative allocation of values"? Purposive decisions no doubt allocate values—they are expressions of what society considers important and what
is going to be done about it. If these decisions are backed by the coercive powers
of the state, they are certainly authoritative. Perhaps a key implication of this line
of reasoning is that the study of public policy is really the study of the reason for,
or the end goals of, politics. If so, it is not at all clear how politics and policy can
be conceptually disentangled. Yet there is also an argument that this conceptualization has causal order backward. Lowi (1964) argued that policy begat politics, not the other way around. It is the nature or the type of purposive action
that shapes the struggle over whose values get authoritatively allocated.

The larger point here is that the lack of conceptual clarity is a big reason why
it is legitimate to question whether policy studies has any legitimate claim to be
a distinct academic enterprise. For the past half-century, it has been mostly content to claim the problem orientation á la Lasswell as its raison d'être, or (more
commonly) to ignore the issue altogether. Given that the field has never fully or
forcefully articulated its reason for being, it is little wonder we are not even sure
what to call it. We have used terms like "policy sciences" as synonyms throughout
this book as handy descriptive terms for the general field of policy studies. Yet it
is not at all clear that these terms should be treated as interchangeable. A term
like "policy sciences," for example, may carry epistemological and philosophical

implications that some policy scholars (especially if they are of a post-positivist bent) are at odds with.

Our approach to the conceptual fuzziness lurking at the heart of policy studies is to seek more clarity by looking at key research questions and using these as a basis for defining such terms as "policy analysis" and "policy evaluation." Obviously we believe this is at least a partially effective way to impose theoretical and epistemological coherence onto policy studies. Yet these terms are not always used in the way we describe them, and in some ways we have drawn artificially clear conceptual lines. The ex ante and ex post division we use to distinguish analysis and evaluation, for example, is blurred in practice by a considerable amount of in medias res, studies that by definition blur the pre- and post-decision markers we have used. Perhaps if we had a clearer understanding of the core concept of policy, these divisions could be made sharper and less reliant on the individual perspective of a given researcher or writer.

The bottom line is that public policy must find a way to make the concepts at the heart of the field clearer. At least, it must do so if it is ever to justify itself as an academic undertaking distinct from fields such as political science and public administration.

Epistemology

A running theme throughout this book is a central split in philosophy, a difference over how policy should be studied. This split was virtually ordained by Lasswell's original notion of the "policy sciences of democracy." The key problem with that vision, of course, is that science is not particularly democratic, and democratic values seem to leave little room for the positivist leanings of the scientific approach.

The result has been two camps that often imply the two approaches are contradictory and mutually exclusive, camps we have termed throughout this book rationalists and post-positivists.[4] This is an accurate enough claim within some narrowly defined limits. Rationalists, for the most part, do make assumptions about an objectively knowable state of the world, a world that can be empirically described and analyzed. Post-positivists, for the most part, argue that whatever is objective about the physical world does not imply a similar state of affairs in the political and social world. Reality in those domains is a heavily constructed reality, with "truth" and "fact" varying with perspective and context. These two radically different assumptions about the nature of the political and social world naturally lead to radically different notions of how to go about understanding those worlds.

Yet these differences are sometimes overblown. Many of the self-described post-positivists are not necessarily antirationalist in the sense that they see the whole enterprise as pointless (a good example is deLeon 1997). Mostly what these scholars are arguing for is epistemological pluralism, a place in policy studies where subjective experience is considered at least as meaningful as a regression coefficient. Similarly, self-proclaimed rationalists have recognized that the failure to account for values is a key weakness of their work, and thus they have developed methods to incorporate—or at least account for—subjective values in their work (e.g., Meier and Gill 2000; Smith and Granberg-Rademacker 2003; Smith 2005). In practice, then, what we see in public policy is less two warring camps in a fight to the philosophical death than a general recognition by everybody that effectively studying public policy means figuring out ways to combine values and empiricism.

Still, it has to be said that the differences here are significant and deep enough to act as a brake on the field as a whole moving forward. The harsh truth is that the scientific method that orients the rationalist project is in fundamental ways incompatible with democratic values. Rationalist policy research is not participatory, does not give contradictory outcomes equal weight, and does not submit the validity of its conclusions to a vote. From the post-positivist perspective, this makes the rationalist project misleading (or even dangerous) in democratic terms. Yet in its defense, the rationalist project is enormously informative; it is probably fair to say it has produced more useful knowledge (both in applied and academic senses) than its post-positivist opposite.

Part of the problem for the post-positivists is that the rationalists have a practical and utilitarian epistemology in the scientific method, and the post-positivists simply have no equivalent. The alternate methods of gaining knowledge about public policy pushed from the post-positivist perspective—hermeneutics, discourse theory, and the like—take relativism as a virtue. Pile this on top of the conceptual vagueness that characterizes the policy field, and what we tend to end up with is an approach to public policy that confuses as much as it illuminates (at least it does if our experience teaching graduate students is any guide). Post-positivists recognize this problem and have sought to construct practical approaches to studying public policy. A good example is participatory policy analysis, which springs from the notion of deliberative democracy and is championed by scholars such as Fischer (2003), deLeon (1997), and Durning (1993). In practice, PPA requires creating something like juries: panels of citizens who study a particular policy problem and seek to come to some consensus on what should be done about it. The PPA methodology requires policy analysts to select people "randomly . . . from a broadly defined pool of affected citizens (possibly formulated to take sociocultural variables in account) so as to avoid the stigma of being 'captured' by established interest and stakeholders, to engage in a participatory analytic exercise" (deLeon 1997, 111). Whatever its advantages, this sort of activity is resource intensive and has questionable external validity. Resource limits often make it an impractical research option, and the focus on a specific issue, time, and place (i.e., lack of generalizability) makes it a nonstarter for many rationalists. For reasons such as these, no form of post-positivist–championed methodology has come close to providing a widely used alternative to the mostly quantitative tool kit championed by the rationalists.

When it comes to differences between the rationalist and post-positivist camps, there are clearly strengths and weaknesses on both sides. It is our view that the rationalist project, at least thus far, does the better job of identifying problems, probabilistically assessing the likely effects of alternative responses to those problems, identifying the impact of the alternative chosen, and systematically assessing how and why policy changes. It certainly has the most practical analytical tools. The reasons supporting this perspective are detailed at length in other chapters in this book. The rationalist project, however, has failed miserably in its effort to separate values from facts, and post-positivists are quite right to point out that any notion that the rationalist project can make political decision making less political is, to put it mildly, highly unlikely. Post-positivist approaches embrace the messy, perspective-driven political realm of policy and use the values of the stakeholders as the lenses to examine problems; the relative worth of proposed solutions; and the process of deciding, changing, or implementing policy, as well as assessing what a policy has actually done. In short, the post-positivists provide a considerably richer picture of politics in policy studies. The problem with this approach is that it is comparatively more difficult to put into practice, and it is harder to assess what the end result really means.

Is it possible to find and build from some common ground between these two approaches? Perhaps. This effort is best exemplified by work like that of Jones and McBeth (2010), who give serious thought to—and an empirical demonstration of—how a post-positivist theoretical framework might be employed to generate hypotheses that can be empirically tested using the quantitative tool kit of rationalists. The success of such hybrid platforms—essentially post-positivist theory and rationalist methods—remains to be seen. It is too early to judge whether they will be embraced as a child of both camps or rejected as the monster of neither. What we can say is that post-positivists and rationalists show no sign of withdrawing behind their epistemological walls and raising the drawbridges to keep the other side out. As Jones and McBeth demonstrate, the two camps are actively engaged and, if nothing else, continue to make substantive and informative criticisms of each other.

Conclusion: Whither Policy Studies?

The central conclusions reached thus far are that policy studies has made and continues to make important and lasting contributions to our cumulative understanding of how the political and administrative world works, and that it has struggled and continues to struggle with conceptual and epistemological difficulties that are a long way from being resolved. Efforts are also being made to take a more interdisciplinary approach to public policy in the hopes of providing a richer and more powerful way of conceptualizing how policy decisions are made (see Chapter 9). So where does this leave public policy as a field of study? Does such a thing really exist?

Based on our explorations throughout this book, we believe a strong case can be made for the affirmative. There is such a thing as policy studies and, at least in general terms, we can describe it.

Distilling the message of this book, we propose that the field of policy studies is the systematic search for answers to five core questions:

1) What problems does government pay attention to, and why?
2) What government response is the most effective response to those problems, and why?
3) How are solutions chosen?
4) How are those solutions translated into action?
5) What impact has policy made on those problems?

Out of necessity, these questions demand a theoretical and methodological pluralism; there is no grand theory that ties them all together (though some policy scholars have made pretty good tries, as typologies and the stages heuristic demonstrate). What clearly connects these questions, and the various domains of policy study they generate, is the problem orientation that powered Lasswell's original vision of the policy sciences.

Policy studies is also grappling with disagreements about key conceptual and epistemological issues. Most notably, there is a significant philosophical divide between rationalists and post-positivists, the former favoring objectivism and quantitative methodologies and the latter favoring subjectivism and qualitative methodologies. This rift is not really fatal to the field. The differences are no more serious than they are in most other social science fields. As members of both camps recognize the legitimacy of each other's claims—probably more so than comparable "qual" and "quant" camps that divide other fields—this is less a philosophical fight to the death than a difficult search for common ground.

Policy studies has a strong element of art and craft (as opposed to science), but this is to be expected in a field whose core research questions have such clear applied implications. Public policy is more than a mood, though. Perhaps it is not (yet) a science, but it can stake a legitimate claim to being a field of study.

Notes

1. The one potential exception to this that we can see is the use of the welfare economics paradigm in policy analysis. The welfare economics paradigm, though, is obviously not a unique product of policy studies. And even here, there is strong resistance to using economics-based frameworks as a primary theoretical vehicle to answer "What should we do?"

2. Kingdon's (1995) framework also owes a significant debt to bounded rationality.

3. We could not find a single citation in any major policy, political science, or public administration journal of the past two decades whose primary subject was defining the concept of public policy, much less one that proposed a conceptual distinction between politics and policy that justified a separate academic discipline to focus on the latter. Such articles may exist, but our search makes us confident that they are not a primary focus of policy scholars.

4. This may be another case of the sloppy and unclear labeling so characteristic of policy studies. We suspect many scholars we have lumped under these classifications have rejected the titles, arguing that, for example, "empiricist" or "deconstructionist" is more accurate and descriptive of their particular perspectives.

Alford, John R., and John R. Hibbing. 2004. "The Origin of Politics: An Evolutionary Theory of Political Behavior." *Perspectives on Politics* 2: 707–723.

Anderson, Charles. 1979. "The Place of Principle in Policy Analysis." *American Political Science Review* 73: 711–723.

Anderson, James E. 1974. *Public Policy-Making*. New York: Praeger.

_____. 1994. *Public Policy-Making: An Introduction*. 2nd ed. Geneva, IL: Houghton Mifflin.

_____. 1997. *Public Policy-Making*. 3rd ed. New York: Holt, Rinehart, and Winston.

Angrist, Joshua, and Jorn-Steffen Pischke. 2008. *Mostly Harmless Econometrics*. Princeton, NJ: Princeton University Press.

Ariely, Dan. 2009. *Predictably Irrational: The Hidden Forces That Shape Our Decisions*. New York: HarperCollins.

Avellaneda, Claudia. 2009. "Municipal Performance: Does Mayoral Quality Matter?" *Journal of Public Administration Research and Theory* 19: 285–312.

Axelrod, Robert. 2008. "Political Science and Beyond: Presidential Address to the American Political Science Association." *Perspectives on Politics* 6(1): 3–9.

Bachrach, Peter, and Morton Baratz. 1962. "The Two Faces of Power." *American Political Science Review* 56: 947–952.

Bardach, Eugene. 1977. *The Implementation Game: What Happens After a Bill Becomes Law*. Cambridge, MA: MIT Press.

_____. 2005/2011. *A Practical Guide for Policy Analysis: The Eightfold Path to More Effective Problem Solving*. Washington, DC: CQ Press.

_____. 2006. "Policy Dynamics." In *The Oxford Handbook of Public Policy*, ed. Michael Moran, Martin Rein, and Robert E. Goodin, 336–366. New York: Oxford University Press.

Barkow, Jerome H., Leda Cosmides, and John Tooby. 1992. *The Adapted Mind: Evolutionary Psychology and the Generation of Culture*. New York: Oxford University Press.

Baumgartner, Frank R., and Bryan D. Jones. 1993/2009. *Agendas and Instability in American Politics*. Chicago: University of Chicago Press.

Berman, Paul. 1980. "Thinking About Programmed and Adaptive Implementation: Matching Strategies to Situations." In *Why Policies Succeed or Fail*, ed. Helen Ingram and Dean Mann, 205–227. Beverly Hills, CA: Sage.

Berry, Frances Stokes, and William D. Berry. 1990. "State Lottery Adoptions as Policy Innovations: An Event History Analysis." *American Political Science Review* 84: 395–415.

Bingham, Richard D., and Claire Felbinger. 2002. *Evaluation in Practice: A Methodological Approach*. New York: Seven Bridges Press.

Birkland, Thomas. 2001. *An Introduction to the Policy Process*. Armonk, NY: M. E. Sharpe.

Blomquist, William, and Peter deLeon. 2011. "The Design and Promise of the Institutional Analysis and Development Framework." *Policy Studies Journal* 39(1): 1–6.

Boardman, Anthony E., D. H. Greenberg, A. R. Vining, and D. L. Weimer. 2001. *Cost-Benefit Analysis: Concepts and Practice*. Upper Saddle River, NJ: Prentice Hall.

Boardman, Anthony E., Wendy L. Mallery, and Aidan Vining. 1994. "Learning from *Ex Ante/Ex Post* Cost-Benefit Comparisons: The Coquilhalla Highway Example." *Socio-Economic Planning Sciences* 28: 69–84.

Bobrow, Davis, and John Dryzek. 1987. *Policy Analysis by Design*. Pittsburgh: Pittsburgh University Press.

Boehm, Christopher. 1999. *Hierarchy in the Forest: The Evolution of Egalitarian Behavior*. Boston: Harvard University Press.

_____. 2012. *Moral Origins: The Evolution of Virtue, Altruism, and Shame*. New York: Basic Books.

Bogason, Peter. 2007. "Postmodern Public Administration." In *The Oxford Handbook of Public Management*, ed. Ewan Ferlie, Laurence E. Lynn Jr., and Christopher Pollitt. New York: Oxford University Press. doi: 10.1093/oxfordhb/978019922 6443.001.0001.

Bohte, John. 2007. "Governmental Efficiency in Our Times: Is the 'What' Really More Important than the 'How'?" *Public Administration Review* (September/October): 811–815.

Boscarino, Jessica E. 2009. "Surfing for Problems: Advocacy Group Strategy in U.S. Forestry Policy." *Policy Studies Journal* 37(3): 415–434.

Boushey, Graeme. 2012. "Punctuated Equilibrium Theory and the Diffusion of Innovations." *Policy Studies Journal* 40(1): 127–146.

Brafman, Ori, and Rom Brafman. 2008. *Sway: The Irresistible Pull of Irrational Behavior*. New York: Broadway Books.

Breunig, Christian, and Chris Koski. 2012. "The Tortoise or the Hare? Incrementalism, Punctuations, and Their Consequences." *Policy Studies Journal* 40(1): 45–67.

Brewer, Garry D., and Peter deLeon. 1983. *The Foundations of Policy Analysis*. Homewood, IL: Dorsey Press.

Buchanan, James M., and Gordon Tullock. 1962. *The Calculus of Consent: Logical Foundations of Constitutional Democracy*. Ann Arbor: University of Michigan Press.

Bullock, Charles. 1981. "Implementation of Equal Education Opportunity Programs: A Comparative Analysis." In *Effective Policy Implementation*, ed. Daniel Mazmanian and Paul Sabatier, 89–126. Lexington, MA: D. C. Heath.

Burtless, Gary. 1995. "The Case for Randomized Field Trials in Economic and Policy Research." *Journal of Economic Perspectives* 9: 63–84.

Camerer, Colin F., George Lowenstein, and Matthew Rabin. 2004. *Advances in Behavioral Economics*. Princeton, NJ: Princeton University Press.

Cameron, Lisa. 1999. "Raising the Stakes in the Ultimatum Game: Experimental Evidence from Indonesia." *Economic Inquiry* 37: 47–59.

Campbell, Donald, and Julian Stanley. 1966. *Experimental and Quasi-Experimental Designs for Research*. Chicago: Rand McNally.

Campen, J. T. 1986. *Benefit, Cost, and Beyond: The Political Economy of Benefit-Cost Analysis*. Cambridge, MA: Ballinger.

Carmines, Edward G., and James A. Stimson. 1989. *Issue Evolution: Race and the Transformation of American Politics*. Princeton, NJ: Princeton University Press.

Chiappe, Dan, Adam Brown, Brian Dow, Jennifer Koontz, Marisela Rodriguez, and Kelly McCulloch. 2004. "Cheaters Are Looked at Longer and Remembered Better Than Cooperators in Social Exchange Situations." *Evolutionary Psychology* 2: 108–120.

Chubb, John, and Terry Moe. 1988. "Politics, Markets and the Organization of Schools." *American Political Science Review* 82(4): 1065–1087.

———. 1990. *Politics, Markets and America's Schools*. Washington, DC: Brookings Institution Press.

Cialdini, Robert B., and Melanie R. Trost. 1998. "Social Influence: Social Norms, Conformity, and Compliance." In *The Handbook of Social Psychology*, 4th ed., ed. Daniel T. Gilbert, Susan T. Fiske, and Gardner Lindzey, 151–192. Boston: McGraw-Hill.

Cialdini, Robert B., and Noah J. Goldstein. 2004. "Social Influence: Compliance and Conformity." *Annual Review of Psychology* 55 (February): 591–621.

Cobb, Roger, and Charles Elder. 1983. *Agenda-Building and Democratic Politics*. Baltimore, MD: Johns Hopkins University Press.

Cohen, Michael, James March, and Johan Olsen. 1972. "A Garbage Can Model of Organizational Choice." *Administrative Science Quarterly* 17: 1–25.

Collingridge, D., and C. Reeves. 1986. *Science Speaks to Power: The Role of Experts in Policymaking*. New York: St. Martin's Press.

Congdon, William, Jeffrey Kling, and Sendhil Mullainathan. 2009. "Behavioral Economics and Tax Policy." National Bureau of Economic Research. Working Paper 15328.

Cook, Brian J. 2010. "Arenas of Power in Climate Change Policymaking." *Policy Studies Journal* 38(3): 465–486.

Cook, Thomas, and Donald T. Campbell. 1979. *Quasi-Experimentation: Design and Analysis Issues for Field Settings*. Chicago: Rand McNally.

Cook, Thomas, and William Shadish. 1994. "Social Experiments: Some Developments over the Past Fifteen Years." *Annual Review of Psychology* 45: 545–580.

Cosmides, Leda, and John Tooby. 1992. "Cognitive Adaptations for Social Exchange." In *The Adapted Mind: Evolutionary Psychology and the Generation of Culture*, ed. Jerome H. Barkow, Leda Cosmides, and John Tooby, 163–228. Oxford: Oxford University Press.

———. 1994. "Better Than Rational: Evolutionary Psychology and the Invisible Hand." *American Economic Review* 84(2): 327–332.

Crawford, Charles, and Catherine Salmon. 2004. *Evolutionary Psychology, Public Policy, and Personal Decisions*. Mahwah, NJ: Lawrence Erlbaum Associates.

Cremins, James J. 1983. *Legal and Political Issues in Special Education*. Springfield, IL: Charles C. Thomas.

Damasio, Antonio. 1994. *Descartes' Error: Emotion, Reason, and the Human Brain*. New York: Quill.

Davies, H. T., S. M. Nutley, and P. C. Smith. 2000. *What Works? Evidence-Based Policy and Practice in Public Service*. Bristol, UK: Policy Press.

Davis, Otto A., M. A. H. Dempster, and Aaron Wildavsky. 1966. "A Theory of the Budgetary Process." *American Political Science Review* 60: 529–547.

Dawes, Robyn M., and Richard H. Thaler. 1988. "Cooperation." *Journal of Economic Perspectives* 2: 187–197.

deLeon, Linda, and Robert B. Denhardt. 2000. "The Political Theory of Reinvention." *Public Administration Review* 60: 89–97.

deLeon, Peter. 1988. *Advice and Consent: The Development of the Policy Sciences*. New York: Russell Sage Foundation.

———. 1995. "Democratic Values and the Policy Sciences." *American Political Science Review* (November): 886–905.

———. 1997. *Democracy and the Policy Sciences*. Albany: State University of New York Press.

———. 1999a. "The Missing Link Revisited: Contemporary Implementation Research." *Policy Studies Review* 16: 311–339.

———. 1999b. "The Stages Approach to the Policy Process." In *Theories of the Policy Process*, ed. Paul A. Sabatier, 19–32. Boulder, CO: Westview Press.

———. 1999c. "Cold Comfort Indeed: A Rejoinder to Lester and Goggin." *Policy Currents* 8: 6–8.

———. 2006. "The Historical Roots of the Field." In *The Oxford Handbook of Public Policy*, ed. Michael Moran, Martin Rein, and Robert E. Goodin, 39–57. New York: Oxford University Press.

deLeon, Peter, and Linda deLeon. 2002. "What Ever Happened to Policy Implementation? An Alternative Approach." *Journal of Public Administration Research and Theory* 12: 467–492.

Deniston, O. Lynn. 1972. "Program Planning for Disease Control Programs." Communicable Disease Center, Health Services and Mental Health Administration, Public Health Service, Department of Health, Education and Welfare.

de Quervain, Dominique J.-F., Urs Fischbacher, Valerie Treyer, Melanie Schellhammer, Ulrich Schnyder, Alfred Buck, and Ernst Fehr. 2004. "The Neural Basis of Altruistic Punishment." *Science* 305: 1254–1258.

Derthick, Martha. 1972. *New Towns In-Town: Why a Federal Program Failed*. Washington, DC: The Urban Institute.

Downs, Anthony. 1957. *An Economic Theory of Democracy*. New York: Harper and Row.

———. 1972. "Up and Down with Ecology—The 'Issue-Attention' Cycle." *Public Interest* 28: 39–41.

Dresang, Dennis. 1983. "Foreword." In *The Logic of Policy Inquiry*, ed. David Paris and James Reynolds. New York: Longman.

Dror, Yehezkel. 1968. *Public Policy Making Reexamined*. Scranton, PA: Chandler Publishing.

Druckman, James N. 2004. "Political Preference Formation: Competition, Deliberation, and the (Ir)relevance of Framing Effects." *American Political Science Review* 98: 671–686.

Dryzek, John. 1989. "Policy Sciences of Democracy." *Polity* 22: 97–118.

Dryzek, John, and Douglas Torgerson. 1993. "Democracy and the Policy Sciences." *Policy Sciences* 26: 127–138.

Dubnick, Mel, and Barbara Bardes. 1983. *Thinking About Public Policy*. New York: John Wiley and Sons.

Dunn, William N. 1981/2011. *Public Policy Analysis*. Englewood Cliffs, NJ: Prentice Hall.

Durning, Dan. 1993. "Participatory Policy Analysis in a Social Service Agency: A Case Study." *Journal of Policy Analysis and Management* 12: 231–257.

Dye, Thomas R. 1976. *Policy Analysis: What Governments Do, Why They Do It, and What Difference It Makes*. Tuscaloosa: University of Alabama Press.

———. 1987. *Understanding Public Policy*. Upper Saddle River, NJ: Prentice Hall.

Easton, David. 1953. *The Political System*. New York: Knopf.

———. 1965. *A Systems Analysis of Political Life*. New York: Wiley.

Edelman, Murray. 1964. *The Symbolic Uses of Politics*. Urbana: University of Illinois Press.

———. 1990. *Constructing the Political Spectacle*. Chicago: University of Chicago Press.

Eisenberger, Naomi I., Matthew D. Lieberman, and Kipling D. Williams. 2003. "Does Rejection Hurt? An fMRI Study of Social Exclusion." *Science* 302: 290–292.

Eller, Warren, and Glen Krutz. 2009. "Policy Process, Scholarship and the Road Ahead: An Introduction to the 2008 Policy Shootout!" *The Policy Studies Journal* 37: 1–4.

Ellis, Lee. 2003. "Biosocial Theorizing and Criminal Justice Policy." In *Human Nature and Public Policy: An Evolutionary Approach*, ed. Albert Somit and Steven A. Peterson, 97–120. New York: Palgrave Macmillan.

Ellison, Brian A., and Adam J. Newmark. 2010. "Building the Reservoir to Nowhere: The Role of Agencies in Advocacy Coalitions." *Policy Studies Journal* 38(4): 653–678.

Elmore, Richard. 1985. "Forward and Backward Mapping." In *Policy Implementation in Federal and Unitary Systems*, ed. K. Hanf and T. Toonen. Dordrecht, The Netherlands: Marinus Nijhoff.

Etzioni, Amitai. 2006. "The Unique Methodology of Policy Research." In *The Oxford Handbook of Public Policy*, ed. Michael Moran, Martin Rein, and Robert E. Goodin, 833–843. New York: Oxford University Press.

Eulau, Heinz. 1977. "The Workshop: The Place of Policy Analysis in Political Science: Five Perspectives." *American Journal of Political Science* 23: 415–433.

Eyestone, Robert. 1971. *The Threads of Public Policy: A Study in Policy Leadership.* Indianapolis: Bobbs-Merrill.

Farr, James, Jacob Hacker, and Nicole Kazee. 2006. "The Policy Scientist of Democracy: The Discipline of Harold D. Lasswell." *American Political Science Review* 100: 579–587.

Fehr, Ernst, and Urs Fischbacher. 2004. "Third-Party Punishment and Social Norms." *Evolution and Human Behavior* 25: 63–87.

Fehr, Ernst, Urs Fischbacher, and Elena Tougareva. 2002. "Do High Stakes Competition Undermine Fairness? Evidence from Russia." University of Zurich, Institute for Empirical Research in Economics, Working Paper No. 120.

Fehr, Ernst, and Simon Gächter. 2000. "Cooperation and Punishment in Public Goods Experiments." *American Economic Review* 90: 980–994.

Ferman, Barbara. 1990. "When Failure Is Success: Implementation and Madisonian Government." In *Implementation and the Policy Process: Opening Up the Black Box*, ed. Dennis Palumbo and Donald Calista, 39–50. Westport, CT: Greenwood Press.

Fessler, Daniel T. 2002. "Emotions and Cost-Benefit Assessment: The Role of Shame and Self-Esteem in Risk Taking." In *Bounded Rationality: The Adaptive Toolbox*, ed. Gerd Gigerenzer and Reinhard Selton, 191–214. Cambridge, MA: MIT Press.

Field, Alexander J. 2004. *Altruistically Inclined? The Behavioral Sciences, Evolutionary Theory, and the Origins of Reciprocity*. Ann Arbor: University of Michigan Press.

Fischer, Frank. 1980. *Politics, Values, and Public Policy: The Problem of Methodology.* Boulder, CO: Westview Press.

———. 1995. *Evaluating Public Policy*. Chicago: Nelson Hall.

———. 2003. *Reframing Public Policy: Discursive Politics and Deliberative Practices*. New York: Oxford University Press.

Fischer, Frank, and John Forester. 1993. *The Argumentative Turn in Policy Analysis and Planning*. Durham, NC: Duke University Press.

Fishkin, James S. 1991. *Democracy and Deliberation*. New Haven, CT: Yale University Press.

Fishkin, James, and Peter Laslett. 2003. *Debating Deliberative Democracy*. Malden, MA: Blackwell.

Fishkin, James, and Robert Luskin. 1999. "Bringing Deliberation to the Democratic Dialogue." In *The Poll with a Human Face*, ed. Amy Reynolds and Maxwell McCombs, 3–38. Philadelphia: Lawrence Erlbaum.

Fitzpatrick, Jody L., James R. Sanders, and Blaine Worthen. 2004. *Program Evaluation: Alternative Approaches and Practical Guidelines*. Boston: Pearson.

Flyvbjerg, Bent. 2008. "Curbing Optimism Bias and Strategic Misrepresentation in Planning: Reference Class Forecasting in Practice." *European Planning Studies* 16: 3–21.

Foley, Elise. 2012. "Obama Administration to Stop Deporting Younger Undocumented Immigrants and Grant Work Permits." *The Huffington Post*, June 15. http://www.huffingtonpost.com/2012/06/15/obama-immigration-order-deportation-dream-act_n_1599658.html. Accessed July 17, 2012.

Frank, Robert H. 1988. *Passions Within Reason: The Strategic Role of Emotions*. New York: W.W. Norton.

_____. 2005. *What Price the Moral High Ground? Ethical Dilemmas in Competitive Environments*. Princeton, NJ: Princeton University Press.

Frederickson, H. George. 2007. "Vulgar Accountability." *PA Times* (August): 11.

Frederickson, H. George, and Kevin B. Smith. 2003. *The Public Administration Theory Primer*. Boulder, CO: Westview Press.

Frederickson, H. George, Kevin B. Smith, Christopher W. Larimer, and Michael J. Licari. 2012. *The Public Administration Theory Primer*. 2nd ed. Boulder, CO: Westview Press.

Freedman, David. 2009. *Statistical Models and Causal Inference: A Dialogue with the Social Sciences*, ed. David Collier, Jasjeet S. Sekhon, and Philip B. Stark. New York: Cambridge University Press.

Freeman, J. Leiper. 1965. *The Political Process: Executive Bureau–Legislative Committee Relations*. Rev. ed. New York: Random House.

Friedman, Jeffrey. 1996. *The Rational Choice Controversy: Economic Models of Politics Reconsidered*. New Haven, CT: Yale University Press.

Fuguitt, Diana, and Shanton Wilcox. 1999. *Cost-Benefit Analysis for Public Sector Decision Makers*. Westport, CT: Quorum Books.

Fung, Archon, and Erik O. Wright. 2003a. *Deepening Democracy: Institutional Innovations in Empowered Participatory Governance*. London: Verso.

_____. 2003b. "Thinking About Empowered Participatory Governance." In *Deepening Democracy: Institutional Innovations in Empowered Participatory Governance*, ed. Archon Fung and Erik O. Wright. London: Verso.

Garrett, James E. 1993. "Public Administration and Policy Implementation—A Social Work Perspective." *International Journal of Public Administration* 16: 1247–1263.

George, A. L., and T. J. McKeown. 1985. "Case Studies and Theories of Organizational Decision Making." In *Research on Public Organizations*, ed. R. F. Coulam and R. A. Smith. Greenwich, CT: JAI Press.

Gerber, Alan S., Donald P. Green, and Christopher W. Larimer. 2008. "Social Pressure and Voter Turnout: Evidence from a Large-Scale Field Experiment." *American Political Science Review* 102 (February): 33–48.

Ghuman, Shawn. 2012. "Florida, Iowa Target Voting Rights for Ex-felons." *USA Today*, July 10.

Gigerenzer, Gerd, and Reinhard Selton. 2002. *Bounded Rationality: The Adaptive Toolbox*. Cambridge, MA: MIT Press.

Gigerenzer, Gerd, and Peter M. Todd. 1999a. "Fast and Frugal Heuristics." In *Simple Heuristics That Make Us Smart*, ed. Gerd Gigerenzer and Peter M. Todd, 3–34. New York: Oxford University Press.

———. 1999b. *Simple Heuristics That Make Us Smart*. New York: Oxford University Press.

Gilens, Martin. 2000. *Why Americans Hate Welfare: Race, Media, and the Politics of Antipoverty Policy*. Chicago: University of Chicago Press.

Goggin, Malcolm, Ann O'M. Bowman, James Lester, and Laurence O'Toole Jr. 1990. *Implementation Theory and Practice: Towards a Third Generation*. Glenview, IL: Scott, Foresman/Little, Brown.

Goleman, Daniel. 1995. *Emotional Intelligence: Why It Can Matter More Than IQ*. New York: Bantam.

Goodin, Robert. 1999. "Rationality Redux: Reflections on Herbert A. Simon's Vision of Politics." In *Competition and Cooperation: Conversations with Nobelists About Economics and Political Science*, ed. James E. Alt, Margaret Levi, and Elinor Ostrom, 60–84. New York: Russell Sage Foundation.

Goodin, Robert, Martin Rein, and Michael Moran. 2006. "The Public and Its Policies." In *The Oxford Handbook of Public Policy*, ed. Michael Moran, Martin Rein, and Robert E. Goodin, 3–35. New York: Oxford University Press.

Gormley, William. 1986. "Regulatory Issue Networks in a Federal System." *Polity* 18 (Summer): 595–620.

Government Accountability Office (GAO). 2001. *School Vouchers: Publicly Funded Programs in Cleveland and Milwaukee*. Washington, DC: USGAO.

———. 2002. *School Vouchers: Characteristics of Privately Funded Programs*. Washington, DC: USGAO.

Gravetter, Frederick, and Larry Wallnau. 2004. *Statistics for the Behavioral Sciences*. 6th ed. Belmont, CA: Wadsworth.

Green, Donald P., and Ian Shapiro. 1994. *Pathologies of Rational Choice Theory: A Critique of Applications in Political Science*. New Haven, CT: Yale University Press.

Greenberg, George, Jeffrey Miller, Lawrence Mohr, and Bruce Vladeck. 1977. "Developing Public Policy Theory: Perspectives from Empirical Research." *American Political Science Review* 71(4): 1532–1543.

Gupta, Dipak. 2001. *Analyzing Public Policy: Concepts, Tools, and Techniques*. Washington, DC: CQ Press.

Guth, Werner, and Reinhard Tietz. 1990. "Ultimatum Bargaining Behavior: A Survey and Comparison of Experimental Results." *Journal of Economic Psychology* 11: 417–449.

Hajer, Maarten, and David Laws. 2006. "Ordering Through Discourse." In *The Oxford Handbook of Public Policy*, ed. Michael Moran, Martin Rein, and Robert E. Goodin, 251–268. New York: Oxford University Press.

Hamm, Keith. 1983. "Patterns of Influence Among Committees, Agencies, and Interest Groups." *Legislative Studies Quarterly* 8: 379–426.

Hanushek, Erik. 1997. "Assessing the Effects of School Resources on Student Performance: An Update." *Educational Evaluation and Policy Analysis* 19: 141–164.

Haveman, Robert. 1987. "Policy Evaluation Research After Twenty Years." *Policy Studies Journal* 16: 191–218.

Head, Brian W. 2008. "Three Lenses of Evidence-Based Policy." *Research and Evaluation* 67: 1–11.

Heaney, Michael, and John Mark Hansen. 2006. "Building the Chicago School." *American Political Science Review* 100: 589–596.

Heclo, Hugh. 1977. *A Government of Strangers: Executive Politics in Washington.* Washington, DC: Brookings Institution Press.

_____. 1978. "Issue Networks and the Executive Establishment." In *The New American Political System*, ed. Anthony King, 87–124. Washington, DC: American Enterprise Institute.

Henrich, Joseph, Robert Boyd, Samuel Bowles, Colin Camerer, Ernst Fehr, Herbert Gintis, and Richard McElreath. 2001. "In Search of Homo-Economicus: Behavioral Experiments in 15 Small-Scale Societies." *American Economic Review* 91: 73–78.

Henry, Adam Douglas. 2011. "Ideology, Power, and the Structure of Policy Networks." *Policy Studies Journal* 39(3): 361–384.

Hibbing, John R., and Elizabeth Theiss-Morse. 1995. *Congress as Public Enemy.* Cambridge, MA: Cambridge University Press.

_____. 2002. *Stealth Democracy: Americans' Belief About How Government Should Work.* Cambridge, MA: Cambridge University Press.

_____. 2005. "Citizenship and Civic Engagement." *Annual Review of Political Science* 8: 227–249.

Hicks, J. R. 1939. "The Foundations of Welfare Economics." *Economic Journal* 49: 696–712.

Hicklin, Alisa, and Erik Godwin. 2009. "Agents of Change: The Role of Public Managers in Public Policy." *Policy Studies Journal* 37: 13–20.

Hill, Kim Quaile. 1997. "In Search of Policy Theory." *Policy Currents* 7 (April): 1–9.

Hjern, Benny. 1982. "Implementation Research: The Link Gone Missing." *Journal of Public Policy* 2: 301–308.

Hjern, Benny, and Chriss Hull. 1983. "Implementation Research as Empirical Constitutionalism." *European Journal of Political Research* 10: 105–115.

Hogwood, Brian, and Lewis Gunn. 1984. *Policy Analysis for the Real World.* New York: Oxford University Press.

Howell-Moroney, Michael. 2008. "The Tiebout Hypothesis 50 Years Later: Lessons and Lingering Challenges for Metropolitan Governance in the 21st Century." *Public Administration Review* (January/February): 97–109.

Howlett, Michael, and Adam Wellstead. 2011. "Policy Analysts in the Bureaucracy Revisted: The Nature of Contemporary Government." *Politics & Policy* 4: 613–644.

Huckfeldt, Robert, and John Sprague. 1987. "Networks in Context: The Social Flow of Political Information." *American Political Science Review* 81: 1197–1216.

Imbens, Guido, and Jeffrey Wooldridge. 2008. "Recent Developments in the Econometrics of Program Evaluation." National Bureau of Economic Research, Working Paper 14251.

Ingram, Helen. 1990. "Implementation: A Review and Suggested Framework." In *Public Administration: The State of the Art*, ed. Naomi Lynn and Aaron Wildavsky. Chatham, NJ: Chatham House.

Ingram, Helen M., and Anne L. Schneider. 2005a. *Deserving and Entitled: Social Constructions and Target Populations*. Albany: State University of New York Press.

———. 2005b. "Public Policy and the Social Construction of Deservedness." In *Deserving and Entitled: Social Constructions and Target Populations*, ed. Anne L. Schneider and Helen M. Ingram, 1–28. Albany: State University of New York Press.

———. 2006. "Policy Analysis for Democracy." In *The Oxford Handbook of Public Policy*, ed. Michael Moran, Martin Rein, and Robert E. Goodin, 169–189. New York: Oxford University Press.

Ingram, Helen, Anne L. Schneider, and Peter deLeon. 2007. "Social Construction and Policy Design." In *Theories of the Policy Process*, 2nd ed., ed. Paul A. Sabatier, 93–126. Boulder, CO: Westview Press.

Jenkins-Smith, Hank C., and Paul A. Sabatier. 1993. "The Study of the Public Policy Process." In *Policy Change and Learning: An Advocacy Coalition Approach*, ed. Paul A. Sabatier and Hank C. Jenkins-Smith, 1–12. Boulder, CO: Westview Press.

Jochim, Ashley E., and Peter J. May. 2010. "Beyond Subsystems: Policy Regimes and Governance." *Policy Studies Journal* 38(2): 303–28.

John, Peter. 2003. "Is There Life After Policy Streams, Advocacy Coalitions, and Punctuations? Using Evolutionary Theory to Explain Policy Change." *Policy Studies Journal* 31(4): 481–498.

John, Peter, and Shaun Bevan. 2012. "What Are Policy Punctuations? Large Changes in the Legislative Agenda of the UK Government, 1911–2008." *Policy Studies Journal* 40(1): 89–107.

Jones, Bryan D. 2001. *Politics and the Architecture of Choice: Bounded Rationality and Governance*. Chicago: University of Chicago Press.

———. 2003. "Bounded Rationality and Political Science: Lessons from Public Administration and Public Policy." *Journal of Public Administration Research and Theory* 13: 395–412.

Jones, Bryan D., and Frank R. Baumgartner. 2005. *The Politics of Attention: How Government Prioritizes Problems*. Chicago: University of Chicago Press.

———. 2012. "From There to Here: Punctuated Equilibrium to the General Punctuation Thesis to a Theory of Government Information Processing." *Policy Studies Journal* 40(1): 1–19.

Jones, Bryan D., Frank R. Baumgartner, Christian Breunig, Christopher Wlezien, Stuart Soroka, Martial Foucault, Abel Francois, Christoffer Green-Pederson, Chris

Koski, Peter John, Peter Mortensen, Frederic Varone, and Steffan Walgrave. 2009. "A General Empirical Law of Public Budgets: A Comparative Analysis." *American Journal of Political Science* 53: 855–873.

Jones, Bryan D., Frank R. Baumgartner, and James L. True. 1998. "Policy Punctuations: U.S. Budget Authority, 1947–1995." *Journal of Politics* 60(1): 1–33.

Jones, Bryan D., Tracy Sulkin, and Heather A. Larsen. 2003. "Policy Punctuations in American Political Institutions." *American Political Science Review* 97(1): 151–169.

Jones, Bryan D., and Walter Williams. 2007. *The Politics of Bad Ideas*. New York: Longman.

Jones, Charles O. 1970. *An Introduction to the Study of Public Policy*. Belmont, CA: Wadsworth.

_____. 1976. "Why Congress Can't Do Policy Analysis (Or Words to That Effect)." *Policy Analysis* 2: 251–264.

Jones, Michael D., and Hank C. Jenkins-Smith. 2009. "Trans-Subsystems Dynamics: Policy Topography, Mass Opinion, and Policy Change." *Policy Studies Journal* 37(1): 37–58.

Jones, Michael D., and Mark K. McBeth. 2010. "A Narrative Policy Framework: Clear Enough to be Wrong." *Policy Studies Journal* 38(2): 329–353.

Just, R. E., D. L. Hueth, and A. Schmitz. 2004. *Welfare Economics of Public Policy: A Practical Approach to Project and Policy Evaluation*. Cheltenham: Edward Elgar.

Kahneman, Daniel. 1994. "New Challenges to the Rationality Assumption." *Journal of Institutional and Theoretical Economics* 150: 18–36.

_____. 2011. *Thinking, Fast and Slow*. New York: Farrar, Straus, and Giroux.

Kahneman, Daniel, and Robert Sugden. 2005. "Experienced Utility as a Standard of Policy Evaluation." *Environmental and Resource Economics* 32: 161–181.

Kahneman, Daniel, and Richard H. Thaler. 2006. "Anomalies: Utility Maximization and Experienced Utility." *Journal of Economic Perspectives* 20(1): 221–234.

Kahneman, Daniel, and Amos Tversky. 1978. "Prospect Theory: An Analysis of Decision Under Risk." *Econometrica* 47: 263–291.

_____. 1984. "Choices, Values, and Frames." *American Psychologist* 39(4): 341–350.

Kaldor, N. 1939. "Welfare Propositions of Economics and Interpersonal Comparison of Utility." *Economic Journal* 39: 549–552.

Karch, Andrew. 2007. *Democratic Laboratories: Policy Diffusion Among the American States*. Ann Arbor: University of Michigan Press.

Kathlene, Lyn, and John Martin. 1991. "Enhancing Citizen Participation: Panel Designs, Perspectives, and Policy Formulation." *Journal of Policy Analysis and Management* 10: 46–63.

Kellow, Aynsley. 1988. "Promoting Elegance in Policy Theory: Simplifying Lowi's Arenas of Power." *Policy Studies Journal* 16 (Summer): 713–724.

_____. 1989. "Taking the Long Way Home? A Reply to Spitzer on the Arenas of Power." *Policy Studies Journal* 17 (Spring): 537–546.

Kenny, Christopher B. 1992. "Political Participation and Effects from the Social Environment." *American Journal of Political Science* 36: 259–267.

Kerwin, Cornelius, and Scott Furlong. 2010. *Rulemaking: How Government Agencies Write Law and Make Policy.* Washington, DC: CQ Press.

King, Gary, R. Keohane, and S. Verba. 1994. *Designing Social Inquiry: Scientific Inference in Qualitative Research.* Princeton, NJ: Princeton University Press.

Kingdon, John W. 1995. *Agendas, Alternatives, and Public Policies.* 2nd ed. Boston: Little, Brown.

Kirp, D. 1992. "The End of Policy Analysis." *Journal of Policy Analysis and Management* 11: 693–696.

Kjellberg, Francesco. 1977. "Do Policies (Really) Determine Politics? And Eventually How?" *Policy Studies Journal* (Special Issue): 554–570.

Kluver, L. 1995. "Consensus Conferences at the Danish Board of Technology." In *Public Participation in Science*, ed. S. Joss and J. Durant. London: Science Museum.

Koppell, Jonathan G. S. 2010. *World Rule: Accountability, Legitimacy, and the Design of Global Governance.* Chicago: University of Chicago Press.

Kuhn, Thomas. 1970. *The Structure of Scientific Revolutions.* Chicago: University of Chicago Press.

Kuran, Timur. 1995. *Private Truths, Public Lies: The Social Consequences of Preference Falsification.* Cambridge, MA: Harvard University Press.

Kurzban, Robert. 2010. *Why Everyone (Else) Is a Hypocrite: Evolution and the Modular Mind.* Princeton, NJ: Princeton University Press.

Ladd, Helen F. 2002. "School Vouchers: A Critical View." *Journal of Economic Perspectives* 16: 3–24.

Lasswell, Harold. 1936. *Who Gets What, When, and How?* New York: McGraw Hill.

———. 1951a. "The Immediate Future of Research Policy and Method in Political Science." *American Political Science Review* 45: 133–142.

———. 1951b. "The Policy Orientation." In *The Policy Sciences: Recent Developments in Scope and Method,* ed. Daniel Lerner and Harold Lasswell, 3–15. Stanford, CA: Stanford University Press.

———. 1956. "The Political Science of Science: An Inquiry into the Possible Reconciliation of Mastery and Freedom." *American Political Science Review* 50: 961–979.

———. 1971. *A Pre-View of the Policy Sciences.* New York: American Elsevier.

Leach, William D., and Paul A. Sabatier. 2005. "To Trust an Adversary: Integrating Rational and Psychological Models of Collaborative Policymaking." *American Political Science Review* 99(4): 491–503.

LeDoux, Joseph. 1996. *The Emotional Brain: The Mysterious Underpinnings of Emotional Life.* New York: Simon & Schuster.

———. 2002. *Synaptic Self: How Our Brains Become Who We Are.* New York: Penguin Books.

Lemann, Nicholas. 1995. "The Great Sorting." *The Atlantic Monthly* 276(3): 84–97.

Lester, James. 1990. "A New Federalism? Environmental Policy in the States." In *Environmental Policy in the 1990s*, ed. Norman Vig and Michael Kraft. Washington, DC: Congressional Quarterly Press.

Lester, James, and Malcolm Goggin. 1998. "Back to the Future: The Rediscovery of Implementation Studies. *Policy Currents* (September): 1–7.

Lester, James, and Joseph Stewart Jr. 2000. *Public Policy: An Evolutionary Approach*. Belmont, CA: Wadsworth.

Levin, Henry, and Patrick McEwan. 2001. *Cost-Effectiveness Analysis*. 2nd ed. Thousand Oaks, CA: Sage.

Lin, Ann Chih. 1996. "When Failure Is Better Than Success: Subverted, Aborted, and Non-Implementation." Paper presented at the Annual Meeting of the American Political Science Association.

Lindblom, Charles E. 1959. "The Science of Muddling Through." *Public Administration Review* 19: 79–88.

———. 1979. "Still Muddling: Not Yet Through." *Public Administration Review* 39: 517–526.

Lipsky, Michael. 1971. "Street-Level Bureaucracy and the Analysis of Urban Reform." *Urban Affairs Quarterly* 6: 391–409.

———. 1980. *Street-Level Bureaucracy*. New York: Russell Sage Foundation.

Liu, Xinsberg, Eric Lindquist, Arnold Vedlitz, and Kenneth Vincent. 2010. "Understanding Local Policymaking: Policy Elites' Perceptions of Local Agenda Setting and Alternative Policy Selection." *Policy Studies Journal* 38(1): 69–92.

Lowery, David, W. E. Lyons, and Ruth Hoogland DeHoog. 1995. "The Empirical Evidence for Citizen Information and a Market for Public Goods." *American Political Science Review* 89(3): 705–707.

Lowi, Theodore J. 1964. "American Business, Public Policy, Case Studies, and Political Theory." *World Politics* 16(4): 677–715.

———. 1970. "Decision Making vs. Policy Making: Toward an Antidote for Technocracy." *Public Administration Review* (May/June): 314–325.

———. 1972. "Four Systems of Policy, Politics, and Choice." *Public Administration Review* 33 (July–August): 298–310.

———. 1988. "Comment." *Policy Studies Journal* 16 (Summer): 725–728.

Lyons, W. E., David Lowery, and Ruth Hoogland DeHoog. 1992. *The Politics of Dissatisfaction: Citizens, Services, and Urban Institutions*. New York: M. E. Sharpe.

Macedo, Stephen. 2005. *Democracy at Risk: How Political Choices Undermine Citizen Participation and What We Can Do About It*. Washington, DC: Brookings Institution Press.

Majone, Giandomenico. 2006. "Agenda Setting." In *The Oxford Handbook of Public Policy*, ed. Michael Moran, Martin Rein, and Robert E. Goodin, 228–250. New York: Oxford University Press.

Majone, Giandomenico, and Aaron Wildavsky. 1979. "Implementation as Evolution." In *Implementation*, ed. Jeffrey Pressman and Aaron Wildavsky. Berkeley: University of California Press.

March, James G. 1994. *A Primer on Decision Making: How Decisions Happen*. New York: Free Press.

March, James G., and Johan P. Olsen. 2006. "The Logic of Appropriateness." In *The Oxford Handbook of Public Policy*, ed. Michael Moran, Martin Rein, and Robert E. Goodin, 689–708. New York: Oxford University Press.

Marcus, George E., W. Russell Neuman, and Michael MacKuen. 2000. *Affective Intelligence and Political Judgment*. Chicago: University of Chicago Press.

Mark, M. M., G. T. Henry, and G. Julnes. 1999. "Toward an Integrative Framework for Evaluation Practice." *American Journal of Evaluation* 20: 177–198.

Matland, Richard. 1995. "Synthesizing the Implementation Literature: The Ambiguity-Conflict Model of Policy Implementation." *Journal of Public Administration Research and Theory* 5: 145–174.

Matti, Simon, and Annica Sanstrom. 2011. "The Rationale Determining Advocacy Coalitions: Examining Coordination Networks and Corresponding Beliefs." *Policy Studies Journal* 39(3): 385–410.

May, Peter J. 1991. "Reconsidering Policy Design: Policies and Publics." *Journal of Public Policy* 11(2): 187–206.

_____. 1992. "Policy Learning and Failure." *Journal of Public Policy* 12(4): 331–354.

Mayhew, David R. 1974. *The Electoral Connection*. New Haven, CT: Yale University Press.

Mazmanian, Daniel, and Paul Sabatier. 1983. *Implementation and Public Policy*. Glendale, IL: Scott, Foresman.

McBeth, Mark K., Donna L. Lybecker, and Kacee Garner. 2010. "The Story of Good Citizenship: Framing Public Policy in the Context of Duty-Based Versus Engaged Citizenship." *Politics & Policy* 38(1): 1–23.

McBeth, Mark K., Elizabeth A. Shanahan, and Michael D. Jones. 2005. "The Science of Storytelling: Measuring Policy Beliefs in Greater Yellowstone." *Society & Natural Resources* 18: 413–429.

McBeth, Mark K., Elizabeth A. Shanahan, Ruth J. Arnell, and Paul L. Hathaway. 2007. "The Intersection of Narrative Policy Analysis and Policy Change Theory." *Policy Studies Journal* 35 (1): 87–108.

McCool, Daniel C. 1995a. "Policy Subsystems." In *Public Policy Theories, Models, and Concepts: An Anthology*, ed. Daniel C. McCool, 251–255. Englewood Cliffs, NJ: Prentice Hall.

_____. 1995b. *Public Policy Theories, Models and Concepts: An Anthology*. Englewood Cliffs, NJ: Prentice Hall.

_____. 1995c. "The Theoretical Foundations of Policy Studies." In *Public Policy Theories, Models, and Concepts: An Anthology*, ed. Daniel C. McCool, 1–27. Englewood Cliffs, NJ: Prentice Hall.

_____. 1995d. "Discussion." In *Public Policy Theories, Models, and Concepts: An Anthology*, ed. Daniel C. McCool, 380–389. Englewood Cliffs, NJ: Prentice Hall.

McDermott, Rose. 2004. "The Feeling of Rationality: The Meaning of Neuroscientific Advances for Political Science." *Perspectives on Politics* 2: 691–706.

McDermott, Rose, James Fowler, and Oleg Smirnov. 2008. "On the Evolutionary Origins of Prospect Theory." *Journal of Politics* 70(2): 335–350.

McFarlane, Deborah. 1989. "Test the Statutory Coherence Hypothesis: The Implementation of Federal Family Planning Policy in the States." *Administration & Society* 20: 395–422.

McGinnis, Michael D. 2011. "An Introduction to IAD and the Language of the Ostrom Workshop: A Simple Guide to a Complex Framework." *Policy Studies Journal* 39(1): 169–183.

Meier, Kenneth. 1994. *The Politics of Sin.* New York: M. E. Sharpe.

_____. 1999. "Drugs, Sex, Rock, and Roll: A Theory of Morality Politics." *Policy Studies Journal* 27: 681–695.

_____. 2009. "Policy Theory, Policy Theory Everywhere: Ravings of a Deranged Policy Scholar." *Policy Studies Journal* 37: 5–11.

Meier, Kenneth, and Jeff Gill, eds. 2000. *What Works: A New Approach to Program and Policy Analysis.* Boulder, CO: Westview Press.

Meier, Kenneth, and Deborah McFarlane. 1996. "Statutory Coherence and Policy Implementation: The Case of Family Planning." *Journal of Public Policy* 15(3): 281–298.

Meier, Kenneth, J. L. Polinard, and Robert D. Wrinkle. 2000. "Bureaucracy and Organizational Performance: Causality Arguments About Public Schools." *American Journal of Political Science* 44(3): 590–602.

Melnick, R. Shep. 1994. "Separation of Powers and the Strategy of Rights: The Expansion of Special Education." In *The New Politics of Public Policy*, ed. Marc K. Landy and Martin A. Levin, 23–46. Baltimore, MD: Johns Hopkins University Press.

Meltsner, A. 1976. *Policy Analysts in the Bureaucracy.* Berkeley: University of California Press.

Metcalf, Kim, Ronald Beghetto, and Natalie Legan. 2002. "Interpreting Voucher Research: The Influence of Multiple Comparison Groups and Types." Paper presented at The Promise and Reality of School Choice: The Milwaukee Experience, Milwaukee, WI, October 17–18.

Moe, Terry. 2001. *Schools, Vouchers, and the American Public.* Washington, DC: Brookings Institution Press.

Mohr, Lawrence. 1995. *Impact Analysis for Program Evaluation.* 2nd ed. Thousand Oaks, CA: Sage.

_____. 1999. "The Qualitative Method of Impact Analysis." *American Journal of Evaluation* 99: 69–85.

Mondou, Matthieu, and Eric Montpetit. 2010. "Policy Styles and Degenerative Politics: Poverty Policy Designs in Newfoundland and Quebec." *Policy Studies Journal* 38(4): 703–721.

Mooney, Christopher. 1991. "Information in State Legislative Decision Making." *Legislative Studies Quarterly* 16: 445–455.

_____, ed. 2000. *The Public Clash of Private Values: The Politics of Morality Policy.* Chatham, NJ: Chatham House.

Mooney, Christopher, and Mei-Hsien Lee. 1999. "Morality Policy Reinvention: State Death Penalties." *Annals of the American Academy of Political and Social Sciences* 566 (November): 80–92.

Morgan, Stephen L., and Christopher Winship. 2007. *Counterfactuals and Causal Inference: Methods and Principles for Social Research*. New York: Cambridge University Press.

Morris, Jake Breton, Valentina Tassone, Rudolf de Groot, Marguerite Camilleri, and Stefano Moncada. 2011. "A Framework for Participatory Impact Assessment: Involving Stakeholders in European Policy Making, a Case Study of Land Use Change in Malta." *Ecology and Society* 16: 12–31.

Morton, Rebecca B., and Kenneth C. Williams. 2010. *Experimental Political Science and the Study of Causality: From Nature to the Lab*. New York: Cambridge University Press.

Mucciaroni, Gary. 2011. "Are Debates About 'Morality Policy' Really About Morality? Framing Opposition to Gay and Lesbian Rights." *Policy Studies Journal* 39: 187–216.

Munger, Michael. 2000. *Analyzing Policy: Choices, Conflicts, and Practices*. New York: W. W. Norton.

Nakamura, Robert, and Frank Smallwood. 1980. *The Politics of Policy Implementation*. New York: St. Martin's Press.

Nas, T. F. 1996. *Cost-Benefit Analysis: Theory and Application*. Thousand Oaks, CA: Sage.

Nelson, Barbara J. 1984. *Making an Issue of Child Abuse: Political Agenda Setting for Social Problems*. Chicago: University of Chicago Press.

Newell, Allen, and Herbert A. Simon. 1972. *Human Problem Solving*. Englewood Cliffs, NJ: Prentice Hall.

Nicholson-Crotty, Sean, and Kenneth Meier. 2005. "From Perception to Public Policy: Translating Social Constructions into Policy Designs." In *Deserving and Entitled: Social Constructions and Target Populations*, ed. Anne L. Schneider and Helen M. Ingram, 223–242. Albany: State University of New York Press.

Nicholson-Crotty, Sean, and Laurence O'Toole Jr. 2004. "Public Management and Organizational Performance: The Case of Law Enforcement Agencies." *Journal of Public Administration and Theory* 14: 1–18.

Niskanen, William. 1971. *Bureaucracy and Representative Government*. Hawthorne, NY: Aldine de Gruyter.

Nowak, Martin A., Karen M. Page, and Karl Sigmund. 2000. "Fairness Versus Reason in the Ultimatum Game." *Science* 289: 1773–1775.

Nowlin, Matthew C. 2011. "Theories of the Policy Process: State of the Research and Emerging Trends." *Policy Studies Journal* 39(S1): 41–60.

Orbell, John, Tomonori Morikawa, Jason Hartwig, James Hanley, and Nicholas Allen. 2004. "Machiavellian Intelligence as a Basis for the Evolution of Cooperative Dispositions." *American Political Science Review* 98: 1–16.

Ostrom, Elinor. 1998. "A Behavioral Approach to the Rational Theory of Collective Action, Presidential Address, American Political Science Association, 1997." *American Political Science Review* 92(1): 1–22.

_____. 2005. "Toward a Behavioral Theory Linking Trust, Reciprocity, and Reputation." In *Trust and Reciprocity: Interdisciplinary Lessons from Experimental Research*, ed. Elinor Ostrom and James Walker, 19–79. New York: Russell Sage.

_____. 2007. "Institutional Rational Choice: An Assessment of the Institutional Analysis." In *Theories of the Policy Process*, ed. Paul A. Sabatier, 21–64. Boulder, CO: Westview Press.

_____. 2011. "Background on the Institutional Analysis and Development Framework." *Policy Studies Journal* 39(1): 7–27.

Ostrom, Elinor, Roy Gardner, and James Walker. 1994. *Rules, Games, and Common-Pool Resources*. Ann Arbor: University of Michigan Press.

Ostrom, Elinor, James Walker, and Roy Gardner. 1992. "Covenants with and Without a Sword: Self-Governance Is Possible." *American Political Science Review* 86(2): 404–417.

Ostrom, Vincent. 1973. *The Intellectual Crisis in Public Administration*. Tuscaloosa: University of Alabama Press.

O'Toole, Laurence, and Kenneth J. Meier. 2011. *Public Management: Organizations, Governance and Performance*. New York: Cambridge University Press.

O'Toole, Laurence J., Jr. 1986. "Policy Recommendations for Multi-Actor Implementation: An Assessment of the Field." *Journal of Public Policy* 6(2): 181–210.

_____. 1995. "Rational Choice and Policy Implementation: Implications for Interorganizational Network Management." *American Review of Public Administration* 25: 43–57.

_____. 2000. "Research on Policy Implementation: Assessments and Prospects." *Journal of Public Administration Research and Theory* 20: 263–288.

Page, Edward C. 2006. "The Origins of Policy." In *The Oxford Handbook of Public Policy*, ed. Michael Moran, Martin Rein, and Robert E. Goodin, 207–227. New York: Oxford University Press.

Palumbo, Dennis. 1981. "The State of Policy Studies Research and the Policy of the New Policy Studies Review." *Policy Studies Review* 1: 5–10.

Panksepp, Jaak. 2003. "Feeling the Pain of Social Loss." *Science* 302: 237–239.

Patton, M. Q. 2000. "Overview: Language Matters." *New Directions for Evaluation* 86: 5–16.

Petrovsky, Nicolai. 2006. "Public Management Theory and Federal Programs: A Test Using Part Scores." Paper presented at the conference on Empirical Studies of Organizations and Public Management, Texas A&M University, May 4–6.

Pielke, Roger A. 2004. "What Future for the Policy Sciences?" *Policy Sciences*. 34: 209–225.

Pierce, Jonathan J. 2011. "Coalition Stability and Belief Change: Advocacy Coalitions in U.S. Foreign Policy and the Creation of Israel, 1922–44." *Policy Studies Journal* 39(3): 411–434.

Pressman, Jeffrey, and Aaron Wildavsky. 1973. *Implementation: How Great Expectations in Washington Are Dashed in Oakland*. Berkeley: University of California Press.

Prindle, David F. 2012. "Importing Concepts from Biology into Political Science: The Case of Punctuated Equilibrium." *Policy Studies Journal* 40(1): 21–43.

Pump, Barry. 2011. "Beyond Metaphors: New Research on Agendas in the Policy Process." *Policy Studies Journal* 39(S1): 1–12.

Quade, E. S. 1989. *Analysis for Public Decisions*. 3rd ed. New York: North-Holland.

Radin, Beryl. 1997. "Presidential Address: The Evolution of the Policy Analysis Field: From Conversations to Conversations." *Journal of Policy Analysis and Management* 2: 204–218.

———. 2000. *Beyond Machiavelli: Policy Analysis Comes of Age*. Washington, DC: Georgetown University Press.

Ravitch, Diane. 2011. *The Life and Death of the Great American School System*. New York: Basic Books.

Redford, Emmette S. 1969. *Democracy in the Administrative State*. New York: Oxford University Press.

Reich, Gary, and Jay Barth. 2010. "Educating Citizens or Defying Federal Authority? A Comparative Study of In-State Tuition for Undocumented Students." *Policy Studies Journal* 38(3): 419–445.

Reid, F. 2003. "Evidence-Based Policy: Where Is the Evidence for It?" School for Policy Studies, University of Bristol, Working Paper No. 3.

Renn, Ortwin, Thomas Webber, Horst Rakel, Peter Dienel, and Brenda Johnson. 1993. "Public Participation in Decision Making: A Three-Step Procedure." *Policy Sciences* 26: 189–214.

Rich, Andrew. 2001. "The Politics of Expertise in Congress and the News Media." *Social Science Quarterly* 82: 583–601.

Richardson, H. S. 2000. "The Stupidity of the Cost-Benefit Standard." *Journal of Legal Studies* 29: 971–1003.

Ripley, Randall B. 1985. *Policy Analysis in Political Science*. Chicago: Nelson-Hall.

Robinson, Lisa, and James Hammitt. 2011. "Behavioral Economics and the Conduct of Benefit-Cost Analysis: Towards Principles and Standards." *Journal of Cost-Benefit Analysis*. doi: 0.2202/2152-2812.1059.

Robinson, Scott E., Floun'say Caver, Kenneth J. Meier, and Laurence J. O'Toole Jr. 2007. "Explaining Policy Punctuations: Bureaucratization and Budget Change." *American Journal of Political Science* 51 (January): 140–150.

Robinson, Scott E., and Warren S. Eller. 2010. "Participation in Policy Streams: Testing the Separation of Problems and Solutions in Subnational Policy Systems." *Policy Studies Journal* 38(2): 199–216.

Rose, Richard. 1993. *Lesson-Drawing in Public Policy*. Chatham, NJ: Chatham House.

Rosenbaum, R. 1981. "Statutory Structure and Policy Implementation: The Case of Wetlands Regulation." In *Effective Policy Implementation*, ed. Daniel Mazmanian and Paul Sabatier, 63–85. Lexington, MA: D. C. Heath.

Rossi, Peter H., and Howard E. Freeman. 1993. *Evaluation: A Systematic Approach.* 5th ed. Thousand Oaks, CA: Sage.

Rothstein, Richard. 1997. *What Do We Know About Declining (or Rising) Student Achievement?* Arlington, VA: Educational Research Service.

Rubin, Paul H. 2002. *Darwinian Politics: The Evolutionary Origin of Freedom.* New Brunswick, NJ: Rutgers University Press.

Saad, Gad. 2003. "Evolution and Political Marketing." In *Human Nature and Public Policy: An Evolutionary Approach,* ed. Albert Somit and Steven A. Peterson, 121–138. New York: Palgrave Macmillan.

Sabatier, Paul A. 1988. "An Advocacy Coalition Framework of Policy Change and the Role of Policy-Oriented Learning Therein." *Policy Sciences* 21: 129–168.

_____. 1991a. "Political Science and Public Policy." *PS: Political Science and Politics* 24: 144–147.

_____. 1991b. "Toward Better Theories of the Policy Process." *PS: Political Science and Politics* 24: 147–156.

_____. 1997. "The Status and Development of Policy Theory: A Reply to Hill." *Policy Currents* 7 (December): 1–10.

_____. 1999a. "The Need for Better Theories." In *Theories of the Policy Process,* ed. Paul Sabatier, 3–18. Boulder, CO: Westview Press.

_____, ed. 1999b. *Theories of the Policy Process.* Boulder, CO: Westview Press.

_____. 2007a. "The Need for Better Theories." In *Theories of the Policy Process,* 2nd ed., ed. Paul A. Sabatier, 3–17. Boulder, CO: Westview Press.

_____. 2007b. "Fostering the Development of Policy Theory." In *Theories of the Policy Process,* 2nd ed., ed. Paul A. Sabatier, 321–336. Boulder, CO: Westview Press.

Sabatier, Paul A., and Hank C. Jenkins-Smith. 1999. "The Advocacy Coalition Framework: An Assessment." In *Theories of the Policy Process,* ed. Paul A. Sabatier, 117–166. Boulder, CO: Westview Press.

Saetren, Harald. 2005. "Fact and Myths About Research on Public Policy Implementation: Out-of-Fashion, Allegedly Dead, but Still Very Much Alive and Relevant." *Policy Studies Journal* 33: 559–582.

Sanfey, Alan G., James Billing, Jessica A. Aronson, Leigh E. Nystrom, and Jonathan D. Cohen. 2003. "The Neural Basis of Economic Decision-Making in the Ultimatum Game." *Science* 300: 1755–1758.

Schachter, Hindy Lauer. 2007. "Does Frederick Taylor's Ghost Still Haunt the Halls of Government? A Look at the Concept of Governmental Efficiency in Our Time." *Public Administration Review* (September/October): 800–810.

Schattschneider, E. E. 1965. *The Semi-Sovereign People.* New York: Wadsworth.

Scheberle, Denise. 1997. *Federalism and Environmental Policy: Trust and the Politics of Implementation.* Washington, DC: Georgetown University Press.

Schlager, Edella. 2007. "A Comparison of Frameworks, Theories, and Models of Policy Processes." In *Theories of the Policy Process,* 2nd ed., ed. Paul A. Sabatier, 293–319. Boulder, CO: Westview Press.

Schneider, Anne, and Helen Ingram. 1993. "Social Constructions of Target Populations: Implications for Politics and Policy." *American Political Science Review* (June): 334–347.

———. 1997. *Policy Design for Democracy*. Lawrence: University of Kansas Press.

Schneider, Anne, and Mara Sidney. 2009. "What Is Next for Policy Design and Social Construction Theory?" *Policy Studies Journal* 37(1): 103–119.

Schneider, Mark, and Jack Buckley. 2002. "What Do Parents Want from Schools? Evidence from the Internet." *Educational Evaluation and Policy Analysis* 24(2): 133–144.

Schneider, Mark, Paul Teske, Melissa Marschall, and Christine Roch. 1998. "Shopping for Schools: In the Land of the Blind, the One-Eyed Parent May Be Enough." *American Journal of Political Science* 42(3): 769–793.

Scholz, John T. 1998. "Trust, Taxes, and Compliance." In *Trust and Governance*, ed. Valerie Braithwaite and Margaret Levi, 135–166. New York: Russell Sage Foundation.

Schram, Arthur, and Joep Sonnemans. 1996. "Why People Vote: Experimental Evidence." *Journal of Economic Psychology* 17: 417–442.

Schram, Sanford. 2005. "Putting a Black Face on Welfare: The Good and the Bad." In *Deserving and Entitled: Social Constructions and Target Populations*, ed. Anne L. Schneider and Helen M. Ingram, 261–289. Albany: State University of New York Press.

Scriven, Michael. 1967. "The Methodology of Evaluation." In *Perspectives of Curriculum Evaluation*, ed. Ralph Tyler, Robert Gagane, and Michael Scriven. AERA Monograph Series on Curriculum Evaluation. Chicago: Rand McNally.

———. 1991. *Evaluation Thesaurus*. Newbury Park, CA: Sage.

Shadish, William, Thomas Cook, and Donald Campbell. 2002. *Experimental and Quasi-Experimental Designs for Generalized Causal Inference*. Boston: Houghton Mifflin.

Shadish, William, Thomas Cook, and Laura Leviton. 1991. *Foundations of Program Evaluation: Theories of Practice*. Newbury Park, CA: Sage.

Shanahan, Elizabeth, Michael D. Jones, and Mark K. McBeth. 2011. "Policy Narratives and Policy Processes." *Policy Studies Journal* 39(3): 535–561.

Shipan, Charles R., and Craig Volden. 2008. "The Mechanisms of Policy Diffusion." *American Journal of Political Science* 52(4): 840–857.

Shulock, Nancy. 1997. "The Paradox of Policy Analysis: If It Is Not Used, Why Do We Produce So Much of It?" *Journal of Policy Analysis and Management* 18: 226–244.

Simon, Herbert A. 1947. *Administrative Behavior*. New York: Free Press.

———. 1955. "A Behavioral Model of Rational Choice." *The Quarterly Journal of Economics* 69(1): 99–118.

———. 1985. "Human Nature in Politics: The Dialogue with Psychology and Political Science." *Political Psychology* 16: 45–61.

———. 1997. *Administrative Behavior*. 4th ed. New York: Free Press.

Smirnov, Oleg. 2007. "Altruistic Punishment in Politics and Life Sciences." *Perspectives on Politics* 5(3): 489–501.

Smith, Kevin B. 2002. "Typologies, Taxonomies and the Benefits of Policy Classification." *Policy Studies Journal* 30: 379–395.

_____. 2003. *The Ideology of Education*. Albany: State University of New York Press.

_____. 2005. "Data Don't Matter? Academic Research and School Choice." *Perspectives on Politics* 3(2): 285–299.

_____. 2006a. "Economic Techniques." In *The Oxford Handbook of Public Policy*, ed. Michael Moran, Martin Rein, and Robert E. Goodin, 729–745. New York: Oxford University Press.

_____. 2006b. "Representational Altruism: The Wary Cooperator as Authoritative Decision Maker." *American Journal of Political Science* 50(4): 1013–1022.

Smith, Kevin B., and Scott Granberg-Rademacker. 2003. "Money Only Matters If You Want It To? Exposing the Normative Implications of Empirical Research." *Political Research Quarterly* 56: 223–232.

Smith, Kevin B., and Christopher W. Larimer. 2004. "A Mixed Relationship: Bureaucracy and School Performance." *Public Administration Review* (November/December): 728–736.

Smith, Kevin B., and Michael J. Licari. 2007. *Public Administration: Power and Politics in the Fourth Branch of Government*. New York: Oxford University Press.

Smith, Kevin B., and Kenneth Meier. 1995. *The Case Against School Choice*. New York: M. E. Sharpe.

Smith, V. Kerry, and Eric Moore. 2010. "Behavioral Economics and Benefit Cost Analysis." *Environmental Resource Economics* 46: 217–234.

Somit, Albert, and Steven A. Peterson, eds. 2003a. *Human Nature and Public Policy: An Evolutionary Approach*. New York: Palgrave Macmillan.

_____. 2003b. "From Human Nature to Public Policy: Evolutionary Theory Challenges the 'Standard Model.'" In *Human Nature and Public Policy: An Evolutionary Approach*, ed. Albert Somit and Steven A. Peterson, 3–18. New York: Palgrave Macmillan.

Soss, Joe. 1999. "Lessons of Welfare: Policy Design, Political Learning, and Political Action." *American Political Science Review* 93: 363–380.

_____. 2005. "Making Clients and Citizens: Welfare Policy as a Source of Status, Belief, and Action." In *Deserving and Entitled: Social Constructions and Target Populations*, ed. Anne L. Schneider and Helen M. Ingram, 291–328. Albany: State University of New York Press.

Spitzer, Robert J. 1987. "Promoting Policy Theory: Revising the Arenas of Power." *Policy Studies Journal* (June): 675–689.

_____. 1989. "From Complexity to Simplicity: More on Policy Theory and the Arenas of Power." *Policy Studies Journal* 17 (Spring): 529–536.

Steinberger, Peter J. 1980. "Typologies of Public Policy: Meaning Construction and the Policy Process." *Social Science Quarterly* (September): 185–197.

Stone, Deborah. 1988. *Policy Paradox and Political Reason.* Glenview, IL: Scott, Foresman.

———. 2002. *Policy Paradox: The Art of Political Decision Making.* New York: W. W. Norton.

———. 2005. "Foreword." In *Deserving and Entitled: Social Constructions and Target Populations*, ed. Anne L. Schneider and Helen M. Ingram, xi. Albany: State University of New York Press.

Talmage, H. 1982. "Evaluation of Programs." In *Encyclopedia of Educational Research*, 5th ed., ed. H. E. Mitzel, 592–611. New York: Free Press.

Tatalovich, R., and B. W. Daynes, eds. 1998. *Moral Controversies in American Politics.* New York: M. E. Sharpe.

Teske, Paul, Mark Schneider, Michael Mintrom, and Samuel Best. 1993. "Establishing the Micro Foundations of a Macro Theory: Information, Movers, and the Competitive Local Market for Public Goods." *American Political Science Review* 87: 702–713.

Thacher, D., and M. Rein. 2004. "Managing Value Conflict in Public Policy." *Governance* 17: 457–486.

Theodoulou, Stella. 1995. "The Contemporary Language of Public Policy: A Starting Point." In *Public Policy: The Essential Readings*, ed. Stella Theodoulou and Matthew Cahn, 1–9. Englewood Cliffs, NJ: Prentice Hall.

Tiebout, Charles M. 1956. "A Pure Theory of Local Expenditures." *Journal of Political Economy* 64: 416–424.

Trisko, Karen Sue, and V. C. League. 1978. *Developing Successful Programs.* Oakland, CA: Awareness House.

True, James L., Bryan D. Jones, and Frank R. Baumgartner. 1999. "Punctuated-Equilibrium Theory: Explaining Stability and Change in American Policymaking." In *Theories of Policy Process*, ed. Paul A. Sabatier, 97–116. Boulder, CO: Westview Press.

Truman, David. 1951. *The Governmental Process: Political Interests and Public Opinion.* New York: Knopf.

Turnbull, H. Rutherford, III. 1986. *Free Appropriate Public Education: The Law and Children with Disabilities.* Denver, CO: Love Publishing.

Tversky, Amos, and Daniel Kahneman. 1974. "Judgment Under Uncertainty: Heuristics and Biases." *Science* 185: 1124–1131.

———. 1981. "The Framing of Decisions and the Psychology of Choice." *Science* 211: 453–458.

Tyler, Tom R. 1990. *Why People Obey the Law.* New Haven, CT: Yale University Press.

———. 2001. "The Psychology of Public Dissatisfaction with Government." In *What Is It About Government That Americans Dislike?*, ed. John R. Hibbing and Elizabeth Theiss-Morse, 227–242. Cambridge: Cambridge University Press.

Unnever, James, Allan Kerckhoff, and Timothy Robinson. 2000. "District Variations in Educational Resources and Student Outcomes." *Economics of Education Review* 19: 245–259.

Verstegen, Deborah, and Richard King. 1998. "The Relationship Between School Spending and Student Achievement: A Review and Analysis of 35 Years of Production Function Research." *Journal of Education Economics* 24: 243–262.

Waldo, Dwight. 1946. *The Administrative State*. San Francisco: Chandler.

Walker, Jack L. 1969. "The Diffusion of Innovations Among the American States." *American Political Science Review* 63: 880–889.

Walker, Richard, Laurence O'Toole Jr., and Kenneth Meier. 2007. "It's Where You Are That Matters: An Empirical Analysis of the Networking Behaviour of English Local Government Officers." *Public Administration* 85: 739–756.

Walsh, Anthony. 2006. "Evolutionary Psychology and Criminal Behavior." In *Missing the Revolution: Darwinism for Social Scientists*, ed. Jerome H. Barkow, 225–268. New York: Oxford University Press.

Wanat, John. 1974. "Bases of Budgetary Incrementalism." *American Political Science Review* 68: 1221–1228.

Weber, J. Mark, Shirli Kopelman, and David M. Messick. 2004. "A Conceptual Review of Decision Making in Social Dilemmas: Applying a Logic of Appropriateness." *Personality and Social Psychology Review* 8(3): 281–307.

Weible, Christopher M., Paul A. Sabatier, and Kelly McQueen. 2009. "Themes and Variations: Taking Stock of the Advocacy Coalition Framework." *Policy Studies Journal* 37(1): 121–140.

Weible, Christopher M., Paul A. Sabatier, Hank C. Jenkins-Smith, Daniel Nohrstedt, Adam Douglas Henry, and Peter deLeon. 2011. "A Quarter Century of the Advocacy Coalition Framework: An Introduction to the Special Issue." *Policy Studies Journal* 39(3): 349–360.

Weimer, David L. 2008. "Theories Of and In the Policy Process." *Policy Studies Journal* 36(4): 489–495.

Weimer, David, and Aidan Vining. 2005. *Policy Analysis: Concepts and Practice*. Upper Saddle River, NJ: Prentice Hall.

Weiss, Carol H. 1998. *Evaluation*. Upper Saddle River, NJ: Prentice Hall.

Wenger, Jennie. 2000. "What Do Schools Produce? Implications of Multiple Outputs in Education." *Contemporary Economic Policy* 18(1): 27–36.

Weston, Drew. 2007. *The Political Brain: The Role of Emotion in Deciding the Fate of the Nation*. New York: Public Affairs.

Whatley, Mark A., J. Matthew Webster, Richard H. Smith, and Adele Rhodes. 1999. "The Effect of a Favor on Public and Private Compliance: How Internalized Is the Norm of Reciprocity?" *Basic and Applied Social Psychology* 21(3): 251–259.

Whitaker, Eric A., Mitch N. Herian, Christopher W. Larimer, and Michael Lang. 2012. "Legislative Bills and Ballot Initiatives: Raising the Minimum Wage in the American States, 1997–2006." *Policy Studies Journal*.

Whiten, Andrew, and Richard B. Byrne, eds. 1997. *Machiavellian Intelligence II: Extensions and Applications*. Cambridge: Cambridge University Press.

Wholey, Joseph S., et al. 1970. *Federal Evaluation Policy*. Washington, DC: The Urban Institute.

Wildavsky, Aaron. 1964. *The Politics of the Budgetary Process*. Boston: Little, Brown.

Williams, Walter. 1971. *Social Policy Research and Analysis*. New York: American Elsevier.

———. 1998. *Honest Numbers and Democracy*. Washington, DC: Georgetown University Press.

Wilson, Edward O. 2012. *The Social Conquest of Earth*. New York: Liveright Publishing.

Wilson, James Q. 1973a. "On Pettigrew and Armor." *The Public Interest* 30: 132–134.

———. 1973b. *Political Organizations*. New York: Basic Books.

———. 1980. "The Politics of Regulation." In *The Politics of Regulation*, ed. James Q. Wilson, 357–394. New York: Basic Books.

———. 1983. *American Government: Institutions and Policies*. 2nd ed. Lexington, MA: D. C. Heath.

Wilson, Richard. 2006. "Policy Analysis as Policy Advice." In *The Oxford Handbook of Public Policy*, ed. Michael Moran, Martin Rein, and Robert E. Goodin, 152–168. New York: Oxford University Press.

Winter, Søren. 1999. "New Directions for Implementation Research." *Policy Currents* 8(4): 1–5.

Wolff, Jonathan, and Dirk Haubrich. 2006. "Economism and Its Limits." In *The Oxford Handbook of Public Policy*, ed. Michael Moran, Martin Rein, and Robert E. Goodin, 746–770. New York: Oxford University Press.

Wood, B. Dan, and Alesha Doan. 2003. "The Politics of Problem Definition: Applying and Testing Threshold Models." *American Journal of Political Science* 47(4): 640–653.

Wood, B. Dan, and Arnold Vedlitz. 2007. "Issue Definition, Information Processing, and the Politics of Global Warming." *American Journal of Political Science* 51(3): 552–568.

Workman, Samuel, Bryan D. Jones, and Ashley E. Jochim. 2009. "Information Processing and Policy Dynamics." *Policy Studies Journal* 37(1): 75–92.

Xiao, Erte, and Daniel Houser. 2011. "Punish in Public." *Journal of Public Economics* 95(7–8): 1006–1017.

Yanow, D. 2000. *Conducting Interpretive Policy Analysis*. Newbury Park, CA: Sage.

Zahariadis, Nikolaos. 2007. "The Multiple Streams Framework: Structure, Limitations, Prospects." In *Theories of the Policy Process*, ed. Paul A. Sabatier, 65–92. Boulder, CO: Westview Press.

Zeckhauser, R., and E. Schaefer. 1968. "Public Policy and Normative Economic Theory." In *The Study of Policy Formation*, ed. R. Bauer and K. J. Gergen, 27–101. Glencoe, IL: Free Press.

Goals, 48, 79, 105, 127, 132, 138, 139,
146, 151, 154, 156–157, 171, 177,
178, 184, 185, 189, 193, 230
unclear goals, 133, 176
Goggin, Malcolm, 162–163, 165, 166–
167
Gore, Al, 211
Gould, Stephen Jay, 82, 226
Government Accountability Office, 129
Granberg-Rademacker, Scott, 134, 135
Great Depression, 37
Greenberg, George, 39–40, 44
Gutmann, Amy, 116

Habermas, Jurgen, 116
Hamm, Keith, 77, 78
Hanushek, Erik, 114
Health issues, 83, 89, 90, 115, 211
health care, 11, 13, 134
Heclo, Hugh, 75–77, 81
Hermeneutics, 175, 187, 192, 213, 232
Heuristics, 198–199, 203, 208, 218
Hibbing, John R., 192, 208
Hobbes, Thomas, 7
Hospitals, 134
Houser, Daniel, 216
Howell-Moroney, Michael, 63
Human condition/dignity, 7, 10, 17, 201

IAD. *See* Institutions: institutional
analysis and development
Identifiable individuals, 210–211, 217
Ideology, 13, 79, 91, 119, 147, 173
Immigration policy, 87, 185–186
Impact analysis, 132–139, 140, 142, 147
defined, 126
flagship approach to, 142, 143
logic and theory of, 136–139
and program evaluation, 128–132,
134
quasi-experimental approaches in,
144–145

questions that motivate, 126–127, 131
and research design, 142–146
and statistical control techniques,
145–146
Implementation and Public Policy
(Mazmanian and Sabatier),
157–159
Implementation Game, The (Bardach),
156
*Implementation: How Great Expectations
in Washington Are Dashed in
Oakland* (Pressman and
Wildavsky), 152–154
Implementation studies, 151–152
continuation/reform of, 166–167
demise of, 163, 165, 169
first generation of, 152–155
fourth generation of, 165–169
and perspective issues, 159–162
second generation of, 155–162
third generation of, 162–165, 169
typology of, 165–166
See also Policy implementation
Incrementalism, 50–54, 70, 81, 83, 85,
87, 95, 197, 198
and stability, 82
Infrastructure, 121
Ingram, Helen, 32, 180, 181, 182, 183,
184, 187, 188, 189, 191, 193, 194
Institutions, 48, 83, 84, 85, 96, 198, 219
design flaw of, 64, 70
institutional analysis and
development (IAD), 65–69
institutional design, 87, 212
institutional friction, 85
institutional rational choice, 62–69
institutional reform, 113–114, 139
new institutionalism, 197, 198
Interdisciplinary approach. *See*
Multidisciplinary orientation
Interest groups, 37, 38, 73, 75, 76, 77, 78,
79, 91, 110